THE THEATRE OF
ARISTOPHANES

Kenneth McLeish

THE THEATRE OF ARISTOPHANES

TAPLINGER PUBLISHING COMPANY
NEW YORK

for my parents

First published in the United States in 1980 by
TAPLINGER PUBLISHING CO., INC.
New York, New York

Copyright © 1980 by Kenneth McLeish
All rights reserved.
Printed in Great Britain

Library of Congress Catalog Card Number: 79-3142
ISBN 1-8008-7630-x

Contents

List of Figures

All figures drawn by Sue Ebrahim

The Graces were looking for an everlasting home;
They found it in the soul of Aristophanes.

(attributed to Plato)

Preface

There are many works of textual and historical scholarship which deal with Aristophanes. This book attempts a different task: to examine the plays from the point of view of a dramatic critic, and to try to discover, as closely as possible, what their effect may have been on the original audience.

The book was written with the general reader in mind, and in particular for those students of theatre who are not classical scholars, but who wish to study the unique phenomenon of Greek Old Comedy in some detail, and to relate its performing traditions to comedy of later ages and styles. For this reason, I have tended throughout to assume a larger familiarity with Aristophanes' own work than with the literature of classical criticism, and I have avoided controversy wherever possible. All extracts from the plays are given in translation. I am grateful to Cambridge University Press for permission to quote from my own translation of *Knights*; to Penguin Books Ltd for permission to quote from David Barrett's translations of *Wasps, Women at the Festival* and *Frogs*; and to The University of Michigan Press and New English Library Ltd for permission to quote from William Arrowsmith's translation of *Birds*, and from Douglass Parker's translations of *Acharnians* and *Assemblywomen*. (Where no satisfactory translation has been published, I have used plain versions of my own.) Line references throughout the book are to the Greek text of Hall and Geldart (Oxford, second edition 1906–1907).

In between more general opening and closing chapters, the book is divided into three sections, which cover respectively the circumstances within which Aristophanes worked, some aesthetic matters unique in or crucial to his plays, and a discussion of the creative role played by the actors as they performed the scripts. Except in Chapters 2–4, which contain in part a summary of essential general information, I have tried not to duplicate the content of other books on Aristophanes. The books listed in the bibliography are likely to be of most use to the non-specialist seeking the current state of our knowledge.

My thanks are due first to my father, Professor John McLeish, for help and advice at the start of the project; to Sir Kenneth Dover, who kept a friendly eye on the book from the beginning, and who saved me from much error; to William Arrowsmith, Frederic Raphael, Eric Southern and Walter Stein, who read the

9

manuscript in draft and provided useful criticism; and above all to my wife, Valerie McLeish, for help and encouragement throughout and for indexing the book. It is a pleasure to acknowledge my debts, and my duty to state that faults remaining in the book are the result of my own intransigence rather than of the advice of my friends.

KENNETH MCLEISH
Lincoln, England 1979

Chronological Table

c. 600 BC	Dramatic Choruses at Corinth and Sicyon
c. 550	Thespis introduces first solo speakers
534	Drama introduced to state festivals of Athens
525–456	Aeschylus
c. 500	Precinct of Dionysos becomes site of dramatic presentations in Athens, instead of the *agora*
c. 500–429	Pericles
496–406	Sophocles
490	Battle of Marathon
487	Comedy introduced to Dionysian festivals at Athens
484–406	Euripides
480	Battles of Thermopylae and Salamis
479	Final defeat of Persians
472	Aeschylus: *Persians*
469–399	Socrates
c. 465	Classical *orchestra* built in precinct of Dionysos
458	Aeschylus: *Oresteia*
c. 450–380	Aristophanes
449	Contest of tragic actors introduced
442–429	Great period of Periclean Athens. Parthenon built
442	Contest of comic actors introduced
c. 442	Sophocles: *Antigone*
438	Euripides: *Alcestis*
431	Euripides: *Medea*. Peloponnesian War begins
c. 429	Sophocles: *Oedipus the King*. Death of Pericles
c. 428	Aristophanes' first play produced
425	Aristophanes: *Acharnians* (Lenaia, second prize)
424	Aristophanes: *Knights* (Lenaia, first prize)
423	Aristophanes: *Clouds* (City Dionysia, third prize). This version is lost; ours is a revised and unperformed revision of some six years later
422	Aristophanes: *Wasps* (Lenaia, second prize)
421	Aristophanes: *Peace* (City Dionysia, second prize)
415–413	Disastrous Athenian expedition to Sicily
414	Aristophanes: *Birds* (City Dionysia, second prize)

I

Introduction: the Aristophanic Experience

The excellence of Aristophanes has never been questioned. Critics have argued about this or that detail in his work; but there has never been any doubt that he is a dramatist of the front rank, a comic artist of the highest order. His plays have survived not by accident or for the light they shed on other matters, but for their intrinsic quality. They are a unique, and uniquely important, part of the heritage of Western literature; they offer the reader or spectator an engrossing, enriching experience.

Perhaps because of this excellence, Aristophanes has been fortunate in the calibre of those who have studied his work. This is particularly the case in the fields of textual criticism and commentary. The surviving plays are in an excellent, if not perfect, textual state – certainly bearing comparison with those of Shakespeare. There is a large body of commentary, from the scholiasts of the second century BC to those of our own day. There are still difficulties to be explained and problems to be solved, but by and large we can be confident that we know what Aristophanes said in the extant plays, and what he meant.

The question then arises, how are we to use these texts? How will they help us to discover and define Aristophanes' excellence for ourselves? Is their influence to be as nothing more than texts for study, or will they lead us to savour the Aristophanic experience in other ways?

The method of this book is to treat the texts almost like archaeological evidence: to examine them for clues about how they were first performed in the fifth century BC, and the effect they may have had on fifth-century audiences. For the closer we can relate our own experience of Aristophanes to that of the original spectators, the more we should be able to find out about it. No one is surprised to discover, in tragedy, that we are moved or affected by the same things as the Greeks; we should acknowledge that we may laugh at the same things too.

Of course, it is impossible to be certain that the Greeks laughed at every single joke which amuses us, and found it funny in exactly the same way. But in general it is perfectly clear what reactions Aristophanes wanted from his audience, and how he set about getting them – and also that the greater proportion of his comic effects worked in the same way then as they do now. In fact, the persistence of certain kinds of jokes and routines in the comic tradition after Aristophanes suggests that the essential nature of comedy has changed very little, and its techniques hardly at all.

We should perhaps begin by considering the two groups of spectators whose experience we are hoping to define: those of the fifth century BC and those of today. It was implied above that there is very little difference between them (they laughed then as they laugh now, at the same things and for similar reasons); but in fact there is a huge gulf between the Greek audience and ourselves, and we must begin by considering some of the differences. For a play does not exist primarily as a written text intended for detailed private study: it exists momentarily, as the words and actions of the performers are perceived by the spectators. Bearing on that moment are all the spectators' previous experience of drama, and the circumstances of the particular performance itself, as well as the events of the actual play; a skilful playwright will draw on that experience and those circumstances to help evoke the response he is seeking. And it is obvious that spectators in ancient Athens came to a performance of Aristophanes with radically different expectations and experience from those of today.

The beginning of our task, therefore, is to get as close as possible to the fifth-century spectator. We need to know the physical trappings of his theatre-going: where he sat, what he saw and what else was happening apart from the play itself. We need to know about the previous dramatic experience of spectator and playwright alike, the traditions of comedy, the cultic and ritual significance both of the spectacle as a whole and of specific events within it. We need to know the working conditions of playwright and performers, and their experience and expectations of the performance they were creating. All these matters are of prime importance, and there is clear evidence about them in the texts. They are discussed in Chapters 2–4.

The previous experience of the modern spectator leads us into deeper and murkier regions. He has none of the religious and few of the festive feelings of his ancient Athenian predecessor; he knows much less about the non-literary, phallic comedy that preceded Aristophanes, and even less about Aristophanes' contemporary rivals (both matters of considerable importance to the original spectator). On the other hand, he has a vast accumulation of experience denied to the ancient Athenian. This includes not only an entire dramatic tradition extending over twenty-four centuries and embracing comedies totally different in style and intention from those of Aristophanes, but also a huge available weight of scholarly theorizing, comment and criticism – about Aristophanes, drama, the nature of laughter, the very art of theatre itself. He is accustomed to a style of dramatic performance that is like the Greek in some respects, but totally different in others. Even his view of Aristophanes himself is likely to be more sophisticated. He may, for example, have read the play in advance of the performance; he may have later plays of Aristophanes to compare with it; he may have ideas about Aristophanes' status in the hierarchy of world theatre; his knowledge of Aristophanes' Greek is as a learned, second-hand language, rather than his own. In fact he is like the Greek spectator only in one way, that he is hoping to be entertained rather than bored.

The existence and effects of the twenty-four centuries between the ancient spectators and ourselves determine the major part of this book. In order to understand the Greek experience more fully, we must examine several aspects of our own, not only to consider which of our assumptions about comic theatre are different from those of the Greeks, but also – and more significantly – to consider which are or could be similar.

Categories of comedy (1): 'farce' and 'comedy'

The first matter to be dealt with is the appearance after Aristophanes of several different categories of comedy. The development of character comedy, already begun in late Aristophanes and continued in Greek and Roman New Comedy, led eventually to a critical division of stage comedy into two genres, 'comedy' and 'farce', and two types, literary and non-literary. This division (though sometimes more apparent to critics than real) continued right through the Roman and early Christian periods, was reinforced in the Middle Ages by the distinction drawn between courtly (or 'learned') and popular entertainment, and is still evident today, both in theoretical writings and in comic plays themselves. The result is that Aristophanes' plays fall into none of the existing critical or performing types. These types, therefore, must be consciously removed from our minds when we consider the kind of comedy Aristophanes actually wrote.

Very broadly, the modern distinction between farce and comedy might be summed up as follows. Farce is a type of drama intended almost exclusively to evoke laughter. It depends on action rather than character. The action can be subtle or obvious, complex or simple: but the intrusion of seriousness (for example moral or ethical commentary) tends to defeat the primary objective, and alienate the spectators.[1] The essential ingredient of farce, whether verbal or physical, is incongruity. Either realistic characters are placed in unrealistic situations, or unrealistic characters are faced with the trappings of everyday reality. When realistic characters are used, the plot frequently involves them in a sequence of increasing hysteria and desperation; when the characters are unrealistic (like the heroes of Sennett film comedies), the humour often lies in their unpredictable reactions to and manipulations of the everyday. The realistic hero is challenged and threatened by the world around him; the unrealistic hero uses elements of that world to challenge and threaten others. Exaggeration (to the point of surrealism) and ridicule are the main techniques of the farce-dramatist. In farces of what might be called a 'higher' literary type (such as those of Feydeau) the progression of the ridiculous is organized in a meticulous and well-paced way; in farces of less sophistication (such as some of the films of Jerry Lewis) this control is not in evidence, and the plot employs in a random fashion any and every means of evoking hilarity.

If modern farce regards man as a ridiculous, puppet-like creature, modern comedy tends to treat him with a kind of quiet affection. Because (unlike farce) it springs from character rather than action, its effect is seldom hilarious, but more often a kind of serious pleasure, an inward smile at the frailties and foibles of humanity. Whereas farce distorts and parodies the human predicament, comedy describes and defines it. Irony rather than ridicule is the predominant mode: although exaggeration and parody are used, they are never raised to the ludicrous heights common in farce. And whereas farce eschews serious themes, comedy very often embraces them.

A good illustration of the difference between the two genres is the series of impostures in *Twelfth Night*. The trick played on Malvolio is farcical in intention, execution and result; the imposture of Viola, on the other hand, is comic, and its intention, execution and result are made as realistic as possible. The farce world of Malvolio and his tormentors, and the comedy world of Orsino, Olivia and Viola, are kept separate and distinct throughout the play. Malvolio capering cross-gartered before Olivia meets with as blank a response as Feste confronting Viola. Even Malvolio's outburst in the last scene and Feste's song at the end of the play are external to the mood and action in which they are set.

In *Twelfth Night* structural dramatic use is made of the distinctions between the worlds of farce and comedy. In Aristophanes, by contrast, those distinctions are entirely absent. His world is predominantly like that of farce: that is, his plays involve action more often than character, fantasy more often than realism, ridicule and slapstick more often than irony. But they differ from later farce in a crucial way: they contain, as an essential and integral feature of their style, serious themes, serious characters and serious language, all of which are combined with hilarity and slapstick in a manner characteristic of no other writer. Thus, the plot of *Knights* has two equally important strands: a farcical, slapstick contest in shamelessness and the savage and deeply felt denunciation of a political figure from real life. In *Birds*, *Lysistrata* and *Assemblywomen* the leading characters are serious (like the sons in *Wasps*, *Clouds* and *Wealth*). Their actions take place in a farcical atmosphere and contribute to the development of a farcical plot, but they themselves are generally serious rather than ludicrous, and serve a serious theme within the action as well as the immediate farcical needs of the action itself. In the same way, characters who are predominantly farcical, like Dikaiopolis or Trygaios, utter passages with a serious or lyrical content, without any feeling that they are behaving against type (as would be the case, say, if a Feydeau hero launched into serious, lyrical verse or made a speech genuinely extolling the virtues of chastity). The language of Aristophanes in general follows none of the ground rules of modern drama. Even in *Women at the Festival* and *Frogs*, the most unified and consistently farcical of the plays, there are many passages of a seriousness and lyrical beauty which mesh seamlessly with the slapstick and bawdy around them.

The mixture of slapstick and seriousness, lyric and bawdy, reality and fantasy must be carefully controlled if the resulting play is to have unity and forward movement. Aristophanes achieves this control in two ways. Firstly, he takes particular care to ensure that when surrealism and fantasy take over from truth-to-life within the plot, the change, given the circumstances, seems not only attractive but also logical and inevitable. The majority of his plots are constructed on a logical progression from despair to inspiration to fantasy to glorious fulfilment. The individual steps are small, and each follows inevitably from what has gone before; it is only at the end of the play that we realize that a complete inversion has been achieved of the state of affairs at the start. This progression is analysed, and its didactic function discussed, in Chapter 5.

The second means of control involves Aristophanes' treatment of characters and events taken from real life and inserted in the plays. The way this is done depends partly on the establishment of a precise relationship between performer and spectator – a relationship which has been lost in literary comedy since his time, but which still persists in the relationship between the modern stand-up comedian and his audience. Like such a comedian, Aristophanes invests the people and events taken from real life with a kind of illusory, fantasy existence, often either allegorical (as in the case of Kleonymos, the eternal symbol of cowardice) or burlesqued (as in the cases of Euripides, Socrates or Lamachos). Because both comedian and spectator know that the comic creation is distorted from the original in a particular way, a state of conspiratorial irony is established between them, with the parodied person or event as its butt. (This process, unique to Aristophanes in all literary comedy, is so successful that its creations are still effective and funny today, when all the irony derived from topicality is lacking – a claim which cannot be sustained on behalf of less genial satirists like Juvenal or Swift.) The achievement of this relationship between comedian and audience is at the heart of Aristophanes' uniqueness as a dramatist; it is examined in Chapter 6, and extended into a more general discussion of his character-drawing in Chapter 9.

Categories of comedy (2): literary and non-literary comedy

The nature of the relationship between performer and spectator has changed so radically since Aristophanes' time that knowledge of modern acting techniques can very seriously hinder our appreciation of the original Greek performing styles, and therefore distort a major element in the plays' intended effect. The problem has arisen because of the dichotomy that grew up in Rome between 'cultured' and 'popular' entertainment – a dichotomy still present today, when comic artists of the 'legitimate' theatre are thought of as in some way different from those of more 'popular' forms such as circus, the variety stage, music-hall, television and films. And yet it is in these popular types of entertainment that we shall find a closer approximation to the atmosphere and style of an Aristophanic performance than on the legitimate comic stage of today.

Already in the time of Terence a distinction was being made between literary comedies (in elegant and civilized language, and intended for a *recitatio* or closet-performance to a small, sophisticated audience) and broader comic entertainments intended for the people at large (which had to jostle for attention with rope-walkers, gladiators and animal-hunts, often on makeshift stages in the same arenas). By the time of the closing of the theatres under Justinian, and for several centuries afterwards, when performances of comedy were banned by the Christian Church, literary comedy was entirely the possession of readers. St Jerome, Eusebius and Alcuin, for example, enjoyed Plautus and Terence, but they read the plays instead of seeing them performed. Since a reader looks for humour of language rather than humour of action, it was the language particularly of Terence that made him a favourite comic author in post-classical times. In the tenth century, Hroswitha imitated his Latin style to write biblical 'comedies'; during the Middle Ages Petrarch, Dante and Chaucer, all 'literary' rather than 'popular' writers, both read and – in part – translated him; during the Renaissance he was a favourite teaching vehicle of schoolmasters: the headmasters of Eton, Westminster and St Paul's, for example, or the anonymous Dutch authors of the 'Christian Terence'.[2] Even the incorporation of physical comedy from the *commedia dell'arte* into literary comedy in the sixteenth to eighteenth centuries failed to alter the pre-eminence of language: from Shakespeare and Molière to the present day, authors of 'high comedy' have continued to produce what is essentially a literary vehicle, in which action is generally far less important than speech.

This pre-eminence of language has had a clear influence on the way comedy has come to be performed. Over the centuries, comic acting in the legitimate theatre has come to mean a type of performance in which gesture and movement are used principally to complement the delivery of the text. It is only very recently that physical skills from the non-literary tradition (pratfalls, juggling and the like) have been reintroduced to performances of literary comedy – and when they are (as in Peter Brook's production of *A Midsummer Night's Dream* or Barrault's of *Rabelais*) audiences have reacted with as much astonishment as delight. In short, once the comic situation is set up for him, we expect a gifted comic actor (like Jack Lemmon or Fernandel) to amuse us by vocal histrionics supported by gesture and facial expression; but we do not expect him necessarily to be able to do eccentric dancing, or sing, or perform the split-second, gymnastic slapstick of the clowns of silent films. No one is surprised when Chaplin reveals (in *Modern Times*) that he is outstandingly expert at roller-skating; but we would be extremely taken aback by a similar display from a comic actor in a 'legitimate' play. The techniques of physical comedy are not only inappropriate to the literary medium, but lie in general outside the performing style as well.

In Aristophanes none of these distinctions and boundaries apply. His plays demand from the performers just as many of the skills of non-literary as those of literary comedy. If the plays contain a great deal of humour derived from language (requiring actors at least as skilful in linguistic delivery as those of today[3]), there is also an abundance of lyrical song, and a far greater amount of dancing and physical slapstick than is common in later comedy. This internal evidence, as well as consideration of the sheer size of the festival performance, strongly suggests that actors of fifth-century comedy were trained professionals with a wide repertory of skills, some of which would not today be thought part of the actor's armoury. Many sections of the plays may even have been composed as deliberate showcases for such skills. This matter is discussed in Chapter 8.

The techniques of non-literary comic acting have come down to us in a tradition as clear as that of literary comedy. Many of them probably antedate Aristophanes by many centuries, and arose and were developed in mimes, dances and improvised farces such as are common to all societies.[4] It seems likely that Aristophanes worked traditional routines and performing skills into his plays much as Molière and Goldoni used the same kind of material from the *commedia dell'arte*. With the third-century separation of non-literary farce from literary comedy, these non-literary routines (and the skills they required) returned to their natural home: the simple entertainments of ordinary people. The Phlyax farces of Magna Graecia and the mimes, ballets and short farces of the Romans preserved the tradition and carried it into the Christian era. In the so-called 'Dark' Ages folk-comedy developed in a number of different ways. At one level were the minstrels, troubadours and jesters who travelled the European courts; at another were the groups of folk-dancers and mummers who performed at country fairs, whether amateurs (like wassail-singers) or skilled clowns and acrobats (like those shown performing on carts in medieval and Renaissance paintings[5]). There was also a flourishing and continuous tradition of puppet performances, probably owing their origin to religious bans on live stage shows, and surviving to the present day in such manifestations as Punch and Judy, Karaghiozes, the Tivoli marionettes, or the various Middle Eastern and Moorish shadow-plays. Out of this heterogeneous tradition the *commedia dell'arte* developed. This employed dancing, singing, acrobatics and comic dialogue as well as a huge variety of slapstick routines. From the *commedia dell'arte* these routines were taken over both by literary comedy and by simpler comedy (like that of the touring actors mentioned in literature as late as Thomas Hardy). At the end of the seventeenth century centres were established for such performers (for example in the Tivoli Gardens in Copenhagen or the Vauxhall Gardens in London). Out of these the music-hall developed; 'vaude-ville' survived intact into the present century, and many of its most typical routines are preserved for us, in a remarkably detailed way, in the films of early silent comedy. Recently the techniques and traditions of the music-hall have been revived and adapted both by 'serious' dramatists (such as Beckett or the writers of Absurd Drama) and by the many acting-companies whose work stems from improvisation rather than a written text. Once again, in fact, the non-literary, folk style is being incorporated into what has by now become a completely different genre.

The largely folk nature of this non-literary tradition, and its virtual absence from European comedy of the last five hundred years, has caused it to be undervalued or neglected by critics and writers on drama. But just as it is becoming increasingly important in contemporary theatre, so its techniques and routines are an integral part of the style of Aristophanes, and should be borne in mind whenever Athenian comic acting is discussed.

One of the most important features of these folk performances is their use of *lazzi*, or comic 'routines'. These routines are as old as drama itself; they provide points of familiarity for the audience (which the performer can manipulate as he chooses), and offer the performer a pool of well-tried and successful material ('catch-phrases' or 'catch-gestures') on which he can build each new per-formance. Verbal or physical, they are generally short. The 'I say, I say, I say . . .' joke routine is a modern verbal example, and the 'double-take' (in which a character realizes, with a spectacular start, something which has been said or done earlier without his noticing) is a silent routine common to all comedians, though used by each in a different and individual way. There are *lazzi* of falling, walking, eating and fighting; there are *lazzi* involving almost every conceivable kind of physical object, from phallic jester's poles, through ladders and buckets of water, to single flowers and the flimsiest of lace handkerchiefs.

Although the fact that these routines were unwritten, and were improvised or developed in performance, makes their precise nature difficult to discover, there is clear evidence that they were used in the performance of Aristophanes' plays. To quote a single example, the fact that knocking on a door is carefully prepared in the text, and often gets the same kind of reception (see, for example, *Acharnians* 393ff., *Clouds* 132ff., *Peace* 179ff., *Birds* 54ff., *Lysistrata* 428ff., *Women at the Festival* 25ff., *Frogs* 35ff. and 460ff., *Wealth* 1097ff.) suggests that it was accompanied in each case by variations of a particular series of comic *lazzi*. In the same way, the use of crane, revolve and phallus gives rise to markedly similar dialogue in several plays, which suggests the presence of silent *lazzi*. The effect of fear on the bowels, and the elaborate ways of making oneself sick (into someone else's armour) are *lazzi* as familiar in later comedy as in Aristophanes.

While it is clearly impossible to say for certain that because a particular situation in modern farce gives rise to a particular set of routines, the same situation occasioned the same routines in Aristophanes, the existence in general of such routines in Aristophanes is undeniable. As in the case of the relationship between the Athenian comic actor and his audience, an awareness of the traditions and methods of non-literary comedy is likely to bring us nearer to the fifth-century reality than anything we know of legitimate comic acting today.

The need for caution is obvious, and is particularly great in the case of performing conventions in Aristophanes which persist in modern theatre: for example the doubling of several parts by the same actor, or the performance of female roles by men in travesty. Both are common practice today, and lead to specific types of comic routine which affect modern spectators in specific ways. In Chapter 10 these conventions are considered from the vantage-point of the Athenian spectator, in an attempt to determine whether the effects produced were the same as on the modern stage, or (if not) what difference they made to plays in performance.

The most treacherous area of all is bawdy. Here, because our whole conditioning is so different from that of the ancient Greeks, we are in danger of misunderstanding Aristophanes entirely – as can be seen from a glance at many late nineteenth- and early twentieth-century scholarly editions of his plays. But bawdy is a large and vital ingredient in the art of Aristophanes, and cannot be ignored. As with the conventions mentioned above, we must try to discover not the effect it has now, but the sort of effect it may have had then. This issue is discussed in Chapter 7.

The art of Aristophanes

Aristophanes is one of the finest, funniest dramatists in Western literature. His view of human life is a sideways one: large-ranging, genial, unique. His relevance and importance today (leaving aside the blessed therapy of laughter) are undeniable. One of the main reasons – and one of the main ingredients of Aristophanes' art – is succinctly expressed by the theatre director Alexis Solomos[6] as follows:

Aristophanes' comedy, notwithstanding the playwright's unscrupulous passion for laughter, is fundamentally a serious kind of theatre. And this constitutes the major difference between his kind of entertainment and that produced by modern fun-makers – Chaplin being an outstanding exception. Aristophanes' plays involve three serious elements, unknown to most of our mass entertainers, namely poetry, moral purpose and a determined hero. They combine, in absolute symmetry, light and heavy components, in a manner which is familiar to us through the work of some 'engaged' writers of our time, such as Shaw, Mayakovsky, Brecht, Genet, Frisch, Albee and others, though none of them equals Aristophanes' comic genius. His method is, perhaps, best summed up in two lines of his [*Assemblywomen* 1155–1156, translated by Benjamin Bickley Rogers], written in the years of maturity, as advice from the chorus to the audience:

> Let the wise and philosophic
>   choose me for my wisdom's sake.
> Those who joy in mirth and laughter
>   choose me for the jests I make.

THE PLAYWRIGHT

2

The Practical Playwright

Constraints and opportunities

The purpose of this chapter is to review the practical circumstances in which
Aristophanes wrote, to pinpoint so far as is possible the outside influences
working on him as he prepared each play for its festival. The discussion is
limited to theatrical matters only: consideration of his attitude to other matters
– war conditions, for example, or the religious aspect of his work – is treated at
length by other writers.[7] Our aim is to look at the playwright as a public man, a
professional working under particular circumstances, and to see how he came to
terms with the demands those circumstances made on him.

The production of a comedy for an Athenian festival was not a single creative
act, performed by the artist in a single space of time in his own study (as the
writing of modern plays often is: Noël Coward, for example, wrote *Private Lives*
in three days). It was a long process, perhaps taking up most of a year, and
involved the efforts of many people apart from the author himself. Their
attitudes and decisions materially affected the developing shape of the play, and
it is unlikely that the script reached its final state (the form in which it survives)
until the production was very far advanced, probably only weeks or days before
the festival performance itself. Throughout the period of preparation, from first
idea to final performance, Aristophanes must have been cutting, adding and
adapting material in the light of each new step in the process of production.

Apart from his own wishes, he had four other groups of people to consider,
and their favourable reaction was essential to the success of the performance.
The play had to pass the selection committee; it had to appeal to its backer
enough to secure a worthwhile standard of production; it had to rouse the actors
to give it a dimension above merely mechanical performance (a dimension hard
at times to remember today, when we experience Aristophanes as often in the
study as in the theatre); and, finally, it had to excite audience and judges, and
so fulfil its proper religious and dramatic function.

Personalities apart – and they always play a considerable role in theatrical
production – the principal effect of the need to consider these four groups was
probably on the extent and type of innovation Aristophanes allowed himself. A
play different in content or style from any previously performed would hardly

appeal either to public officials or to the man invited to put money into its production. A play with demands on the actors totally unlike those they were used to would be a risky undertaking, if not necessarily doomed. A play too subtle or controversial for the audience would be unlikely to win a prize or be remembered after the initial production. A certain kind of conservatism, in theme and style, was therefore a prerequisite of a play intended to 'sell'. On the other hand, there was always the possibility of a *succès de scandale* – and this might suggest a particular kind of experiment, like the attacks on Kleon in *The Babylonians* or the reversal of traditional dramatic form in *Frogs*.[8]

The festivals

Apart from the (now totally unknown) opportunities afforded them by small-scale local festivals like the Rural Dionysia, the major opportunities for Athenian dramatists occurred at the festivals of the Lenaia in January and the City Dionysia in late March/early April. The usual number of comedies (one per writer) at each festival was five; but throughout Aristophanes' most productive years, probably because of the exigencies of war, this number was reduced to three (between 423 and 414 in the City Dionysia; between 425 and 405 in the Lenaia). Thus, in 425 and 424 there were eight annual chances of performance for an individual dramatist; between 423 and 414 there were six; between 414 and 405 there were eight; after 405 there were ten – though a gradual change in theatre practice (which also saw a change in the role of the Chorus) may have caused this number again to be reduced during the rest of Aristophanes' lifetime.

Assuming the free population of Athens to have numbered about 100,000, an output of six to ten new comedies each year is strikingly high: far higher, for example, than in London, New York or Paris today. It was rare for the same playwright to be given two Choruses out of the available total: Aristophanes' double appearance in 411 (with *Lysistrata* and *Women at the Festival*: see below), was not so far as we know repeated in his lifetime.

There is no trustworthy information on the actual standard of the comedies selected. Apart from Aristophanes' own work and his scathing remarks about his rivals, we know only that public opinion was less one-sided: his derided rivals often beat him in the competitions. (Whether this was due to excellence, or to other factors, for example professional infighting or such imponderables as sentiment for the aged Kratinos (who beat Aristophanes in 423), is a matter for conjecture.) The lists of writers, and frequency of selection, seem to indicate that most writers were what we might call 'Sunday authors' only, and submitted one or perhaps two plays in a whole lifetime. But there was also a small group whose names appear frequently (Kratinos twenty-one times, for example). Including Aristophanes himself, there were perhaps half a dozen regular, 'professional' authors, whose names, we may presume, would weigh heavily with the festival selectors. If this is so, then Aristophanes, with some forty comedies in a writing life of forty or fifty years, is typical of a small group rather than of the writing population as a whole.

These 'professionals' must have known each other well. Aristophanes' references to Kratinos in *Knights* 400 and 526ff., and *Frogs* 357, for example, have none of the heavy sarcasm used against lesser writers like Karkinos, Morsimos and Melanthios in *Peace* 781ff. We know from Plato's *Symposium* that Aristophanes was on good terms with at least two of his butts, Socrates and Agathon; we also know that he collaborated with his near-contemporary Eupolis, although they quarrelled and the partnership was dissolved during the preparation of *Knights*.[9] It seems likely enough that he belonged to a tightly knit group of professionals, that they created a standard of comic writing for the festivals, and that they all therefore knew not only the sort of thing required, but also the sort of thing they would be competing against.

The two main festivals, Lenaia and City Dionysia, were markedly different in style. The Lenaia, because of the difficulty of sea travel in January, was a domestic Athenian occasion, on a comparatively modest scale. In contrast, the City Dionysia, linked with the annual arrival of tribute from the allies, was a large-scale, formal festival attended by many non-Athenians. The balance of tragedy and comedy was very different at each festival. Two tragedians entered two plays each at the Lenaia (giving a tragedy-comedy ratio of 4:3), and three tragedians entered four plays each at the City Dionysia (giving a tragedy-comedy ratio of 12:3). Perhaps on account of the colder weather, each drama day at the Lenaia would be shorter. Certainly sitting on one day at the City Dionysia through three tragedies and one satyr-play before each comedy would make the audience's response to the comedy far different from that at the Lenaia. (The best-known modern parallel is the Oberammergau Passion-play, the audience of which exhibits, as the hours wear on, a unique mixture of devotional concentration and boisterous relaxation at the slightest humorous incident.)

If this factor – the different nature of each festival – influenced the playwright at all, it would make him write less dense, complex stories for the City Dionysia. The Lenaia was the festival for subtlety; spectacle or slapstick were a surer guarantee of success at the City Dionysia. Such a division would suit the political atmosphere too. At the Lenaia the playwright might concentrate on local politics, themes affecting Athens alone; this would be an appropriate occasion for free speech about the city, its enemies and its allies. At the City Dionysia the politics would be more general, broader and all-embracing. Finally, the different amounts of money available for each production would affect an author's style. At the City Dionysia lavish costumes, spectacular music and dancing would carry audience interest; at the less extravagant Lenaia the actual words spoken, the text itself, would be more important.

27

This balance of probabilities is supported by the evidence of those plays of Aristophanes for which a specific festival is known. Here is Dikaiopolis' famous comment on the Lenaia (*Acharnians* 502–508, in Douglass Parker's expanded translation):

> The further to ease your minds, I note in passing
> that we are, so to speak, in closed session here.
> A year ago, Kleon charged that I had slandered
> the State in the presence of strangers, by presenting my play,
> *The Babylonians*, at our Great Festival of Dionysos.
> I do not admit the truth of this charge even now,
> but I point out that it cannot apply to the present:
> This is the Lenaia – our personal, private feast –
> Athenians Only; Foreigners Please Keep Out –
> and neither troops nor tribute have yet arrived
> from our Noble Allies. The whole great harvest of Empire
> is winnowed, the chaff and straw are scattered abroad,
> and only the citizens of Athens, the fine kernels
> of grain, remain.
>   – Not to forget, of course,
> our Loyal Resident Aliens, whom, in completion
> of a metaphor, I might term the nourishing bran.
> My criticisms, then, are strictly *entre nous*.

This speech, occurring as it does in a political context (Dikaiopolis has just announced that he is going to say something 'fearful but just' on the city's affairs), shows a concentration on (often fairly obscure) local matters which is repeated in all the plays written for the Lenaia: *Acharnians* itself, *Knights*, *Wasps* and *Frogs*. The themes and undertones of *Clouds*, *Peace* and *Birds*, on the other hand, are large, general, simpler, far more appropriate to the heterogeneous audience of the City Dionysia.

The same is true of spectacle. The costumes required for *Wasps* and *Frogs* (Lenaia) would be spectacular enough, but in a different category of magnificence entirely from those of *Birds* (City Dionysia). The intimate style of the humour in Lenaian plays like *Acharnians* or *Knights* contrasts sharply with the easily comprehensible, broad theme of the Dionysian *Clouds* or the pan-Hellenic message of *Peace*. Socrates' students and Trygaios' beetle are stage ideas comprehensible by even the Greekless visitor; in contrast, the Euripides scene in *Acharnians*, the political undertones of *Knights*, or the debates in *Wasps* and *Frogs* require a level of concentration in the theatre and of background knowledge more likely to be found in the local audience of the Lenaia.

The two plays of 411 are an apparent exception to these remarks. *Lysistrata*, with an easily comprehended and pan-Hellenic message, seems more suited to the City Dionysia; *Women at the Festival* deals with purely local matters, and is full of private jokes and specialized humour more suited to the audience at the

Lenaia – chamber music rather than a symphony concert. And yet each play was exhibited at the 'wrong' festival.

There are four possible explanations. (1) The unusual fact that the same author was selected twice in the same year may have meant fitting the plays in as they came along. (2) The placing of the plays may support those scholars who say that there was, in fact, no difference in style in plays written for the two festivals: Aristophanes entered his plays indifferently for either festival, taking no thought at all for his potential audience. (3) The reason may be theatrical: the actor needed for the difficult part of Mnesilochos (see Chapter 9, pp. 133–140) may not have been allocated to Aristophanes for the Lenaia, and so *Women at the Festival* was kept back until he was available; or the success of *Lysistrata* at the Lenaia may have caused a new play, with sexual ambivalence again at its heart, to be commissioned for the later festival the same year. (4) The reasons are political: the appearance of Spartans on stage during the City Dionysia would have been unpopular with the allies, and the upheavals of 411 between oligarchs and democrats may have led Aristophanes to enter *Women at the Festival* (after *Wealth* his least political play) for the larger, more public festival.

Once again the evidence is slight and inconclusive. The most that can be said is that the two festivals did have different characteristics, and that most of the surviving plays, where they can be attributed to one festival or the other, exhibit traits in common with the apparent 'style' of their festival. Certainly it would be surprising if Aristophanes, otherwise so sensitive to the atmosphere and climate of contemporary thought, took no account whatever of the different styles and standards of the festivals where his plays were to be first performed.

Selection and finance

In order to be selected for a festival production, dramatists made application to one of the city archons: for the Lenaia to the *archon basileus*, for the City Dionysia to the more important *archon eponymos*. The *archon eponymos* was the busier of these officials. His job covered the general administration of all aspects of city life save religious ceremonies and military matters. The position was held for a year, and the archon gave his name to the year in which he held office. The *archon basileus*, in the same way, had complete oversight of all public religious ceremonies during his year of office.

It is improbable that such busy officials performed all their duties themselves. They are far more likely to have rubber-stamped decisions made by designated members of their staffs. About such minor officials we know nothing. Their very existence is a matter for conjecture, let alone such details as whether they were permanent civil servants, with expert knowledge in the fields they supervised, or not. But the balance of probability is that anyone deputed to

29

oversee dramatic selection would have at least some interest in the task, and would be *au fait* not only with the successes and failures of previous years (for the job of archon was above all a political one), but also with current trends in drama, public feeling, the gossip of the stage community, and the status of the various writers who submitted plays.

The archon's year of office began in the middle of summer. This meant that the dramatic festivals of the following spring occurred late in his year, and would therefore have considerable political importance (for example on his chances of election for a later year). The choice of poets was therefore not merely an artistic matter. Very probably the names of intending competitors would be known when the archon first took office, and the final selection was one of his first public decisions, to allow time for backers to be chosen and financial and other preparations made. A dramatist would therefore need to have at least a synopsis of his play ready some six months before the time of performance. He would deliver this – perhaps reading sample scenes to the officials – as early as possible; but he would be unlikely to complete a full draft before his leading actor and financial backer were chosen.[10]

We may imagine, then, taking *Peace* as an example, that some time in the late summer of 422 Aristophanes would inform the officials of the *archon eponymos*-elect for 422/421 that he was hoping for a Chorus at the City Dionysia of 421. He would explain the general theme of the play and its generating idea, the journey of a mortal to heaven in search of a god. Some of the central scenes in heaven were probably ready at this stage; but he would be unlikely to have taken up the officials' time by reading less vital passages in traditional style, such as the opening section or the knockabout scenes that close the play. Official interest, after all, would focus on what was novel rather than what was not. At this meeting he would also give the officials some idea of any extra costs – not many in *Peace*, compared with the extravagant demands of *Birds* or the second Chorus in *Frogs* – a factor of some importance when they came to nominate a backer.

Armed with all this knowledge, the officials would proceed to selection. Their job might be politically sensitive. In the case of *Peace*, for example, they must have been aware of the likelihood of peace (the Peace of Nikias) being ratified during their year of office, and the theme of the play may have appealed because of that. Plays like *Knights*, on the other hand, where an important and dangerous man was lampooned, must have provoked anxious and lively debate among the officials. They seem (as institutions continue to do) to have treated plays by established writers with more sympathy than those by newcomers: this may be one reason why novice playwrights often submitted their plays in someone else's name. (Although he did it regularly throughout his career, Aristophanes was most consistent in this practice at the very beginning, submitting three plays in the name of Kallistratos, and at the end, when his last two plays were submitted in the name of his son Araros, presumably to give the young man a flying start.)

Once formal approval was granted, the archon appointed a backer (the *choregos*) to carry the expense of the production. This could be heavy: in 406/405 money was so short, and expenses so great, that two backers shared the cost of each production. There were rich men who specialized in this form of public service: we hear for example (in Lysias xxi) of a man in the last years of the fifth century who underwrote eight productions in nine years. (The passage gives 3,000 drachmas as the amount required for a tragedy, and 1,600 for a comedy. To give a perspective, the price of an adult male slave at about this time varied between 150 and 300 drachmas.[11])

The success or failure of the production depended almost as much on the backer as on the author. A large-scale play like *Birds*, say, written for a major festival, could hardly have made its proper effect with the indifferent Chorusmen and second-hand costumes some backers were content to provide. It would be important to a playwright that his appointed backer was sympathetic as well as rich. The provision of special effects (like the crane in *Peace* or the twin Choruses of *Lysistrata* – both needing the expense of extra rehearsal) would be entirely at the discretion of the backer. The fact that so many surviving plays do contain special effects supports the view that it was considered a matter of pride and civic duty to provide as lavish a production as possible. It is in this context that we should read the following series of jokes against Antimachos, backer of *Acharnians* (lines 1150–1173, in Parker's version):

> A compact prayer *in re* that greediest of civil servants,
> that blubber-lipped bard of blather,
> > ANTIMACHOS, son of Spittoon:
> BLAST HIM, ZEUS! He conducted our Chorus
> > in last year's performance,
> and barred us from the post-play supper.
> > We didn't get a bite – not one!
>
> We've planned a little dinner for Antimachos.
> We'll sit down and watch him salivate,
> impatient for our subtle dish,
> a finely roasted cuttlefish
> *au gras, au jus* – and oh, so very late!
>
> We've planned a little dinner for Antimachos;
> at last we'll bring it, sizzling, sweet, and brown.
> The sight of squid will ravage him;
> he'll reach – but, by our stratagem,
> a dog will get there first and gulp it down –
> *Yes, a dog will get there first and gulp it down!*
>
> So much for his gluttony, Gentlemen;
> > now to do his lechery justice.

31

> Some night, when this boudoir cavalier
>   dismounts from the mattress for home,
> on the way we envision him, shaken
>   with ague, meeting ORESTES
> the madman, drunk, who will smash in his skull
>   with a satisfying *boom*.
>
> We've planned some entertainment for Antimachos.
> He'll venture to avenge his broken head;
> the moment that he topples prone,
> he'll fumble for a cobblestone –
> but grab a newly minted turd instead.
>
> We've planned some entertainment for Antimachos.
> He'll struggle up and give Orestes chase.
> He'll draw his deadly pellet back
> and launch his aerial attack –
> and miss, and hit KRATINOS in the face –
> *Yes, he'll miss and hit* Kratinos *in the face!*

This chapter of comic accidents is probably not meant to be taken any more seriously than a modern comedian's jokes against his agent or producer. The frequency of references to feasts for the performers (for example *Clouds* 339ff. or *Peace* 1355ff.) might indicate wishful thinking in wartime; but it may equally well show that they were a standard part of the backer's outgoings – in which case they set a standard of generosity from which the style of a whole production may be inferred.

As well as providing costumes, scenery (if any) and special effects, the backer would have the final say in matters such as the quality of the Chorus and the number of rehearsals it was allowed, the provision of musicians, and the supply of the extra, non-speaking characters with which Aristophanes' plays abound. Perhaps the very abundance of such characters is an indication of good relations between Aristophanes and his backers. Certainly, apart from *Knights* (whose dramatic style precludes extravagance in dress or hordes of extras, and which could have been produced far more cheaply than any other of his plays), the surviving comedies imply very considerable generosity on the part of the backers, a willingness in fact to provide whatever the poet might demand. Our evidence suggests that such generosity was not rare: the only criticism of a lavish backer comes late in the fourth century (in Aristotle, *Nicomachean Ethics* 1123ª 20), and concerns lack of taste rather than extravagance.

The performers

The relationship of the author to members of his acting-company is discussed in detail in Chapters 8 and 9. It will suffice here to mention a few details about the selection and training of the performers generally.

It is well established that the leading actor for a tragedy was chosen by lot, and appeared in each of the sequence of tragedies by 'his' author. There is no evidence for comic practice; but it is most likely to have followed the custom of tragedy, with the leading actor chosen by lot – the purpose of this, as in the case of all other selections by lot, being to allow the gods a part in the selection process.

Even so, it is not unlikely that the choice of outsiders, whether officials or gods, might well be 'assisted' in special cases. It would probably be hard for the archons to resist strong unofficial pressure from an influential playwright to ensure that a particular actor was allotted to him. (I am assuming that the acting styles of different comedians were distinct, and that they had obvious stage personalities which came across in their performances: see Chapter 8. If they did not, then of course the result of the lots would be a matter of indifference to poet and officials alike.) There cannot have been many more great comic actors than there were 'professional' authors. If their styles were distinct, then Aristophanes had two choices. He could either write a part with a particular actor in mind, and then exert pressure to have that actor allocated to him; or he could wait to complete his play until he knew which actor was available. Neither practice accords ill with the known methods of selection; neither is detrimental to the final quality of a play.

The second, third and subsequent actors were probably not chosen by lot, but were appointed by playwright, backer and leading actor working together. Though the backer had no financial stake in the actors (who were paid by the state), his investment in the production as a whole would tend to make him concerned that suitable men were chosen. There is some evidence[12] that in the fourth century the orator Aeschines began his career by hiring himself out as a freelance third actor, though this was for revivals at the Rural Dionysia, not the major city festivals. Possibly each leading actor had a pool of actors out of which he could form a 'company' – some of them possibly full-time professionals, touring in the summer months when no Athenian performances were being given, or taking part in the private recitations and other performances that were a feature of at any rate aristocratic relaxation. (On the professional status of actors, see Chapter 8.) Such a company of actors would include musicians as well. The flautist Chairis, for example, appears in several of Aristophanes' plays, and is mentioned by name and joked about as if he was a figure familiar to acting-company and audience alike (for example *Acharnians* 16, *Peace* 951, *Birds* 857).

The job of auditioning and selecting a Chorus was the responsibility of the backer. Once again we should imagine him working in sympathy with the author, and possibly with the leading actor as well. At about this stage, as the performers were first brought together, the preparation of the play ceased to concern public officials and became the sole responsibility of author, backer and leading actor. As the character of the company became apparent, the playwright would be able to give his play a more definite shape, leaving little for later addition except the felicities discovered in rehearsal (a fruitful part of any stage comedy), and topical allusions which would need to be left until as near the performance as possible.

Thus, in the late autumn and early winter months, preparations would be going on in two areas at once. The backer, helped by flautist and Chorus-trainer (who might be the author himself), would begin training the Chorus. For this a complete script of all the choral sections would be essential. The leading actor would begin to rehearse with his assistants (except for such 'extras' as would only appear briefly, and who would not be required for rehearsal until the play moved into the theatre itself). For this work a full outline of the script and a large proportion of finished dialogue would be required – though (because fewer people, and individual actors rather than groups, were involved) there was more room to cut, adapt and add than in the choral sections.

Throughout this period the author must have divided his time between both groups, writing, rewriting, adapting and encouraging. If the theory[13] that Aristophanes played the leading role in some of his early plays is correct, then his efforts at this stage in trying to keep the whole production in order must have been herculean. (He must also have been allotted to his own plays as leading actor, a matter which could certainly not have been left to the sole discretion of the gods.)

At some date not too far from the start of the festival, the performers must have had access to the theatre for rehearsals. At this point – which need not have been until two or three weeks before the production – stage machinery, extras, props and costumes would be brought in, and the whole play 'run through' in its proper setting. If modern stage practice is any guide, this was a crucial period, and probably resulted in a fair amount of alteration and adaptation. (Two factors contributing to alteration would be such knowledge as the company had gleaned about the other comedies entered for the festival, and the possible visit of one or more of the archon's officials. Neither is reported in our evidence, but both seem likely.)

The final script (possibly only existing in the actors' memories, not fully written down) would now be fixed, to remain largely unchanged until after the performance, when it might be revised and published, taken on tour by the actors, shelved and later revived, or – like *Clouds* – rewritten for revival but not produced.

Judges and audience

While preparing his play, a comic poet must constantly have had at the back of his mind the fact of competition, and the need to please the audience and impress the judges. To an extent this would restrict his options. He would know what had been successful and unsuccessful in previous years, and the sort of play expected from him personally, based on his previous work. He would need either to conform to this expectation or to depart from it in a significant and admirably daring way.

There has been long and fierce controversy over the composition of festival audiences.[14] The balance of probability is that most spectators were male, of all ages; they were mainly free citizens, with a scattering of slaves. The fourth-century theatre held between 14,000 and 17,000 spectators, and it is likely that the fifth-century audience was roughly of this size too. At the City Dionysia the large number of visitors from abroad would swell the crowd to a size greater than that at the Lenaia. In years of plague or intense military effort the audience would naturally have been smaller (possibly smaller 'houses' were another reason, apart from lack of money, for reducing the number of festival days during so much of the war). The presence of outsiders at the City Dionysia, or the absence at war of many of the city's menfolk, would be factors to be borne in mind by the playwright. (A good example is the joke in *Clouds* 323ff., where Socrates invites Strepsiades to 'look towards Parnes' to see the Clouds. Every Athenian would know that the Acropolis was in the way, and so would every visitor – after the joke. The summons to 'everyone in Greece' to help rescue Peace in *Peace* 292ff., and the ensuing scene, gain great force with an audience of diverse nationality. Similarly, scenes like Dikaiopolis' confrontation with the venal and extravagant peace envoy (*Acharnians* 65ff.) gain tremendously in effect if an immediate contrast is possible with the audience's experience of actual war conditions.)

The choice of the judges, and the method by which they reached a decision, show a desire both to ensure impartiality and to allow the gods a place in the deliberations. The names of those men proposed as judges by each of the ten tribes were sifted in advance (by a committee of the council, including the backers for that year); a pool of possible names was drawn up, and placed in ten sealed jars, which were kept under guard until the contest. At the start of the contest the jars were opened, and the archon selected one name from each jar. Thus, the chances of any one backer's nominee being finally chosen were small, and the gods were permitted to 'guide' a random choice at both initial and final selection.

At the end of the festival each of the ten judges wrote an order of merit on a tablet, and placed it in another jar. From this jar the archon chose five tablets at random, and those five decided the result. Thus, again, a random element was introduced. It would be numerically possible, for example, to win by a majority of the ten judges, and still lose because the right five tablets were not chosen from the jar. We have no information on what happened if the five tablets chosen did not give a conclusive result.

35

The judges seem to have had no special expertise – and in fact the less they possessed, the more impartial their decision would be. They must have been aware of the feelings both of the crowd and of influential supporters of one poet or another. Between the opening of the festival and the final verdict there was plenty of time for bribery or coercion, however carefully the judges were protected. It seems unlikely that they would vote in the teeth of audience opinion; apparently, however, this did happen, strikingly so in the case of *Clouds*, where the spectators demanded a first prize and the judges awarded a third prize.[15] The fact that the personal choice of each judge could be discovered afterwards by an examination of the tablets must have increased the likelihood of corruption. It is however notable that (except in the case of Euripides) the decisions of the fifth-century judges are very often in line with later critical opinion, and those abuses of the system which resulted in court cases are mainly later than the fifth century, and belong to a period of revivals rather than original plays.

The decision of judges and spectators alike would be considerably affected by the position of each play during the festival. The effect of a comedy in particular would depend very much on the tone of the other plays performed that day. Seeing *Birds* (for example) after the *Oresteia* (for example) would be a different experience from seeing it after *Philoctetes* or *Alcestis*. To be the first or last performed comic author in the festival might be an advantage or a disadvantage, depending on the mood of the crowd and the nature of the other competing plays. (We may wonder, for example, what the effect on the reception of *Clouds* was of having two other comedies about the Socratic circle performed at the same festival.) It is not known how plays were allocated to days. But the planning and layout of a day at the City Dionysia in particular (where five plays would be seen one after another) are unlikely to have been left entirely to chance. In this matter too the effects of an influential lobby for one author or another would almost certainly be felt, whether the decision was taken by the archon's officials *in camera* or in public committee open to the solicitations of all interested parties.

Practical matters like these apart, the poet would still have to consider carefully what he was going to offer a large crowd on an important religious and ceremonial occasion. Aristophanes' protestations about his own originality, his political wisdom, and his avoidance of low burlesque and slapstick are one thing; the evidence of the plays themselves, and the prizes they won, is sometimes another. *Clouds*, for example (which must have seemed well in tune with contemporary public attitudes to sophism), was markedly less successful than Aristophanes expected; at other times, if a first prize is a sufficient indication, he caught the public mood exactly (for example in the parabasis of *Frogs* or – more unexpectedly – with the baiting of Kleon in *Knights*).

It is impossible to say exactly what qualities in a play appealed to or repelled an audience. The parabasis of *Frogs* (lines 675–737), for example, which is often cited as the reason for its success, occurs nearly an hour before the end of the play, certainly long enough for the immediate effect of its political acuteness to have been blunted by what followed; we should perhaps wonder if some parts of the poetic contest were not equally well liked. The general theme of *Peace*, the expression of happiness in rural surroundings and the harmony between man and nature, may not have been obvious or effective enough to carry the play through the second half, which perhaps seemed to its first audience as routine and uninspired as it does to some critics today.

Certain themes do, however, stand out from the plays, and may show what did succeed with most audiences. Frequency of repetition is a good guide: no ambitious playwright would go on for years writing material which his public totally disliked. Predictably slapstick, bawdy and the lampooning of notorious individuals like Kleonymos or Theoros come first; a marked vein of surrealist fantasy runs through all the plays; less predictably successful – but no less common, and therefore presumably what the audience wanted – are political caricature (often extremely subtle) and tragic parody, both of which need an audience of some sophistication. Two elements central to Aristophanes' comedy, at whose total effect we can only guess today, are the deep religious feeling apparent in even the smallest sections of the plays, and the lyricism, music and spectacle of which our texts offer only a tantalizing glimpse. The Aristophanic mixture is unique, and the juxtaposition of themes and styles can seem surprising to us. But the facts that it is much the same in all the surviving plays, and that Aristophanes was anything but unsuccessful as a public playwright, indicate that, to a large extent at least, he understood exactly what he had to provide, if he was to fulfil the differing requirements of each of the groups who came into contact with his work as it proceeded from conception to performance.

3
The Theatre of Dionysos

'Blocking'

Before a director can 'block' a play (that is, work out the movements and disposition of the actors about the stage), he needs precise knowledge of the size and shape of the stage, its entrances, its advantages and its drawbacks. In the same way, a playwright writing for a specific theatre (as Aristophanes did) will 'block' the action as he writes, taking account of the opportunities and restrictions the building possesses. This is most important for a writer of comedy, where physical action is usually a vital part of the conception, and where the fact of performance itself is often treated in a precise, ironical way (see pp. 79ff.), something rare indeed in tragedy. Both of these essential elements are latent in the scripts as we have them today, and in order to discover them we, the readers, must ourselves 'block' the plays as we read. To do this, we need as clear a picture as possible of the dimensions and layout of the theatre for which they were written.

No other subject in the study of Greek drama arouses more controversy. The problems arise chiefly because in the fourth century there were radical alterations in production practice, and the design of existing theatres was modified to suit them. Thus, the extant remains (often in any case further altered or crumbled by time) are at best misleading evidence for fifth-century theatre practice. Many of the problems have been satisfactorily solved; but on a number of vital issues (including the height of the stage above the theatre floor, the size and shape of the stage buildings, and the nature of the revolve) there is deep and continuing scholarly disagreement. For those who wish to explore these choppy waters, excellent guides exist;[16] the brief outline that follows is aimed solely at assisting the reader in the 'blocking' process described above.

The theatre

It is likely that all Aristophanes' plays were written for performance in the Theatre of Dionysos at the foot of the Acropolis. There was some kind of performing area on this site from early times; in Aristophanes' boyhood, under Pericles, extensive improvements were begun, and the building work may well have been continued during the Peace of Nikias (421–416), and completed between 410 and 404, a period when other substantial buildings on and around the Acropolis (for example the Erechtheum) were also finished.

Although there are substantial and important differences in detail, the Romanized remains that visitors see today preserve something at least of the original theatre: the main acting area (the *orchestra* or dancing-circle, which was a complete circle in Aristophanes' time), the *parodoi* or walkways which led into it, and the layout of the audience seats. Above all, the size and openness of the theatre remain unchanged – and make a striking contrast with the closed, formal design of later theatres like the nearby Theatre of Herodes Atticus.

The plan in Figure 1[17] shows a possible reconstruction of the theatre in Aristophanes' time. The heart of the building was the dancing-circle (*orchestra*), of hard packed earth inside a circle of squared stone, and 60 feet in diameter. This was the principal acting area, used always by the Chorus and often by the actors. A low altar (perhaps 3 or 4 feet high) stood in the centre. The dancing-circle was approached by two walkways (*parodoi*), wide entrance paths which gave access not only to spectators, but also to Chorus and sometimes actors during the performance – indeed, the first entry of the Chorus-men, marching or dancing along the walkways into the dancing-circle, was a spectacular feature of many Greek plays.

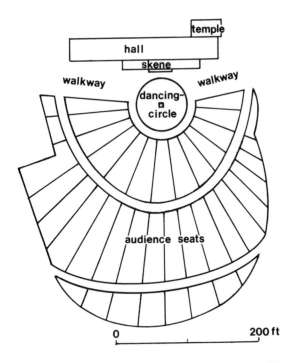

Figure 1. Plan of the Aristophanic Theatre of Dionysos and ancillary buildings, looking down from the Acropolis.

39

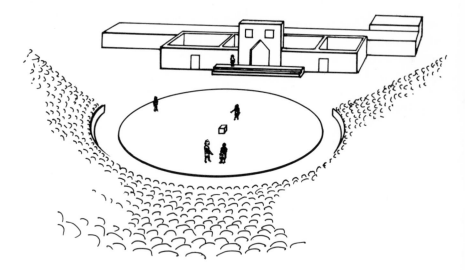

Figure 2. Spectator's-eye view of the Theatre of Dionysos and ancillary buildings.

Looking down on the dancing-circle were tiers of audience seats. These were probably solidly made (of wood), and were raised up partly on the natural slope of the hill and partly on terraces of earth and rubble contained by supporting walls. In Aristophanes' time these seats covered a vastly greater area than do the extant remains: they held upwards of 14,000 spectators, and we should envisage an audience area stretching back up the hill right to the foot of the Acropolis wall itself. (The theatre at Epidaurus, though slightly larger, gives some idea of the huge area required.)

Across the dancing-circle, facing the spectators, was the wooden *skene* or stage building (for details, see below). Behind this was a long hall. Its wall on the theatre side was blank; on the other side it was open, perhaps for use as a colonnade in wet or hot weather. One end of the hall was divided off into a separate room. This connected with a small temple of Dionysos, and may have been a room used by the archon and his staff, a vestry for priests, or a storeroom for religious or theatrical paraphernalia. The floor of both hall and temple was approximately 8 feet below the level of the main theatre floor (owing partly to the natural slope of the hillside, partly to building work). It is not known how high the hall and temple were. Thus, although they were part of the theatre complex and were visible to the theatre audience, neither hall nor temple were part of the actual theatre itself.

Thus, from the centre front seats of the auditorium, a spectator would look across the 60-foot dancing-circle (with an altar in the middle) to an acting area incorporating the circle itself and the ends of the walkways, and backed by a wooden *skene* perhaps 12 feet high. (The *skene* would partially screen from view the hall, temple of Dionysos and visitors to the shrine beyond.) To left and right his view would meet the spectators, rising in tiered rows until the retaining wall cut off all view of the ends of the walkways leading out of the theatre. (Preparations to enter from these walkways could in fact be made out of sight of all spectators except those highest up on the opposite side.)

A spectator on the centre back row would have an elongated version of the same view. He would be no less than 300 feet from the front of the *skene*, and his added height would give him a clear view of the roof of the *skene*, and possibly the hall and ground level beyond. Acoustics apart – and there is no reason to suppose them any less clear than in later Greek theatres – the seats at the back must have been far less coveted than those at the front. Webster, *GTP**, p. 4, for example, calculates that an actor 6 feet tall would look 3½ inches high to a spectator at the front (as compared with 5 inches from the dress-circle in a large modern theatre), but only ¾ of an inch high to a spectator at the back.

The acting area visible to all spectators would include the dancing-circle, the whole area at ground level in front of the *skene*, and about 20 feet of the walkway at each side. In this area a Chorus of twenty-four, plus actors and extras, was accommodated. There are surprisingly few problems of visibility. Even if the members of the Chorus were standing up, the fact that the vast majority of spectators were looking *down* at the performance would mean that the actors were not seriously hidden from view. (In modern productions in Athens and Epidaurus the Chorus-men separate, and move into inconspicuous groups during the non-choral portions of the plays; sometimes they even crouch down or kneel. There is no reason to suppose that fifth-century practice was radically different. Even in modern theatre-in-the-round, visibility is seldom a problem.)

The skene

Position. Between the edge of the dancing-circle and the back wall of the hall there was a rectangle of ground 19 feet wide and over 200 feet long. This ground was on the same level as the dancing-circle, that is, 8 feet above the floor level of the hall behind. Because of this difference in height the wall of the hall was probably not high enough to provide an adequate backdrop for the actors or to prevent the audience being distracted by people moving about in the shrine area on the other side of the hall. It seems likely, therefore, that some kind of structure was put up to act as a screen, to form a backdrop for the actors, and to hide the operators of stage machinery from the audience. This structure was the *skene*, and the question to be answered is, what was it like?[18]

It seems that there was access to the acting area from the hall below: a flight of steps leading up to a wide doorway in the centre of the wall of the hall. This

*Full details of books referred to in the text by their initials will be found in the bibliography on pp. 177–178.

41

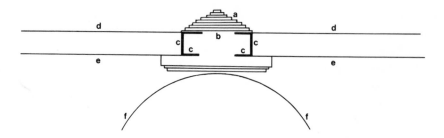

Figure 3. Plan of the skene. **a** = *steps down to hall;* **b** = *doorway;* **c** = *stone foundations supporting wooden building;* **d** = *hall wall;* **e** = *wicker wall of skene;* **f** = *edge of dancing-circle.*

doorway was in the central, focal point of the entire acting area, from the audience's point of view. It is here, around and in front of the doorway, that the *skene* was built. (For a suggested plan, see Figure 3.)

The only archaeological evidence about the *skene* lies just in front of the probable site of this doorway. It is a rectangular stone foundation 26 feet long and 9 feet wide, with slots set into it, possibly for wooden floor beams. Apart from that, there is no surviving evidence of any kind at all, except for the meaning of the word *skene* itself: a tent or booth, a temporary building with walls of wickerwork or cloth.[19]

Length. The archaeological evidence suggests that, at the very least, a wooden structure of some kind was built up round the doorway and steps from the floor level of the dancing-circle down to the floor level of the hall, and that it was at least 9 feet wide and 26 feet long. But it must have been much longer than this, for a variety of theatrical reasons. A 'building' only 26 feet long, however imposingly constructed, would look extremely short from most parts of the auditorium; the actors would have no backdrop save the (possibly low) wall of the hall for at least 50 feet on either side of it; people moving about on the other side of the hall would not be completely screened off; acoustics might well be unsatisfactory, with nothing behind the actors to throw their voices forwards; the whole structure would be out of proportion with the size of the dancing-circle, thus diminishing the actors' stature whenever they moved towards it, and making such scenes as the choral attacks in *Acharnians* and *Birds* look ludicrous. Considerations such as these have led scholars to assume a much larger structure, anything up to 105 feet long (that is, extending for about 50 feet on either side of the central doorway).

Width and floor height. As has been said, the width of this structure need have been no greater than the 9 feet of the stone foundation; equally, it cannot have been greater than the 19 feet between the dancing-circle and the edge of the hall. Most authorities allow it about 12 feet. The acting area in front of the central doorway was probably slightly raised, with one or two steps leading up to it:[20] the palace doorway required in so many tragedies would thus be more imposing, and the actors would have another performing level apart from that of the walkways and dancing-circle.

Construction. It seems unlikely that a building 105 feet long by 12 feet wide was of solid wood, roofed in, throughout its length. (Other considerations apart, the shortage of wood caused by war would preclude this for much of our period.) It would be sufficient for only the central section, the 'house' on stone foundations, to be a solid, roofed structure. The rest could well have been genuine *skene*, that is wickerwork or cloth over a wooden frame, like modern theatre flats today.

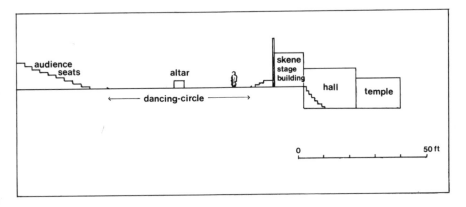

Figure 4. Side elevation of theatre buildings and acting areas.

Roof. Many extant plays, both tragedies and comedies, require an upper level, a 'roof' on which one or more characters can sit or stand. (The Watchman in *Agamemnon* 1ff. and Dikaiopolis' wife in *Acharnians* 262ff. are examples of characters who stay still; the ending of *Clouds* requires at least one character to move about on the roof of Socrates' Blaboratory.) If no part of the stage building had been roofed, an upper level would have had to be built especially for such characters – they could not have stood still on the crane, which is associated with movement from side to side. It is much easier to say that there was probably a flat or gently pitched roof on the stage house itself, covering at least the stone-founded centre section built over the main doorway.

Doorways. If the mid-section of the *skene* was a kind of roofed 'house', more solidly constructed than the rest, then the main doorway would be made as strong and decorated as elaborately as the play demanded. An entrance doorway is a standard requirement in almost every extant play; this suggests that it could have been a permanent feature of the *skene*, which could be disguised or adapted by painted scenery, but not ignored entirely. These entrances had to be strong enough to put up with a considerable amount of knocking and kicking in comedy, and wide enough to show tableaux in tragedy.

43

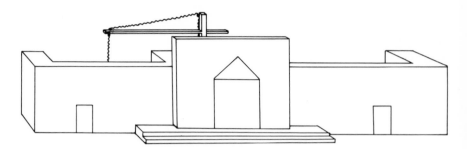

Figure 5. Possible reconstruction of the skene.[21] *The drawing also shows a possible siting of the crane (see pp. 46–48).*

In Aristophanes a single opening of this kind – whether it represents house door, cave, or the Propylaea of the Acropolis – is sufficient for six plays (*Knights, Wasps, Peace, Birds, Lysistrata* and *Wealth*). Three plays (*Clouds, Women at the Festival* and *Assemblywomen*) require two doorways, and two plays (*Acharnians* and *Frogs*) require three. It seems likely that the central, permanent doorway was used as the main house door in each of the plays, and that second and third doors were put up as needed, in the form of small booths, of openings in the *skene*, or of simple door flats like those used in the modern theatre. Such an arrangement preserves the symmetry of the *skene*, and also makes it possible for each of the five plays performed on any given festival day to use different scenery from the others – an obvious advantage in comedy, where more scenery (and especially more doors) might well be needed than in tragedy.

Summary. Although the archaeological evidence is slight, other factors suggest that the *skene* was a structure just over 100 feet long and (in part) about 12 feet wide. The central section at least was of solid wood; the rest may have been wickerwork or cloth over a wooden frame. The central section was probably roofed in, strongly enough to take the weight of one or more actors. If the *skene* as a whole is thought of as a kind of screen or wall, this central section was more like a one-roomed house, at least 22 feet long by 9 feet wide. The central doorway was wide, and may have had a low dais in front of it, with a few steps leading up to it. Other entrances could be provided as required, in a less permanent form. Scenery (perhaps in the form of painted screens) could be placed in front of the *skene*. The whole structure was large and high enough to provide a visual and acoustic background for both actors and Chorus, and solid enough in the centre to make possible the use of stage machinery. Although no certainty is possible, Figure 5 gives an idea of what such a structure may have been like.

Machinery

It is apparent from the texts that two special effects requiring machinery were used by Aristophanes. A crane was certainly available, and was used to swing at least one actor, and possibly more, out from the *skene* across the front of the dancing-circle. Less certain is the nature and even the existence of the revolve, or *ekkuklema*, which enabled interior scenes to be revealed.

The theories for the revolve are three. (1) It was a section of the front of the *skene* which could be revolved on its axis, revealing on a platform whatever had occurred 'inside'. (This kind of structure would particularly suit such scenes as the revelation of Eurydice's corpse in *Antigone* 1293ff.). (2) It was a simple sofa on wheels, which could be rolled out of the doors of the *skene*, with one or more characters on it. (This version would suit such scenes as the appearance of Euripides in *Achamians* 407ff., on which see below.) (3) It was a larger platform on wheels, which could be rolled out through the doors of the *skene*. (This would suit appearances involving more than one character, such as Ajax and the slaughtered sheep (*Ajax* 346ff.) or the disciples of Socrates in *Clouds* 183ff., on which see below.)

The details of the revolve scene in *Achamians* 407ff. are almost exactly duplicated in *Women at the Festival* 95ff. In both plays a visit is paid to a tragic dramatist, who is engrossed in composition. In *Achamians* Euripides says, 'All right, I'll have myself rolled out; I've no time to come down' (409), and in *Women at the Festival* the following dialogue takes place (95–96):

EURIPIDES: Shh!
MNESILOCHOS: What is it?
EURIPIDES: Agathon's coming out.
MNESILOCHOS: Agathon? How d'you mean?
EURIPIDES: Here: they're just rolling him out.

At the end of their appearances both poets have themselves wheeled back. Euripides says, 'Close the bulwarks of the house' (*Achamians* 479), and Agathon says, 'Someone roll me in right away' (*Women at the Festival* 265); in both cases the instruction is given to a single person.

Neither of these scenes requires a large platform: in fact a sofa, or table and chair, would be more appropriate. Agathon is accompanied in song by a Chorus, but its members could have remained unseen; Euripides is surrounded by a pile of ragged costumes, but this hardly requires much space. In both scenes at least one slave is in attendance. The references to height in the Euripides scene ('I haven't time to come down', 409, and 'You write raised up', 410) can refer either to some extravagant body position (as a modern civil servant might be portrayed in comedy with his feet on the desk), or may have sexual overtones.[22] If a sofa, or a platform with a table and chair on it, were not employed, it would be possible to show the scenes by removing screens (in

45

which case Agathon's Chorus might appear with him). However, that explanation makes the use of the first and second persons of the verb *ekkuklein* difficult to explain: 'I'll be rolled out'; 'have yourself rolled out'. A piece of furniture on wheels seems the most likely explanation.

The appearance on the revolve of a larger number of characters is not affected by grammar: in *Clouds* 183 (immediately preceding the unveiling of Socrates' students) the verb is not *ekkuklein* but *anoignunai*, 'to open'.[23] The exact nature of a wheeled platform large enough to hold half a dozen people in ludicrous attitudes (as postulated by Webster, *GTP*, p. 9) is difficult to imagine. We need to ask how large it was (at least 10 feet by 6 feet, according to Webster), how stable it was, and how it was manoeuvred. It is open to question, too, whether the use of such a revolve in *Clouds* would detract from or enhance the appearance of Socrates on another machine only 40 lines later (218). It seems more likely here that the students were hidden by screens, which were rolled away at line 183,[24] and that they made their exit either when the Student ordered them to go (195) or when Strepsiades threatened them with sexual violence (197). The scenery at the beginning of *Clouds* would look bizarre enough to the audience: it represents not only Strepsiades' house with its Herm, but also another large doorway with a large earthenware pot (*dinos*) outside it. The further bizarrerie of having that door – the one before the central entrance of the *skene* – several feet further forward than usual, in the form of one or more wheeled screens, would add to rather than detract from the incongruity and would intrigue the audience in a way characteristic of the opening scenery of Aristophanes' plays (cf. *Acharnians*, *Wasps*, *Peace*, *Birds* and *Lysistrata*, all of which present variations on the standard single door setting).

Other instances in Aristophanes where the revolve may have been used are less conclusive. They are *Knights* 1389 (the appearance of the Spondai), *Birds* 666 (the appearance of the nightingale) and *Lysistrata* 1114 (the appearance of Reconciliation). In each case a revolve of type (1) above (rotating scenery) would be most effective. But the verbs used in *Knights* and *Birds* ('come out'), and the line in *Lysistrata* ('Where's Reconciliation?') lack the tone of preparation and build-up to the revolve appearances in *Acharnians* and *Women at the Festival* quoted above, and it seems wishful thinking on the part of commentators that these scenes should have made use of it. The references in *Acharnians*, *Clouds* and *Women at the Festival*, on the other hand, seem definitely to indicate that some sort of machine was used, either movable screens (possibly on wheels) or wheeled furniture. It is possible that both methods were available. But the infrequency of its use (and the shortness of its appearance even in plays where it does occur) suggests that whatever it was, the revolve was a cumbersome and inelegant device, offering the playwright none of the possibilities of variation and comic exploitation inherent in other effects, such as the crane.[25]

The crane has a less problematical and better attested existence. Its use dates back to Aeschylus, and it is likely that the Periclean reconstruction of the Theatre of Dionysos included a strengthening of the mechanism (perhaps anchoring it in some way to the stone foundations of the stage house). The crane was a wooden beam, probably pivoted in the centre, and with a counterweight behind the *skene*. It projected out in front of the *skene* – for reasons of weight and manoeuvrability, probably not more than a few feet – and could be swung laterally across the edge of the dancing-circle. A machine of considerable size is indicated. Uses of the crane such as for Medea's appearance in *Medea* 1317ff. (the chariot of the Sun) suggest that it could swing high up, and perhaps round and over the *skene*, out of sight of the audience. Its uses in Aristophanes require it also to touch the floor at the level of the dancing-circle, and perhaps to pick characters up from the central door of the *skene*. The actors wore a harness, which was attached to the end of the crane by a hook.

The crane seems to have been widely used by Euripides. This is certainly the inference from the parodies in Aristophanes, where its use is associated with his name in every case but that of Socrates' sling in *Clouds*.[26] It is used in Aristophanes either to 'fly' single actors (for example Iris in *Birds* 1199ff., a passage which may parody Iris' appearance in Euripides' *The Madness of Herakles*, produced about four years earlier), or to lift complicated contrivances like Socrates' sling in *Clouds* or Trygaios' dung-beetle in *Peace*. The rescue scenes in *Women at the Festival* almost certainly used the crane as well, particularly the scene parodying Euripides' *Andromeda* (*Women at the Festival* 1001ff.). If the frog-Chorus in *Frogs* leapt up to full height, it is even possible that Charon's boat was swung across the dancing-circle on the end of the crane, rather than wheeled (or carried by the actors) at ground level.

There is a hint of ricketiness and unpredictability about the crane in Aristophanes. Only Socrates appears to move slowly and with ease – and all he has to do is drop gently from mid-air to the ground. The entrance of Iris in *Birds* 1199ff. is clearly as comic and flustered as possible: Peisetairos' words could be extended ad lib to cover any amount of comic business, stressing the awkwardness of the mechanism:

PEISETAIROS: Hey, you, where are you flying? Where next? Eh?
Keep still . . . stop fluttering . . . stay there . . . slow down, can't you?

In the same way, Euripides' rescue flight in *Women at the Festival* 1009ff. would gain greatly in effect if it was as clumsy in operation as it was misconceived in intention:

MNESILOCHOS: Aha! Gods! Saviour Zeus! My hopes are high:
The man will not forsake me: lo! a sign
Vouchsafed by Perseus as he hurried by –
I must be Andromeda. I've got the chains
Already. Now it's clear: he's on his way
To rescue me: he didn't just fly by.

47

The impression here is of an impassioned overflight by Euripides, with suitable gestures to prepare Mnesilochos for his second entrance at ground level, as Perseus (1016). As well as indicating to the audience which tragedy was about to be parodied, the passage offers the actors the opportunity for some splendid knockabout involving the crane.

The crane and its operator reach their greatest comic heights during the flight of the beetle in *Peace*. Trygaios first appears, on the beetle but not flying high, at 82. Even there he is having trouble controlling the beast ('Gently, gently, calmly, my beetle', 82). He keeps it in order for most of the ensuing Euripides parody (save for a lunge at the slave in 110), and finally takes off on his epic flight at 154. The flight itself lasts for 22 lines of the text as we have it (anything up to 2 minutes). The lines are general, and exclusively to do with the flight. They are also of the sort that any actor of ability can improvise at will, to cover and encourage audience reaction. The likelihood is that this flight (although actually only from one part of the stage, in an arc, across to another) was a *tour de force* of comic business, and that the actor playing Trygaios was allowed to cut, adapt or add lines, depending on the way the mechanism functioned, and on the comic inspiration of the moment. Fixed 'cues' are provided at each end of the flight ('Farewell', 149, and 'But this is Zeus' place, methinks', 177); in between, the text is a brilliant – and easily adaptable – farrago of comic nonsense. Possibly the length of the flight is intended (like Dionysos' voyage in *Frogs*) to symbolize the great distance from one world to another. But very likely much of the business is put in simply for its own sake. (The passage is quoted in full on pp. 85–86.)

Conclusion

So far from being a crude and primitive stage in the development of theatre building, the Theatre of Dionysos in the late fifth century was a remarkably functional building, excellently designed for the job of presenting plays to a mass audience at a religious festival. The buildings themselves were plain; it was left to the performers to provide colour and spectacle. In particular, the theatre layout was ideally suited for a drama centred on mass choral effects; even in the fourth century, when the actors began to retreat from the dancing-circle towards the *skene*, the contrast between them and the Chorus (fundamental to the structure of the plays themselves) was retained, even heightened.

Whereas tragedy achieved its effects with language, or with *coups de théâtre* like those of Aeschylus (the stirring of the Eumenides, or the moment when Prometheus' statue actually spoke), comedy set against the formal, fairly static Chorus a type of action that was fast and busy, full of running and falling, 'gags' and slapstick routines. Even where language dominates (as in the second half of *Frogs*) visual effects still make an instant, hilarious impression (the scales;

Euripides' Muse; the drum; the wrestling parodies). A multitude of 'hand props' and an ingenious use of traditional routines combine to produce an effect which is (unlike that for the reader in the study today) comic before it is political, farcical before it is satirical, perhaps even slapstick before it is subtle. Everything rests on the abilities and practical skills of the actors; the stage setting is left bare and simple to allow them the greatest possible flexibility in performance.

4
The Role of Tradition

As well as the circumstances within which he worked, an Athenian dramatist
would have had to take notice of the earlier traditions of his art. All creative
artists are affected, consciously or unconsciously, by what has gone before,
whether they follow received tradition or alter and extend it to suit their own
requirements.

The origins of Attic comedy are very obscure indeed. In particular, it is
impossible to say with any certainty when a literary shape was first imposed on
the heterogeneous mass of non-literary comic formulae inherited from earliest
times. The problems are further increased by the lack of evidence, whether
anthropological or literary. Hence (as in the previous chapter) it seems best to
eschew controversy[27] and concentrate on matters directly relevant to, and
apparent in, the work of Aristophanes himself.

Dramatic form

The unique form of Old Comedy is the result of an amalgamation of a number
of traditional structures. It used to be thought that Aristophanes was confined,
and his work even vitiated, by the need to conform to a tight inherited structure.
That this theory is nonsense can be seen at once simply by comparing the plays
with one another. None of them is uninfluenced by traditional structures; but in
each case the structures used are chosen to suit the needs of the particular play,
and where total adherence to any given formula would be artistically undesir-
able, the structure is always modified to suit the play, never the other way
round. The most striking example of this is *Frogs*, where the traditional
argument (the *agon*) is placed after rather than before the parabasis. This gives
the scenes that follow (1099–1499) a markedly agonistic character, quite
different from the usual sequence of knockabout scenes that ends a play. The
knockabout scenes are brilliantly adapted into (1) the early dialogues with the
Corpse and Charon, and (2) the various arrivals and departures before
Dionysos and Xanthias are finally admitted to the Underworld (460–673).

Underlying each of Aristophanes' plots is a loose basic shape, which can be
described simply as *problem stated – solution sought – rejoicing*. Usually the problem

has serious rather than comic overtones, the solution is unexpected, often surreal, and the rejoicing is earthy and simple, a reaffirmation of the simple human pleasures which the problem has been hampering.

This basic plot shape is overlaid by another traditional element, again tripartite. Three formal structures, of a complex and patterned metrical construction, appear in whole or in part in most of the plays.[28] They are: (1) *The Choral Entry*. The entrance of the Chorus, though performed in formal metres, is usually flustered, angry or bewildered. It is preceded by a scene of preparation, and often presents in a visual and audible form the effects of the problem underlying the whole action of the play. (2) *The Argument*. This again is in metres not used for 'ordinary' comic scenes. There is metrical response, and often the formal structuring is some of the most rigid in the play. The argument is between hero and Chorus, or opposing halves of the same Chorus, or two allegorical champions speaking for one side or the other. (3) *The Parabasis*. In this the Chorus-men make a direct address to the audience, either in their stage characters, or speaking as comic actors, or speaking on behalf of Aristophanes himself.[29] Metrical response and tight formal organization characterize this section in the same way as they do the argument.

Reading the plays today, we can find it hard to appreciate the full force of these three structures. Indeed, in hastier modern productions they are the first sections to be cut. In the Athenian theatre they must have stood out from the rest of the play in a very marked manner: they involved more people; they used music and varied rhythm; they provided the opportunity for lavish spectacle in such matters as costume, musical accompaniment and the use of balletic movement. In plays where traditional structures are used in full, they can occupy over half the total performance time.

Other elements derived from traditional sources are smaller in scale and of less importance. Most of them are survivals from a non-literary heritage, and are inserted in the plays in a loose way, sometimes with little relevance to the plot. They must have provided the audience with comfortable resting points, or a feeling of satisfaction as each appeared, as though ticked off on a list of the elements usual at festivals. (This impression is also gained from the way some of these passages seem to be inserted willy-nilly into the surviving texts.) They are always short, and seldom developed beyond the needs of the moment in which they appear. The most obvious examples are the feasts, sacrifices and prayers with which the plays abound. *Peace* offers excellent examples. The beetle's feast at the start is paralleled by the preparation for the wedding feast at the end; there is a sacrifice, expanded into the lively Hierokles scene; prayers range from the lyrical invocation of Peace in 974–1016 to the partly ludicrous apostrophe of the Comic Muse in 774–816.

In the same way, hymns and other lyrical interludes are introduced, often with only slight plot justification, but clearly serving an important function in performance. Tereus' invocation of the nightingale (*Birds* 209–222) is typical. It is unnecessary for the plot (the nightingale could be brought onstage without it), but – apart from being beautiful in its own right, one of the finest of Aristophanes' lyrics – it has an important part to play in establishing the magic, timeless atmosphere which pervades the whole play. A similar passage, though rather longer, is the Chorus of Initiates in *Frogs* 372–416 and 449–459. Its purpose is to establish a particular atmosphere, a dimension (like that in *Birds*) totally removed from everyday mortal experience; apart from that, it has no part in the direct advancement of the plot. In fact, passages of this type are generally used to establish mood[30] – obviously as important a function in the effect of the whole play as the monologues, dialogues and slapstick which directly propel the comic action. The fact that passages which could be sung independently as hymns are so integral to a play's effect shows Aristophanes' subtlety in using even the least dramatic of traditional structures.

An interesting survival from the non-literary tradition lies in the numerous short interludes which lampoon known individuals, picking on eccentric character traits and demolishing by ridicule, rather in the manner of Archilochos. In Aristophanes such passages are often very short, and the characters are integrated into the text as metaphors or similes (for example Kleonymos in *Wasps* 818–823[31]). Sometimes they are given apparent relevance to the plot, like the Antimachos passage in *Acharnians* (1150–1173, quoted on pp. 31–32) or the many attacks on rival poets in the parabases and elsewhere. But in a few cases they remain isolated from the surrounding action, as a kind of short *divertissement* in their own right. The three best examples are all in *Birds* (1470–1493, 1553–1564 and 1694). These have no point except their own intrinsic humour, and (like some of the lyrical interludes) could be added to a play or removed from it without significantly changing its effect. Sometimes in modern productions they are replaced with passages of contemporary satire, and although there is a brief moment of surprise, the audience is normally amused by them, and seldom feels that the mood of the play has been affected or even interrupted. This passage from *Birds* is characteristic of Aristophanes' originals (1553–1564, translated by William Arrowsmith[32]):

> There lies a marsh in Webfoot Land,
> the Swamp of Dismal Dread,
> and there we saw foul SOCRATES
> come calling up the dead.
>
> And there that cur PEISANDROS came
> to see if he could see
> the soul he'd lost while still alive
> by dying cowardly.
>
> He brought a special sacrifice,
> a little camel lamb;

then, like Odysseus, slit its throat –
   he slit its throat and ran!

And then a phantom shape flew down,
   a spectre cold and wan,
and on the camel's blood he pounced –
   the vampire CHAIREPHON!

The hero and his adversary

Nearly all the traditional elements discussed above are taken over bodily into
the plays. Where adaptation occurs, it is in the form of altering their length or
varying their position in the play. A different way of handling tradition occurs
with character types. Here the traditional types are modified and developed
into something very different indeed. If comic typology before Aristophanes was
primitive, then in and after his work it became complex and sophisticated.[33]

The development of the hero type is particularly marked. This is probably
because of the didactic and disquisitional nature of Greek drama generally.
Whereas in other literary forms the author can allow himself space to comment
on the events of his story, in drama – both for conciseness and because it is a
form of literature meant to be seen and heard instantaneously, not read and
pondered at leisure – any commentary on the events must be made by the
characters as they perform the events. When Kostia in *The Seagull* tears up his
manuscripts, the action is not merely one more event in the story: it carries its
own burden of interpretation with it.

In Greek drama some of this commentary is given to the Chorus, which is
able to stand apart from the action in a way not generally permitted to the
characters. In addition, however, the leading characters in the drama speak and
act in a way which has both a primary function within the plot and a secondary
function concerned with the general message of the play. In tragedy this
commentary is often inward-looking, and concerns the main moral or religious
theme which the action is illustrating; it is achieved by simple dramatic means
such as the use of irony. In comedy, which is outward-looking (that is,
incorporating comment not only on a central theme, but on anything and
everything as well), the choice of a particular hero type determines the author's
stance to his material, and is therefore a critical and didactic act on his part.

In simpler comedy, such as the rustic farce out of which much of the Greek
tradition evolved, the issues would be clear-cut and the moral commentary
either of small importance or completely absent. Two basic hero types were
used (their presence is first noted by Aristotle). They are the *eiron* (a man who –
ironically – dissembles his real qualities and abilities) and the *alazon* (a man
who loudly lays claim to qualities and abilities not rightly his). These types

53

adequately cover many of the minor figures in Aristophanes. The *alazon* scenes in particular (the knockabout scenes which close many of the plays) seem to lie close to the tradition. In them, the hero plays the *eiron* until the time comes to expel each bragging *alazon*, and the expulsion is short and slapstick, usually turning the *alazon*'s own weapons against himself. The types in these scenes exist on one level only, and moral commentary (if any) is short and explicit, a direct comparison of the hero's humanity with the sterile pretensions of the *alazon*.

At a more developed level, the *alazon* becomes a major character in the action. This is usually the case in plays whose origin is in another cultic tradition, that involving a god hero and his eventual victory over an awesome, blustering rival. The religious aspect of this tradition survives only on the periphery (in the sense, for example, that characters like Dikaiopolis are on the side of divine order, and their adversaries are not); but the *alazon* adversary is a recurring character. The most developed adversaries in Aristophanes are Socrates in *Clouds*, the Paphlagonian in *Knights* and Lamachos in *Acharnians*; what distinguishes them from less developed adversaries (such as War, Herakles, the Athenian Official, Poseidon or Poverty) is that they are rounded characters, whose function is moral as well as dramatic. (We are only amused, not edified, when Poseidon is defeated in *Birds* or Poverty in *Wealth*; but the defeats of Lamachos or Socrates contain a clear moral message, related not just to them but to the underlying message of the play.)

It is possible to divide Aristophanes' heroes into three broad types. Like all comic heroes, they are by nature protean, and suit their response to the demands of each particular encounter. Even so, their individual characteristics are perfectly clear, and enable us to see that their stance in the face of the world is a moral one, meant to inform as well as to entertain. Entertainment clearly comes first, and everything else is subordinate to it; but the particular genius of Aristophanes lies in his ability to make strikingly serious points without long departing from the primary aim of amusing his audience.

The first hero type may be called the *spoudaios* ('sober person'). He is basically serious and earnest, funny not so much in his own right as in the events which happen around him. His stance is not however that of a spectator: what happens happens because he makes it happen. His actions lead to comedy because the other characters react to them in a comic way; but they are serious actions, and could in other circumstances equally well result in a serious play. Lysistrata, Praxagora and Chremylos are the outstanding examples of this type, but Peisetairos and Bdelykleon conform to it, as well as secondary characters like Pheidippides and Blepsidemos. The *spoudaios* in Aristophanes is a kind of visionary, not remote from ordinary life, but adopting a detached stance not shared by the other characters. (The type is rare in modern comedy: Harold Lloyd and Jacques Tati come perhaps nearest to it.) Although these characters follow the ludicrous paths others open up, their motives are essentially un-comic: Lysistrata and Praxagora are earnest moral reformers; Chremylos wants to benefit mankind; Bdelykleon, Pheidippides and Blepsidemos are loving and dutiful sons willing to indulge errant fathers providing the indulging does the old men no harm. The journey from the *spoudaios* in Aristophanes to the young hero or elderly slave of New Comedy is a short one.

The second hero type may be called the *bomolochos* (literally, 'hanger-about for scraps'). He is a buffoon, characterized by loud, irrelevant and often ludicrous remarks. Euelpides in *Birds* is the best developed secondary character of this type. His interjections as Peisetairos discloses his plan to the birds (for example at 492–498, 501–503, 570, 598) reveal the *bomolochos* par excellence, the first of a long line which culminates in the 'comic' half of many modern double-acts (Jimmy James, Lou Costello, Gracie Allen, Eric Morecambe). When he is not a secondary character, but the hero of the play, the function of the *bomolochos* is rather subtler. Aristophanes often uses him in plays dealing with quite abstruse intellectual matters, and his assertive humour either serves to punctuate complicated exposition (as in the *Birds* scene mentioned above), or else makes a very clear commentary on the pretensions of his learned interlocutor. (For example, if Socrates fails to take in even a *bomolochos* like Strepsiades, how can he ever hope to fool an intelligent audience?) Two of Aristophanes' most striking characters are primarily of the *bomolochos* type, and both occur in plays involving literature. They are Dionysos in *Frogs* (whose interjections at 1028–1029, 1067–1068, 1074–1076, and especially 1051–1052 and 1466 are those of a *bomolochos* like Euelpides, but also offer a pointed moral commentary) and Mnesilochos in *Women at the Festival*, one of Aristophanes' finest creations. (Both parts are discussed in Chapter 9.)

The third hero type is familiar not only in Aristophanes, but in comedy of any age, from Odysseus to Falstaff, from the slaves of New Comedy to Scapino, Figaro or Groucho Marx. He may be called by his modern Greek title, *poneros* ('sly person').[34] He is ingenuity personified. He will win any battle, dominate any situation, and do so by the most delightful means possible. He is excessive, and admires himself for his excess; he is subtle, and applauds his own subtlety. No pretentious officials and no pretty girls are safe from him; the world is there for him to enjoy, and he enjoys his own enjoyment of it. The type has been seen by some modern writers (for example Lawrence Durrell and Nikos Kazantzakis) as quintessentially Greek: but in fact it is present in every age and every culture – Man personified, a human being glorying in his own humanity. Dikaiopolis, Agorakritos, Trygaios, and above all Philokleon – Aristophanes' supreme *poneros* – show a zest for living, and for watching their own antics with approval, which is not only particularly well suited to the phallic, regenerative side of the Dionysos cult, but also offers a pointed commentary on the sterility of those who oppose or try to restrain them.

The three basic character types are set out in a simple and schematic fashion in the table below. They are not Aristophanes' invention (they occur in Homer, for example), but they are developed in his plays to a level of sophistication remarkable in an age so innocent of dramatic theorizing. We can see today the excellence of the character-drawing in *Wasps*, *Women at the Festival* and *Frogs* because we have all comedy later than Aristophanes to compare with him; in his own day both he and his audience may have thought no more about it than that the plays were different from received tradition, and different in a satisfying manner.

PLAY	HERO	ASSOCIATE OF HERO	CHIEF ADVERSARY
Acharnians	*poneros* (Dikaiopolis)	—	*alazon* (Lamachos)
Knights	*poneros* (Sausage-seller)	—	*alazon* (Paphlagonian)
Wasps	*poneros* (Philokleon)	—	*spoudaios* (Bdelykleon)
Clouds	*bomolochos* (Strepsiades)	*spoudaios* (Pheidippides)	*alazon* (Socrates)
Peace	*poneros* (Trygaios)	—	*alazon* (War)
Birds	*spoudaios* (Peisetairos)	*bomolochos* (Euelpides)	—
Lysistrata	*spoudaios* (Lysistrata)	—	*alazon/bomolochos* (Athenian Official)
Women at the Festival	*poneros/bomolochos* (Mnesilochos)	*bomolochos/poneros* (Euripides)	—
Frogs	*bomolochos* (Dionysos)	*poneros* (Xanthias)	—
Assembly-women	*spoudaios* (Praxagora)	—	—
Wealth	*poneros* (Karion)/ *spoudaios* (Chremylos)	*spoudaios* (Blepsidemos)	*alazon* (Poverty)

Role of the comic dramatist

It is possible, by assembling a collage of half-lines, snippets and hints separated from their contexts and regrouped (rather like modern 'collage' versions of Shakespeare, but without always acknowledging, as they do, that the selection is deliberately made to illustrate a particular critical point), to make out an excellent case for Aristophanes being anything at all, from high priest of the Eleusinian mysteries to a paid right-wing propagandist.

The problem with any dramatist is sorting out his own voice from those of his characters. Even when a playwright deliberately sets out to discuss a particular topic (as Ibsen or Shaw often did), it is still not always easy, or valuable, to discover his own personal point of view. For plays, unlike essays or sermons, are intended to make an immediate effect, and to entertain as well as convince. The viewpoint expressed by a character is the character's, not necessarily the author's; dramatists are precisely imprecise, and the better the playwright, the better drawn his characters, the more this is the case. It is also more true of comedy than serious drama (whatever claims comedians may make to the contrary): for unless comedy entertains, it fails in its essential purpose.

Aristophanes needs to be approached with especial caution, because of the large amount of first-person comment in his plays, both in the parabases and elsewhere. For example, in *Acharnians* 496–501 Dikaiopolis says:

> Gentlemen of the audience, don't be annoyed
> To see me, dressed in rags, presuming to address
> The Athenians about our own city's affairs
> In the middle of a comedy. Even comedy
> Knows what is just. My message is hard, but fair.

Is he speaking here as Dikaiopolis or Aristophanes (or both)? Does the whole of his speech retain the same character? If not, where does it change? If it does – if, for example, he speaks as Aristophanes throughout – is not the political commentary which follows surprisingly selective, naïve, inept? Would it not be best, in short, to take the passage as no more Aristophanes' own true voice than this one (*Peace* 765–774), where the comic exaggeration is immediately apparent?

> That's why you must all side with me,
> Men and boys alike –
> I advise all the baldheads especially
> To work together to bring me victory:
> For as soon as I win, at the feast
> And the drinking afterwards, everyone will say,
> 'Feed Baldy first; give all the titbits
> To Baldy; refuse nothing to anyone
> With a brow like Baldy's here,
> The finest poet we've ever had!'

There were, however, two extra-dramatic functions inherent in the profession of dramatist in Athens which were part of the tradition within which Aristophanes worked: those of servant of Dionysos and 'instructor' of the people. The religious function of a playwright was implicit in the nature of the dramatic festivals themselves. If the vast majority of the words spoken on three days of a religious festival occurred in plays, then those words would have to carry

57

religious significance. Certainly there was never any move to make drama secular, and take it out of the religious context altogether. The role of teacher is less obvious; but Aristophanes makes the claim too often for us to ignore it, or dismiss it as comic wish-fulfilment, the clown affecting to play Hamlet.

Aristophanes (like Euripides) has often been considered anti-religious, or at any rate opposed to the continued supremacy of the Olympian gods. Evidence for this has been found in the plays themselves. The gods who appear onstage are buffoons imbued with the lowest human qualities, and their priests are liars and charlatans. In *Peace* and *Wealth* Hermes is a contemptible creature, interested only in his own skin (*Peace* 362ff.; *Wealth* 1099ff.) or in creature comforts (*Peace* 192f., 416ff.; *Wealth* 1118ff.). War is a foolish, blustering bugbear-figure (*Peace* 236ff.), and Poseidon a pompous fool who swears by his own name (*Birds* 1565ff., 1614). Zeus himself abdicates to find food (*Wealth* 1171ff.), or is dethroned by a flock of birds, again because of food (*Birds* 1685ff.). Even Dionysos is turned, in *Frogs*, into a coward in a yellow dress (a transformation very different indeed from that in Euripides' *Bacchae*). Priests and oracle-sellers are exactly what Oedipus (in *King Oedipus*) accuses Teiresias of being: venal impostors, beggars with a peculiarly offensive line in persuasion. The priests in *Birds* (851ff.) and *Wealth* (676ff. and 1171ff.) are more successful at cheating than their lowly associates, the oracle-mongers of *Peace* (1052ff.) and *Birds* (959ff.); but none of the four is a shining monument to those who administer religion.

The truth is simply that – just as in the case of 'real' figures like Euripides or Socrates – Aristophanes is dealing here not with reality, but with popular stereotypes. The villainous are funnier than the virtuous; beggar-priests (like comic policemen) are figures of fun; the buffoon Dionysos (in *Frogs*) is no more intended to mock religion than the buffoon Meton (in *Birds*) mocks science. Part of the catharsis provided by comedy arises from the debunking of authority – but it does not follow that real authority is seriously weakened by such debunking, or that the playwright intended it to be. (To some extent the same thing is true of political lampoon. Kleon's silence after the production of *Knights* is no miscalculation, no fearful impotence: it is a far wiser acceptance of the nature of comic lampoon, and the respective standing of himself as demagogue and Aristophanes as playwright, than was his hysterical and abortive lawsuit after *The Babylonians*.)

In fact Aristophanes' plays are instinct with deep religious feeling. His sympathy is with the gods as natural powers, part of the ordered natural world with which the machinations of men are so often in conflict. Dikaiopolis' private festival (*Acharnians* 237ff.) is the celebration of a return to order, and god-in-order; the sacrifices in *Peace* (956ff.), *Birds* (1565ff.), *Lysistrata* (209ff.), *Women at the Festival* (295ff.) and *Wealth* (788ff.), like the religious endings of many of the plays (*Acharnians*, *Peace*, *Birds*, *Lysistrata*, *Women at the Festival*, *Frogs* and *Wealth*), restore religion to its proper place: the hearts and homes of ordinary people. In each case the formality and hymnic style of the language is most marked, and contrasts strongly with that of the *alazones* and others who try to interrupt the progress of the plot.

Not only that, but a subordinate strand in several plays relates directly to the rites and rituals of one or more specific gods. In *Acharnians* the god is Phales-Dionysos, and the language is appropriately phallic; in *Clouds* Zeus battles with Dinos in Strepsiades' mind, and an Olympian – Hermes – finally resolves his dilemma for him; Peace is present both in person (as a statue) and in much of the rural imagery of *Peace*; *Birds* pays homage to Apollo and Pan, and is also full of the desire for peace and plenty, a feeling as rooted in late fifth-century religion as in its politics;[35] *Lysistrata* is filled throughout with the awe and power of Athene; *Women at the Festival* has its cake and eats it by overlaying a 'real' Thesmophoria (complete with hymns and invocations to the appropriate deities) with a comic 'mirror-image' Thesmophoria, a man's-eye view of women's religion, ideally suited to the sexually ambivalent character of this complex play; in *Frogs* the buffoon Dionysos performs before the wooden statue of his real namesake in the *orchestra*, mystic hymns of great seriousness are sung to Iacchos-Dionysos, and some allusion, however secret, is made to the solemn rituals of the Eleusinian Mysteries;[36] Aphrodite is the guiding spirit of *Assemblywomen*; Athene and Apollo share honours with Wealth himself in *Wealth*. And above all, running through all the plays is a theme of serious invocation of the gods and spirits connected with poetry, from Apollo and the Muses to the Graces (with whom Aristophanes was so memorably linked in the lines quoted as the epigraph of this book).

The association of religion with a serious face is a peculiarly modern phenomenon. It would not have occurred to a Greek in 405 that it was blasphemous to laugh at Dionysos in *Frogs* – he would not have made the dichotomy we now see between the god in the *orchestra* and the god on the stage. Religion was part of a man's outlook on life, and involved the whole man, his comic as well as his serious side. Both Aristophanes and his audience would know the religious obligations of a poet writing for an Athenian festival; Aristophanes fulfils those obligations particularly by his constant association of worship with the simplest, deepest urges in man, the times when by moving in harmony with natural order he discovers his own true self.[37]

This idea, that man should act in harmony with natural order, is the basis of the message propagated by Aristophanes in his other traditional role, that of teacher. While he was content to leave his priestly function implicit, he constantly reiterates claims such as that 'grown-ups have poets to teach them, just as children have tutors' (*Frogs* 1054–1056), and that his own work is valuable precisely because of its didactic element (*Acharnians* 650–655). This function is reserved especially for the parabasis, where 'it is right for the holy

59

Chorus to teach and advise the city for the best' (*Frogs* 686–687). In particular it is concerned with saving the city of Athens, restoring the state to the true path from which evil men have diverted it. That is the direct aim of Lysistrata and Praxagora; the Choruses of *Clouds* and *Wasps* pray that Athenian affairs will improve; Dikaiopolis, Agorakritos, Trygaios and Chremylos are all hailed as saviours of Athens.

There is, therefore, a moral intention in Aristophanes' work which goes further than the pious protestations he might have felt obliged to make on a religious occasion. It is typical of his method that he hardly ever specifically states what makes a good citizen: once again there is more fun to be had from castigating the bad than from defining and praising the good. In his preference of peace to war, quietness to busyness, country to town, perhaps even old to new, he mirrors and makes explicit the corporate feelings of a large wartime audience.

In fact a consistent philosophy can be traced throughout his work. Happiness and security are to be found when the natural balance of life is maintained; whenever natural order is upset (whether by corrupt politicians, blinkered jurymen, sophists or pedlars of oracles), unhappiness results. Restoration of natural order is achieved usually by individual initiative. The message is the same as in much Greek tragedy – though the gods in comedy are seldom thought of as the guardians of natural order, and a man reaffirms natural order by self-assertion rather than self-sacrifice.

This philosophy is articulated very aptly by the tripartite structure of many comic plots. The *problem* is whatever is upsetting natural order; the *solution* proposed is a restoration of natural balance; the final *rejoicing* celebrates the return of natural order in human affairs. The plot of *Clouds* shows the theme developed in a clear way. In their own different ways, Strepsiades, Pheidippides and Socrates all disturb the natural order of daily life. Sons should know their duty and keep to it – therefore, Pheidippides' bankrupting of his father by racing horses is bad enough, but his behaviour after visiting Socrates (beating his father, and proposing to justify the same treatment of his mother) is infinitely worse. A man should be honest and neighbourly – therefore, Strepsiades' wish to cheat his creditors is one thing, but his ill-treatment of Pasias, a fellow-demesman, outrages every standard of civilized and conventional behaviour. Neither father nor son follow the natural canon advocating modesty and self-restraint. Instead of 'knowing themselves' they 'test themselves', and the possibilities for action are left infinite – a shocking notion. Socrates questions natural order by his experiments, and seeks to explain them in a rational way. He challenges the supremacy of the divine in human life, replacing it by the supremacy of human intellect (*Clouds* 316–318: compare *Frogs* 885–894). Legality, too, is made a matter for subjective interpretation (a different version of the charge made against jurors in *Wasps* and *Birds*, that they

60

are acting out of motives which have nothing to do with the concept of 'natural' law). Education, in the Right–Wrong argument, is turned into a subject for intellectual debate; neither Right nor Wrong (because both are the children of sophistry) mention the place of natural instinct, obedience to the claims of order. The restoration of natural order in *Clouds* is brought about by super-natural beings: the Chorus of Clouds (who reveal in 1452ff., better late than never, that their mission is to punish those who seek after evil, and make them learn to fear the gods) and Hermes, whose statue by Strepsiades' door has stood throughout the play, as potent a symbol of the acceptance of natural order as the pot 'Dinos' outside the Blaboratory is of the violation of that order.

There are several reasons why Aristophanes adopts this broad philosophy. It is characteristic of comedians that they prefer a conservative stance. Since audiences approach what is new with caution, sometimes even with fear, the comedian finds favour more by mocking new ideas than by advocating them. In the particular situation of the Peloponnesian War, a nostalgic approach to the great days of the past (with its corollary, an attack on those who have ended that greatness) was likely to win favour with the crowd. However people voted in the Assembly (and it is significant that the majority never actually *obeyed* Aristophanes' injunctions), their inner longings were for peace and stability, the unflustered enjoyment of ordinary life, summed up by Euelpides in *Birds* 128–134, and by the Chorus in *Peace* 1127–1139:

> Happiness! Happiness!
> No more army rations,
> No more onions, no more cheese.
> I never cared for fighting.
> I like to sit round the fire,
> Drinking deep with a few dear friends
> While the logs we chopped in summer
> Crackle and blaze,
> Roast nuts and acorns,
> And while the wife has a bath
> Find a slave-girl and snatch a kiss.

Above all, Aristophanes never forgot that his main role was not priest or pamphleteer, but comic dramatist. One of his main purposes was to make people laugh, and his means were the interaction of dramatic characters in a theatre. What those characters said and did, and the feelings they evoked in the audience, were conditioned by all manner of religious, philosophical and political considerations, as well as by the expectations created by the existing traditions of comedy. But didactic purpose was only one of several aims in Aristophanes' mind; had it not been so, he might have written tragedy, history or philosophy instead of comedy. Instruction and amusement are inseparably and uniquely linked in all his work. Even in a passage as open and personal as

61

the parabasis of *Peace* (where he seems to be talking directly about himself, his aims and intentions) a sense of the ridiculous is never far away (*Peace* 759–764, translated by Rogers):

> But I recked not the least for the look of the beast;
>   I never desponded or quailed,
> And I fought for the safety of you and the Isles;
>   I gallantly fought and prevailed.
> You therefore should heed and remember the deed,
>   and afford me my guerdon to-day,
> For I never went off to make love to the boys
>   in the schools of athletic display
> Heretofore when I gained the theatrical prize:
>   but I packed up my traps and departed,
> Having caused you great joy and but little annoy,
>   and mightily pleased the true-hearted.

AESTHETICS

5
The Real World and the Fantasy World

Summary

Like many tragedies, the comedies of Aristophanes have themes concerned, among other things, with the restoration of true cosmic order. In tragedy the hero is often the one who has perverted cosmic order, and its restoration involves him in suffering. In comedy the perversion of natural order has been caused by others; the hero is often the only 'sane' being in an insane world, and his restoration of order leads to rejoicing.

The comedies begin with the hero in dismay, alienated from the rest of the world. His dismay leads him to formulate and carry out a 'strange and mighty deed'. This carries the plot from reality to fantasy, and inverts the natural laws by which the other characters operate.

In the hero's fantastic universe the laws are his to make. Figures from the 'real' world try to stake a claim to part of his success, but almost invariably fail. The plays end with a celebration of the restored world-order, now shown to be morally superior to that at the beginning of the action. The celebration is often a feast, sometimes a wedding or a religious ritual. These celebrations not only closed the comedies, but were also the final acts of the day's performance in the theatre, and so had a religious and festive function outside of their place in the comedies themselves.

The unifying theme

Unless what he sees is to seem merely chaotic, the spectator of a play must be aware – at least subliminally – of some sort of unifying formal structure. Surface style and the pyrotechnics of the actors may make greater claims on his attention during the performance itself; but if the play lacks a sound formal armature, it will appear as random as a series of circus acts.

Usually this underlying structure is bound up with the main philosophical theme of the play, and the events of the plot serve as a particular demonstration of that theme applied to human affairs. In the theatre we watch a succession of scenes, each one of which takes another step towards final resolution; but it is often only on reflection afterwards that we perceive the general theme of which those actions and that resolution were a demonstration. The emotional reaction in the theatre can thus be completed by a parallel intellectual satisfaction.

For instance, in *Othello* the immediate action is concerned with ambition, jealousy and the corruption of nobility, and with their instruments: handkerchiefs, oaths and strangling. The mind is certainly aware of a unifying element in this diversity, but it is not always possible to decide at once, in the theatre, what that element is. In *King Oedipus* the events of a particular story unfold before the spectator in a logical, inexorable and satisfying manner. During the performance we are partially aware that the play concerns deeper themes – the nature of knowledge, or the relationship between men and the gods – but it is usually on reflection, outside the theatre performance, that we finally perceive the inner meanings (for us) of the play. This is so even today, when we approach *King Oedipus* with the hindsight of those who have read it and explanations of it before; the spectator for whom it was originally written was seeing it for the first and possibly the only time.[38]

The underlying theme of many Greek tragedies (and some later ones) is didactic; it concerns the nature of cosmic order, its upsetting and its restoration. Often the hero, who begins the play apparently blessed and secure, is shown to be in conflict with natural order, and his downfall is essential for its restoration. The unfolding of the story involves him personally in a progression from (apparent) light to (apparent) darkness. In some plays the spectator is ironically aware of the hero's dilemma from the start of the action, and his pleasure in the play is in watching the hero's progression towards that same awareness. In other plays spectator and hero make the journey towards final knowledge together and in step. By the end of the play, hero and spectator alike understand more about cosmic order and how it should be maintained; the difference between them is that the hero's physical plight has materially worsened to bring about this knowledge, while the spectator, physically unscathed, is left to ponder on what he has seen and to learn from it.[39]

In most comedies, from Menander to the present day, this kind of progression is lacking. The primary function of comedy is less didactic, less philosophical and generally more deictic than tragedy: its purpose is more often to demonstrate or parody the human situation than to probe or analyse it. The fulcrum of comedy, as with tragedy, may well be cosmic order, the tension between 'natural' and 'unnatural' action. But whereas tragedy often analyses the causes and effects of that tension, comedy is usually concerned with the moment of tension itself.

The plots of most comedies concern obstacles to happiness (in 'serious' comedy often defects of character or awkward circumstances; in 'lighter' comedy often stern authority or lack of cash), and the attempts of the characters to get round them, sometimes successful (in which case the happy outcome provides catharsis for the spectators) and sometimes unsuccessful (in which case the catharsis for the spectator is in watching hilarious disaster, or the ironical satisfaction of seeing characters who have failed to reach manifestly impossible goals accept their alternatives). Another kind of comic plot is concerned with temporary imposture, a delightful fantasy which works for the duration of the play but disappears at the end when normality is restored. (*The Merry Wives of Windsor* and *The Government Inspector* are good examples of this genre. The end of the play leaves matters much as they were at the start; characters and audience have been diverted for the length of the action, and that is the main purpose of the play.)

The comedies of Aristophanes conform to none of these types: they are, in fact, closer to the style of tragedy than to that of any post-Menandrian comedy. Underlying all the hilarious incidents of each plot is a unifying philosophical idea, as didactic as that of a tragedy, and, like tragedy, concerned with cosmic order and the change in attitude required of those who are opposed to it. Sometimes, as in tragedy, it is the hero who is out of line; but more often it is other characters, and the hero is the person who brings about the necessary change. Unlike a tragic hero, he does so not by personal suffering, but by the use of magic or fantasy. He has a vision and powers not shared by the rest of us, an oblique view of the world which is often expressed in words or actions as extravagantly funny as those of a tragic hero are extravagantly pitiable or terrifying. The tragic hero moves from light to darkness, and arouses compassion; the hero in Aristophanes moves from darkness to light, and arouses delighted admiration.

In most tragedies the events which befall the hero are 'real': that is, possible in the world of the audience. The restoration of cosmic order is achieved by extreme but essentially human means: death, fall from eminence, self-torture, banishment. The circumstances of the play, however, are often 'unreal': we are never for example concerned with such matters as what Hamlet had for breakfast or whether Oedipus suffered from toothache. The action of many tragedies requires no precise location, in time or space. The dramatist selects only those trappings of 'reality' which are necessary to his plot. Everyday objects are either vital to the action (like Desdemona's handkerchief) or are not mentioned at all.

Exactly the opposite happens in Aristophanes' comedy. The deed which will ultimately restore cosmic order is 'unreal', impossible in the world of the audience. (No man, for example, could really fly, or argue with Zeus, or make a private peace treaty.) In contrast, the circumstances surrounding the deed are deliberately made as 'real' as possible (see below, pp. 72ff.). A list of the everyday objects necessary in *Peace*, to take as an example a play whose plot is almost entirely surrealist, would fill a page of this book. In the same way, comic heroes speak for the most part in natural, 'real' language, not in the heightened, almost shorthand diction of tragedy.[40]

Saturnalia

This blend of the fantastic and the everyday requires a special atmosphere to succeed. Comedies (of all types and ages) generally take place in a topsy-turvy world where anything at all can happen. Sometimes the laws of causality are in operation, sometimes not. The 'possible' and the 'impossible' jostle each other, sometimes in the same sequence of thought; everything is allowed, providing that it works within the confines of the plot. And most important, everything that happens, possible and impossible alike, is treated with exactly the same gravity by every character in the action.

A good example of this spirit of Saturnalia in action is the atmosphere in Roman New Comedy. The detail is 'realistic' – so much so that Plautus and Terence have been mined for information on 'Roman' life of the third and second centuries BC. But 'reality' (that is, the actual world of the audience) has no place either in the circumstances surrounding the dramatic action or in the action itself. The real world, in Bergson's phrase, is turned inside-out: slaves outwit their masters; slave-girl prostitutes are revealed to be freeborn virgins; poor men become rich, and rich men poor; the humble are exalted and the mighty laid low. In such a world, we cease to question truth-to-life. We never ask, for example, why in *Menaechmi* Menaechmus II, as soon as he arrives in Epidamnus, abandons all his stern moral principles, and not only accepts a free meal and a night of love from a complete stranger but proposes to steal a dress and some jewellery into the bargain; nor do we ask why, although he has been searching Greece for his identical twin brother, and although for most of the play people keep mistaking him for Menaechmus I, he should fail in such a particularly dense manner to put two and two together. All of this is quite unreal, yet we accept it as natural within the confines and conditions of the plot.[41]

The inversion in Aristophanes follows the same pattern, but also introduces another element (one not exploited so fully again until the Absurd Drama of our own century). What happens is that an initially absurd deed is done (absurd meaning rather 'out of keeping with its surroundings' than 'ridiculous'), and turns the 'reality' of the 'real' world inside-out. But as soon as the deed is done, the ordinary laws of causality are once again applied. Although the beginning of the progression is absurd (the founding of a city in the sky, for example), every subsequent event follows logically from the one before. Only the strange and mighty deed inverts reality: subsequent events are absurd not in their own right, but because they arise naturally out of an absurd deed.

Not only that, but very often the situation created by the deed, although logically absurd, is in absolute terms preferable to its alternative (for example peace not war, love not hate, universal justice not injustice). Thus, the whole nature of 'reality' and 'unreality' is challenged: in absolute terms the absurd hero is arguably wiser, saner and better off than his real-life audience. The illusion the spectators see is rendered more desirable than their own reality. This fact relates the hilarious incidents of the play to its serious underlying theme, and leaves the spectators not merely diverted (as they might be by Roman comedy) but also changed (as they might be by tragedy).

This change is symbolized in the change of status which the hero undergoes during the play. At the start he is normally isolated or alone (often indeed, like some tragic heroes, regarded as ill or mad); by the end, however, he is surrounded by well-wishers, the focal point of a feast or wedding. He has been poor, downtrodden and impotent; he becomes successful, despotic and potent. The didactic point about maintaining cosmic balance is thus linked with the theme of regeneration which was fundamental to the whole cult of Dionysos.[42]

Alienation of the hero

Every one of Aristophanes' plays begins with an expression of dissatisfaction. Where the character who will do the deed opens the play, that dissatisfaction is with the state the world is in, and the opening dialogue articulates it into expressions of disgust, despair or impatience. Dikaiopolis in *Acharnians*, Strepsiades in *Clouds*, Lysistrata in *Lysistrata*, Praxagora in *Assemblywomen*, and the pairs of characters who open *Knights*, *Birds*, *Women at the Festival* and *Frogs* all conform to this pattern. In the other plays, where the character who opens the play is not the doer of the deed, the impatience or despair expressed is against that doer, because he is acting in a strange and unnatural manner. The slaves in *Wasps* and *Peace* dislike what they are doing, and the behaviour of their master which causes them to do it. The attitude of Karion in *Wealth*, and to some extent that of Xanthias in *Frogs*, is more relaxed: neither of them knows exactly what his master intends, but goes along with him in a spirit of rather self-aware amusement.

In several of the plays the heroes are given associates, and their first task is to win them over. These associates are almost always either reluctant to help or stupid. The slaves in *Wasps*, *Peace*, *Frogs* and *Wealth* are the least formidable (because they have no freedom of choice): they understand none of the reasons for their masters' discontent, and obey their instructions with varying degrees of willingness or grumbling. Lysistrata's and Praxagora's first task, in the 'real' world portrayed at the start of their respective plays, is to win over a group of giggling, empty-headed women, the majority of whom take part in the schemes out of curiosity rather than conviction. Dikaiopolis' only ally at the start of *Acharnians* is the grotesque demigod Amphitheos; Peisetairos' progress at the start of *Birds* is hampered by the buffoon Euelpides.

Nine of the plays open with expressions of pain or exhaustion: the characters' philosophical separation from the 'real' world is matched by actual physical discomfort. Euelpides, Xanthias, Mnesilochos and Karion have been travelling until they are worn out (in Xanthias' case, admittedly, travelling on ass-back). Dikaiopolis, the slaves in *Knights* and Strepsiades use images of physical pain – smarting eyes, beaten backs, deathly agony – to describe the way the world is treating them. The slaves in *Wasps* and *Peace* find their tasks both pointless and laborious.

In *Wasps*, *Birds* and *Frogs* the image of disease is used. Philokleon is suffering from 'the most unusual disease' of litigious mania (*Wasps* 87–88[43]); Dionysos has a longing that is 'eating him away' (*Frogs* 59); Peisetairos and Euelpides are suffering 'the opposite disease from Sakas' (*Birds* 31) – a longing to leave Athens rather than to be accepted there. Madness is conjured up in two plays: Karion can think of nothing worse than his own fate, serving a 'master out of his wits' (*Wealth* 1–2); Trygaios' slaves tell the audience that their master is mad 'in a strange new way, not like you at all' (*Peace* 54–55).

By these means, long before the deed is done, the doer is usually presented as (a) separate from the society round him; (b) hard to understand, even by his own associates; (c) in distress, mental, physical or both; (d) either sick or mad. This alienation is well established before the deed is done – and in fact is important to our acceptance of the deed as a possible course of action. If one purpose of the play is to show that 'reality' is wrong and its inversion right, then the wrong situation must be seen from the beginning of the action to be dominant, the evil for which the deed is the only antidote.

Progression to the deed

The dissociation of the hero from 'reality' soon leads him to action. Usually he begins by trying to operate within the 'reality' of the other characters, to steer that reality back in line with his own idea of cosmic order. This attempt always fails, and its failure leads inevitably to the doing of the deed. The initial attempt loosens the bonds of 'reality'; the deed inverts reality or sweeps it away for ever.

This progression from reality to non-reality is particularly clear in *Acharnians*. At the start of the play, the world around Dikaiopolis is presented in considerable naturalistic detail. Because it is Dikaiopolis himself who is speaking, the details are selected to articulate his own dissatisfaction; but despite these hostile overtones, they are made to appear 'normal' enough. The everyday world of attendance at civic functions and the contrast between town and country markets are presented in 'realistic' terms. Even Dikaiopolis' grumbling is what anyone might expect, given the circumstances.

Only when the Assembly begins does unreality take over. Here the 'normal' isolation of Dikaiopolis during his soliloquy ('normal', because waiting for latecomers is a familiar experience in our own, 'real' world) is developed in such a way that it becomes unreal, an allegory for the kind of corruption he senses in society. He is, as his name reminds us, a just man and a citizen; but he is allowed to play no part in the democratic gathering which should exhibit justice and citizenship. First his protest about Amphitheos' expulsion is abruptly snubbed and his ensuing comments are ignored (56–64); then, although his cross-examination of Pseudartabas is allowed, its conclusion is ignored and the frauds are invited to the Prytaneion (110–128).

At this point Dikaiopolis decides to perform his strange and mighty deed. His earlier plan of interrupting the Assembly whenever peace was not discussed (37–39) has only served to isolate him further. Democratic methods having failed, he resorts to autarky; Amphitheos leaves to fetch the private treaty, and the plot abandons 'reality' forever. In the new inverted reality Dikaiopolis finds the power he has lacked up till now; the simple announcement of a drop of rain sends the 'real' characters away in confusion (173–174), and we enter with the hero into a fantastic dimension where a treaty is a skin of wine, an elected general is a blustering impostor from the tragic stage, and a one-man Common Market can flourish in a war-torn city filled with spies and informers.

Whether consciously used by Aristophanes or not, the pattern of the 'possible' action followed by the 'impossible' deed appears in many of the extant plays. The slaves in *Knights* first think of running away, then decide to fight the Paphlagonian with his own weapons and in his own inverted world, where the lower you sink the higher you rise. Strepsiades' original intention in *Clouds*, of cheating his creditors, is soon swallowed up in the gigantic perversion of nature which Socrates' Blaboratory represents. *Wasps* begins with a whole series of impostures by Philokleon; Bdelykleon's first, 'real' solution is to imprison him, but when this fails he inverts reality by bringing the court to the old man instead of the old man to the court. In *Peace* Trygaios' original intention is merely to rail at Zeus from the ground; but he soon develops this, first into the voyage to heaven, and then into the bid to rescue Peace. (Not only is this plot an inversion of 'reality', but the whole idea is an inversion of a standard literary theme, the descent of the gods to earth in quest of men.)

In *Birds* the heroes' original intention was simply to emigrate from Athens. The whole conception of Cloudcuckooland is the result of a gradual but inevitable progress, and the final deed, usurping Zeus' throne and marrying Basileia, represents a reversal of the entire perceived structure of the universe. In *Lysistrata* and *Assemblywomen*, although the deeds themselves are possible in the real world, they are surrounded from the start with all the trappings of unreality, as the women depart in a startling and unprecedented manner from their conventional roles in the real world.[44.]

In *Women at the Festival* Euripides' action (sending Mnesilochos to the Thesmophoria, disguised as a woman) is unreal enough; but the whole idea of using tragic rescue scenes to effect a 'real-life' rescue pushes normal stage illusion further than is usual even in Aristophanes. In *Frogs* everything that happens is 'unreal': the quest for Euripides is surpassed only by the poetic contest itself. (In fact, *Women at the Festival* and *Frogs* share a type of organically developing plot which is less concerned than the other plays with great deeds and their consequences. It is notable that both are fantasy plays, where political and topical comment plays a less prominent role than usual.) In *Wealth* the earlier type of plot is used again: a simple action (the consultation of the oracle) leads to an inversion of the real world by a strange and mighty deed, the restoration of Wealth's sight.

Circumstances of the deed

The deed has not only a structural function within the plot (it acts as the hinge between possible and impossible, reality and fantasy), but it also serves the overall didactic purpose of the play (the demonstration that 'reality' is not in tune with cosmic order). Hence it is essential that each spectator should accept it, without question, as a logical and inevitable step in the sequence of events he is watching. If a man walked on to the stage and announced baldly, 'This is a giant dung-beetle, and I'm flying up on it to see Zeus', we might well accept what he said, but our feelings would be very different from those we have when the same deed is prepared and performed in the manner actually used in *Peace*, where great care is taken to make it seem not only possible, but inevitable. We do not need to feel that *we* could fly to Zeus; but we need to feel not only that Trygaios *can*, but that he *must*.

Aristophanes achieves this impression of inevitability and rightness in four ways. Firstly, he not only makes the deed an attractive piece of wish-fulfilment, but also strongly emphasizes its justness and rightness, its harmony with cosmic order. Secondly, he uses a standard stage convention to limit and define the boundaries of his fantastic universe: anything not actually mentioned simply does not exist.[45] In *Lysistrata*, for example, we accept the statements made about the situation entirely on their own terms. We never ask about Lysistrata's own husband; we never wonder how Myrrhine's husband, after seven months away, can turn up so opportunely and in such a desperate state; we never think of whores, masturbation or boys as a means of sexual release for the men; we never question the freedom of movement allowed to Athens' bitterest enemies in wartime, or the fact that unescorted women are freely able to travel there from Boeotia or Sparta. Aristophanes chooses the 'real' facts he wants us to accept, and we not only accept them, but ignore any other facts not mentioned, however relevant to the action.

The third means by which we are made to feel that the deed is inevitable is the care with which it is prepared. A private peace at the start of *Acharnians* would be a startling and therefore incredible idea. As it is, we approach it by a succession of small but logical steps. The situation at the start of the play is wholly

71

realistic; gradually, as the action develops, the characters and events become less and less real, and we are drawn into and accept the new 'reality' of the stage illusion. When the deed comes it is still a surprise, but now it delights us instead of startling us. Something 'strange and mighty' was inevitable, and the particular deed chosen caps that inevitability in a way which is as fresh and unexpected as it is obvious and right. The self-assertion of the hero in his deed is, in fact, a characteristic example of his protean nature at work.

The fourth means by which we are made to accept the deed as right (that is, as possible and inevitable within the play, however bizarre outside it) is the use made of its immediate surroundings. Aristophanes does not merely rub a lamp and produce a genie. He surrounds the fantastic deed with as much ordinary, everyday circumstance as possible. Because we have all experienced the same kind of circumstance, because the hero appears to share in the detail of our humanity, we more easily accept the superhuman nature of what he is actually doing.

Often this is done simply and with little elaboration. All Dikaiopolis gets from Amphitheos is a skin of wine; to share his private peace (as the farmer and bridegroom realize) all that is needed is a drop or two of that wine. In order to restore the sight of Wealth, you do the obvious thing: take him to the temple of Asklepios. Praxagora's amazing performance in the Assembly, and the imposture that makes it possible, are prepared for by a long and detailed description of the real problems of making such an imposture: borrowing men's clothes and stealing unnoticed out of the house. The bizarre domestic court of *Wasps* is filled with everyday objects: a bowl of soup, a kneading-trough, some wooden dishes, a potty.

Where the deed is particularly fantastic, the ordinariness of the surrounding detail is even more important. Aristophanes inextricably blends reality and fantasy; we are diverted by the incongruous mixture, and when we have finished laughing the deed is done and fantasy realized. In Trygaios' flight in *Peace* (154–178, quoted on pp. 85–86) this mixture is particularly effective. Every spectator in a Greek theatre would know what a dung-beetle was like; every spectator would know what the theatre crane was like, and how apprehensive actors could be about using it. Every spectator would know the effect of fear on the bowels (in comedy if not in real life). Aristophanes simply magnifies these everyday aspects to fantastic proportions. The beetle is huge (and therefore, logically, its hunger is also huge); we are invited to share the simple vision that a real flight from one side of the stage to the other can stand for a flight from earth to heaven. At the most fantastic moments of the flight – the most remote from real-life experience – we are explicitly reminded of a whorehouse in Piraeus (165) and a careless crane-operator in the theatre (174ff.). The flight takes place in two dimensions of reality at once; but once it is over, the fantastic dimension is in complete control, and we have no problem in believing

Trygaios' matter-of-fact statement of what is actually impossible (178–179):

> And now I think I see the house of Zeus.
> Anyone inside the house of Zeus? Open up!

One of the most fantastic deeds in Aristophanes is the building of Cloud-cuckooland in *Birds*. By its very nature the city is ethereal and insubstantial. Its foundations are in air, and its sovereignty is over the atmosphere, the 'middle air'. But right from its first appearance the city is given a solid, everyday structure, based on the use of real-life materials (*Birds* 550–552):

PEISETAIROS: The first thing to do is build one single bird-city;
Next, surround the atmosphere and the middle air
With a wall of huge, baked bricks – like Babylon.

Later Peisetairos (now equipped with wings – as a result of the everyday practice of chewing a root) gives Euelpides burlesque but clear and everyday instructions on how to supervise the building work (*Birds* 837–847, in Arrowsmith's translation):

PEISETAIROS: Hop it, man!
Quick, up the rigging of the air!
Hurry! Done? Now, supervise the workers on the wall.
Run the rubble up!
Quick, mix the mortar, man!
Up the ladder with your hod – and then fall down!
Don't stop!
Post the sentries!
Bank the furnace!
Now the watchman's round.
All right, catch two winks.
Rise and shine!
Now, send your heralds off,
one to the gods above, one to the mortals below.
Then scurry back.

EUELPIDES: As for you, just stay right here –
and I hope you choke.

PEISETAIROS: Obey your orders, friend.
Unless you do your share, we shan't get done.

The messenger who reports that the work is completed blends ordinary and fantastic images in the same way as is done in Trygaios' flight, or in Karion's description of the healing of Wealth (*Birds* 1122–1147, in Arrowsmith's translation):

MESSENGER: Where anh where hoo where uh where can he be?
Where is Peisetairos hanh?

PEISETAIROS: Here hunh here.

MESSENGER: Whew! The wall's all up! The wall's done!

PEISETAIROS: Splendid!

MESSENGER: What a wonderful, whopping, well-built wall! Whew!
Why, that wall's so wide that if you hitched up
four Trojan Horses to two huge chariots
with those braggarts Proxenides in one and Theagenes in the
                                                                        other,
they could pass head-on. *That's* the width of your wall!
PEISETAIROS: Wow, what a width!
MESSENGER: And what a height! Measured it myself.
Six hundred feet high!
PEISETAIROS: Poseidon, what a height!
Who in the world could have built a wall like that?
MESSENGER: The birds.
                    Nobody but Birds.
                                        Not one Egyptian,
No bricklayers. No carpenters. Or masons.
Only the birds. I couldn't credit my eyes.
What a sight it was:
                              Thirty thousand Cranes
whose crops were all loaded with boulders and stones,
while the Rails with their beaks blocked out the rocks
and thousands of Storks came bringing up bricks
and Plovers and Terns and seabirds by billions
transported the water right up to the sky!
PEISETAIROS: Heavens!
But which Birds hauled the mortar up?
MESSENGER: Herons,
in hods.
PEISETAIROS: But how was the mortar heaped in the hods?
MESSENGER: Gods, now *that* was a triumph of engineering skill!
Geese burrowed their feet like shovels beneath
and heaved it over their heads to the hods.
PEISETAIROS: They did?
Ah Feet! Ah Feet! O incredible feat!
What can compare with a pair of feet?

Fantasy reinforced: the alazon *scenes*

As soon as the deed is done and accepted, the ordinary laws of causality come into operation again. Natural order has been set right again, and the misconceived 'reality' of the old world turned upside-down. What was formerly regarded as right is now seen to be wrong; characters (like the hero) who were formerly out of step are now seen to have been completely right.

This moral rightness is symbolized by a kind of surreal inviolability, invincibility. As soon as the deed is done, Dikaiopolis becomes a kind of despot in a country of his own making; Trygaios talks with Hermes and outwits him; Peisetairos offers not only to rape the goddess Iris but also to execute her, despite her immortality; Lysistrata and Praxagora, though women, are treated with the deference due to leaders of state; Strepsiades and Karion commit assault (and in Strepsiades' case arson) with impunity.

Real logic and fantasy logic are brought face to face and do battle in the *alazon* scenes. Here characters from the 'real' world try to share the benefits of the hero's fantasy world, without first participating in his strange and mighty deed. Predictably, fantasy not only triumphs over reality, but also sends it packing. The *alazones* try either to apply the rules of real life to the fantasy situation, or to lay claim to a position within the fantasy. In either case, they fail.

There are over forty *alazon* scenes in the extant plays. They vary in length and importance from the 7-line appearance of Kleonymos' son in *Peace* (1298ff.) to the magnificent scene in *Wealth* (823–958) between Karion, the Just Man and the Informer. In most of the scenes the pattern is the same. The *alazon* comes in to beg for or demand preferential treatment, and is rejected. Often the normal pattern of 'real' life is inverted: instead of the citizen hero going for favour to officials, priests or intellectuals, they come to him.

Aristotle considered the *alazon* one of the three main character types in comedy (the others being the *bomolochos* and the *eiron*: see Chapter 4).[46] Certainly there is at least an element of *alazoneia* in all Aristophanes' comic characters: Dikaiopolis begging from Euripides, for example, or Strepsiades faced with the Blaboratory, show the characteristic loudness, assertiveness and denseness that belong to the type. But Aristophanes' heroes have freedom of will, and that is the crucial difference between them and his *alazones*, who are sterile, cardboard figures. Their *alazoneia* is not creative, like the hero's. It arises from a mistaken view of the new, inverted world-order; it is explicit, short-lived, and doomed to failure from the start.

The hero's reaction to each *alazon* varies according to the approach that *alazon* makes to him. The success of his deed has given him a protean ability to adapt to any and every circumstance. The inversion of reality equips him with an especially functional form of *poneria* (see p. 55), an outrageous but good-hearted and creative force, very different from the pallid negativism of his opponents. Reassertion of human values is the didactic point of every *alazon* scene – a striking moral point in view of the inverted world in which they take place.

However, in these scenes more than most, the primary purpose is not didactic: it is to entertain. The commonest weapon for dealing with an *alazon* is the stock-in-trade of every comedian, however lowly or elevated: physical or verbal abuse. This is *poneria* at its most primitive and popular level, that of Mr Punch or the bladderman at a medieval fair. With slightly more elevated *alazones*, like sellers of laws or oracles, more elevated *poneria* is used: the hero either inverts the *alazon*'s oracles so that they recoil in his face (as Trygaios does in the Hierokles scene in *Peace* 1052–1121), or produces rival laws or oracles of his own (as Peisetairos does with the Overseer, Decree-seller and Delinquent Son in *Birds* 1021ff., 1035ff. and 1337ff.).

Fantasy triumphant

The progress of the play is nearly over. The natural world (or rather, man's previous view of it) has been shown to be unsatisfactory; the old order has been inverted by the strange and mighty deed; the inverted order has been tested and proved sound, morally superior to that existing before the deed. All that is needed to provide the final comic catharsis is a celebration.

The harmony at the end of each comedy – harmony of man with cosmic order – is in direct contrast to the alienation at the beginning. The celebration that ends the play reasserts the positive in human life, just as the beginning of the play concerned the negative. With the celebration, fantasy ends: the happiness at the close of a play (though caused by a fantastic act) is once again 'real' and everyday: dancing, feasting and singing, the simple pleasures of ordinary men. These celebrations fulfilled a religious function outside of the comedies themselves: each one ended not just its own comedy, but a whole day of the theatrical festival as well.

Of Aristophanes' extant plays, only *Clouds* (which survives in an unperformed and possibly unpolished revision) ends without a celebration. The bustle and confusion attendant on the burning of the Blaboratory is cathartic enough – inevitable, didactic and satisfying – but it is hardly good-humoured, quite unlike the genial revels which end the other plays. It is hard not to detect a sour note, as the Chorus turns from the burning Blaboratory and the sophists scattering in all directions, with these words from its leader (1510–1511):

> Lead the way out. We've danced
> Enough now, for this one day.

More functional celebrations end the other plays. There are elements of religious ceremonial in *Acharnians, Wealth, Women at the Festival* (which turns the ending of the play into the ending of the Thesmophoria itself) and *Frogs*. *Lysistrata* ends with singing and dancing, and *Wasps* ends with drunken old Philokleon dancing the obscene and comic *kordax*. In *Knights* the final chorus is lost; but the play ends with the Sausage-seller going off to a public banquet. *Assemblywomen* ends by promising a feast of truly Gargantuan proportions. *Birds* and *Peace* end with wedding celebrations.

At one level, these celebratory endings are clearly a remnant of the bacchanalian excitement of old, pre-literary comedy. At another, they provide the culmination of the whole dramatic action, the moment of catharsis which clinches the entire performance. But they also serve the didactic theme underlying the plot, and point a clear moral: the celebrations are 'real' and human (despite the fantastic events which brought them about); their geniality is in sharp contrast with the glum 'reality' in force at the start of the play. If the only way to achieve this happy ending is to invert the order of the world, then there is something seriously wrong with world-order as it stands.

This didactic point is not placed starkly before us (as it is, for example, in the epilogues to many of Jonson's comedies). Just as the serious theme has underlain and unified the comic superstructure throughout the play, so it remains latent to the end. Catharsis, not a moral lesson, is the true dramatic and theatrical function of each final celebration. The primacy of the festive element is nowhere better exemplified than in *Birds*. Here the sheer gusto of the wedding celebration carries all before it, and the moral point of the play unites with our enjoyment of theatre spectacle to produce a delirious and truly satisfying effect. Here are the closing lines of the play (*Birds* 1720–1765), in Arrowsmith's translation:

CHORUS: Make way! Make way!
                    Fall back for the dancers!
Welcome your King with beating wings!
Dance, dance!
            Praise this happy Prince!
Sing the praise of handsome youth,
sing the loveliness of brides!
Weave with circling feet, weave and dance
in honour of the King, in honour of his bride!
Now let the Golden Age of Birds begin
by lovely marriage ushered in,
    Hymen, Hymenaios O!

To such a song as this
the weaving Fates once led
the universal King,
Zeus the lord of all,
to lovely Hera's bed.
    O Hymen, Hymenaios O!

And blooming Love was there,
Love with shimmering wings,
Love the charioteer!
Love once held the reins,
Love drove the happy pair!
    O Hymen! Hymenaios O!

PEISETAIROS: I thank you for your songs and dance.
    Thank you, thank you, one and all.
CHORUS: Now praise the lightnings of your King!
Sing his thunders crashing on the world!
Sing the blazing bolts of Zeus, praise the man
who hurls them!
           Sing the flare of lightning;
praise, praise the crashing of its awful fire!
    O lightning, flash of livid fire,
    O javelin of Zeus,
              everliving light!

O thunders breaking on this lovely world,
rumble majestic that runs before the rain!
O Lightning and Thunders,
                    bow low, bow down,
bow before this man, bow to the lord of all!
He wields the thunder as his very own.
Lightnings flare at the touch of his hand,
            winning, achieving
the Bride of Heaven and the Crown of God!
    O Hymen, Hymenaios O!

PEISETAIROS: Now follow our bridal party, one and all.
Soar on high, you happy breed of Birds,
to the halls of Zeus, to the bed of love!
    Reach me your hand, dear bride.
    Now take me by my wings,
    oh my lovely,
                my sweet,
    and let me lift you up,
    and soar beside you
    through the buoyant air!

CHORUS: *Alalalai!*
        Io!
            Paion!
O greatest of the gods!
Tenella Kallinikos O!

6
Stage Illusion

Summary

The spectator is an essential participant in the creation of stage illusion. A show is not a show unless it is shown to someone. In a sense, actor and spectator conspire together to create a specific kind of effect. This is done in other fields – by a preacher and his congregation, or by a lecturer and his audience – but the link made in the theatre is of a special kind, involving on the actor's part a double role-playing (that of a performer and that of the part he is performing), and on the spectator's part both an awareness of his own expectation and a continual, willing participation in the role-playing of the actor. The French phrase *assister au théâtre* defines the role of the audience more accurately than corresponding English expressions such as 'going to the theatre' or 'watching a play'.

The 'bridge' between actor and spectator, the moment of performance, is handled in different ways in the theatre of convention (like Greek theatre) and the theatre of illusion (like the work of Ibsen or Chekhov). In particular, the spectator's awareness of the fact of performance itself is a continuous element in the theatre of convention; in the theatre of illusion, on the other hand, the spectator is often invited to absorb himself so thoroughly in the illusion the actors create that he becomes oblivious of the fact of performance or the theatre round him. In comedy, actors in literary comedy tend to remain in character throughout their performance; non-literary, 'stand-up' performers constantly step out of their assigned roles in order to entertain.

Aristophanes handles the bridge between actor and spectator in a unique way, which takes in every one of the features described above. His characters constantly move in and out of their assigned roles, and they regularly treat the people and events of real life as characters or symbols within the illusion of the plot. This dynamic fusion of fiction and fact, plot reality and performance reality, is seen at its most marked in the parabasis; its purpose, there as elsewhere, is to serve the underlying satirical or moral point of the show as a whole.

Realism and convention

The way in which spectators 'assist at' the creation of a stage performance today is different from that in ancient Greece.[47] On the modern proscenium stage the effect aimed at is often as close an approximation to reality as possible. Sets, costumes and lighting are designed to simulate real life (at least within the bounds of theatrical necessity, which insists for example that all the furniture in a proscenium-fronted set is placed facing outwards, looking towards the invisible 'fourth wall' through which the audience perceives the play). In the same way, for the duration of the performance, the actors lay aside their own real-life characters and assume those of the parts they are playing. The intrusion of genuine reality (such as a fire alarm or a plea for silence) into performances of naturalistic plays like those of Chekhov would destroy the illusory reality of the stage spectacle and seriously hinder our enjoyment.

In theatre of this kind, empathy between actor and spectator can be very great indeed. Queen Victoria, for example, was genuinely distressed by Irving's 'suffering' in *The Bells*, and moved by Sarah Bernhardt's 'bravery' in *La Dame aux Camélias*; in the same way today we may accept the 'mystery' of a Garbo and the 'toughness' or 'cynicism' of a Bogart as if they belonged to the real actor rather than to the parts he played. Radio and television actors receive abusive or sympathetic letters, addressed to them by name but treating them according to their illusory characters. To a modern actor, the perils of type-casting are all too familiar.

No illusion of reality was created in the Greek theatre. The conditions and circumstances of performance were such that depiction of reality was hardly possible. If the characters said it was dark or stormy, or described their surroundings are desert, mountain peak, or marsh, the spectators accepted what they said, and were untroubled by the fact that no attempt was made physically to represent these things. Masks, costumes and movements all had conventional associations; verse rhythms and musical modes were each given a specific conventional significance. In the theatre of illusion the effects *simulate* reality; in the theatre of convention the effects *symbolize* reality. The prologue to *Henry V* requests the same kind of 'assistance' in the performance from the Elizabethan audience as was expected from audiences in the Greek theatre.

In the theatre of convention, use is made by actors and audience of what Brecht described as the 'alienation effect'.[48] That is, the performers and audience both stand apart from the events of the story being represented. They connive together in the representation, but no attempt is made to pretend that its events, emotions or effects are real. In fact, the opposite is often the case. The audience are asked, so to speak, to stand aside from the stage action, to think about it and evaluate it as it happens, rather than to absorb themselves in it (as they would in the theatre of illusion). To assist this process the Brechtian author will interrupt the action for parenthetical comment, sometimes by introducing performers not involved in the show itself, or even by appearing onstage himself. This process stresses the theatricality of the performance, but does not invalidate its dramatic meaning or power. A good example of the alienation technique at work is the part of the Common Man in Robert Bolt's *A Man for All Seasons*. He takes part in the performance of scenes from the life of Thomas More, obeying the same rules of illusion as the other characters for the duration of each scene; but he changes his character and costume from scene to scene, and makes these changes in full view of the audience, discussing meanwhile (in his character as Common Man) the meaning of the scenes just past and those to come, or the general point of the play as it is developing.

Two types of illusion in comedy

Thus, whereas actors and spectators in the realistic theatre do their best to disguise the theatricality of the performance, this theatricality is an essential and creative ingredient in performances of the theatre of convention. Even so, the full alienation technique as practised by Brecht and his followers is a comparatively late development. Earlier plays of the conventional theatre often 'frame' the action with material outside the illusion (such as prologues and epilogues), but the main action itself generally observes similar rules to those of the theatre of illusion. That is, the actors hide their real-life characters for the duration of the performance, and completely assume that of the characters they are playing. In Shakespeare, for example, soliloquies and asides are the nearest the characters ever come to a direct rupture of illusion, and even in them the actor speaking remains in character throughout. When we 'assist at' a soliloquy from Iago or Edmund, we never for a moment believe that it is the actor revealing his feelings or intentions rather than the character. In Greek tragedy soliloquies even as open as Shakespeare's are rare: the prologue in Euripides is the nearest single actors (as opposed to the Chorus) come to direct address alienated from the stage action.

In most literary comedy the same principle is observed. Direct addresses to the audience are certainly made, in the form of asides, soliloquies, and even apparent question and answer (for example, in the conventional prologue, 'Are you sitting comfortably? Good. Then the story will begin . . .'). But the convention of tragedy is usually observed here as well: such addresses are almost always made in character, and not in the actor's own real person. This passage from Molière's *L'Avare* (IV, 7) is characteristic:

HARPAGON: Thieves! Thieves! Assassins! Murderers! Justice! Merciful heaven, I'm done for! Murdered! They've cut my throat; they've walked off with my money! Who was it? What's happened to him? Where is he? Where's he hiding? How can I find him? Where should I run? Isn't he there? Isn't he here? Who's that? Stop! Give me back my money, you swine . . . Oh, it's me. What a lot of people there are here. Everyone I clap eyes on looks suspicious to me; they all look like my thief. Hey! What are you talking about down there? My thief? What's that noise up there? Is *that* my thief? Please, if you know anything about my thief, I beg you to tell me. He's not hiding out there, is he? They're all looking at me; they're all laughing. You see they're all part of it, all accomplices . . .

Because the speaker remains 'in character', a soliloquy of that type has its boundaries fixed by the requirements of the plot. It is hard to see, for example, how Harpagon in the speech above could have made any meaningful reference to events outside the theatre (like the political or financial state of France). When such topical comments do occur, they are usually in the form of metaphors. In *Tartuffe*, for example, Tartuffe – while remaining a genuine fictional character, whose actions and words are completely explainable in terms of the stage illusion – also stands as an example of a particular kind of rogue, common in the society of his day. Characters like Ancient Pistol, Face, the Surfaces or Figaro can be viewed as contemporary 'types'; but the spectator who is historically uninformed can also enjoy them simply as characters inside the action, whose behaviour and utterances are satisfactorily (if not completely) explained by the mechanics of the plot.

The illusion in non-literary comedy (of the sort described in Chapter 1) is completely different from this. Very often, in fact, non-literary performers come very close to using the full Brechtian alienation technique. In such performances the performer is for most of the time an 'actor' in a 'play', just like his literary counterpart. But (like a medieval Fool) he can also use topical comment, verbal ingenuity, slapstick, insult and inconsequential routines (W. C. Fields' juggling, for example), or 'running gags', all of which cut directly across the illusion established by the general plot. The technique reached its apogee in film musicals and modern film and television comedy. We expect Gene Kelly to dance, and are not affronted when the (photographically realistic) illusion is ruptured to let him do so. We expected Jack Benny not only to assume roles in sketches, but also – in those same sketches – to keep the well established features of his own public personality. In the same way, such performers as Bob Hope and the Marx Brothers were accustomed to have scripts written or adapted especially for them, rather than appearing in 'straight' comedies. They retained certain well-known personal traits in every performance, instead of assuming ready-made parts in a separately existing script. In short, such performers were 'comedians' first and 'actors' (bound by the plot) second.

To performers of this type, anything at all can be grist to the humorous mill. A clear example is the following extract (written for the English television comedian Frankie Howerd). Here the performer is playing the part of a Viking, and what he has to say concerns this illusory role, at least in part. But the script is also filled with remarks made outside the Viking character. References are made to the studio audience, to Howerd's employers (the BBC), to comic rivals and to the political situation then current. Above all, Howerd's own 'real' persona overrides everything; his 'naughty boy', suggestive manner governs the style of every word said:

HOWERD: Yes. Well. Oh. You see, then? (*pause; he listens off-camera*) Eh? Ehh? Oh. Ah. Yes. That's it, is it? I should say so. (*to camera*) Thought you'd all gone home. Oh, you *are* at home? What? Mmmm. No, don't laugh . . . State the country's in, laughs are rationed to three a night. (*to studio audience*) I said, rationed to three . . . oh, never mind. Please yourselves. (*to camera*) No no, not you. This lot here. The usual set-up. Rent-a-crowd. Six stage-hands, two tea-ladies, and fifteen people who couldn't get tickets for Bruce Forsyth. (*to studio audience*) Couldn't get one, could you, dear? (*to camera*) Deaf as a post. (*to audience*) I said, couldn't get one. For Brucie. Couldn't get . . . oh, forget it. (*to camera*) Anyway, we're all here, in this Viking settlement. Oh yes, I know what you're thinking . . . I *know* what you're thinking. (*to audience*) No dear, not that. (*to camera*) We all know what *she's* thinking. Eighty-seven yesterday, and a mind like a sewer. A sew-*er*. Yes. Now then . . .

Illusion in Aristophanes

The opening monologue of *Acharnians* not only makes use of the conventions of Greek theatre and gratifies the spectator's expectation of a particular kind of comic spectacle, but is absolutely typical of Aristophanes' style, and in particular of the unique way in which he handles stage illusion. A lone, elderly figure (who will remain unnamed until line 406, over half an hour into the play) comes onstage and indicates that he is waiting, rather impatiently (1–42):

> Really! The shocks my system's had!
> Not much to smile at . . . no, not much at all,
> Compared with shocks as numberless as sand.
> Let's see, what *did* I like? What really made
> Me sit up and cheer? I know – just one good thing:
> That massive fine puked up by Kleon! Yes,
> That really was a tonic; thank you, Knights,
> For doing that – worthy of Greece, it was.
> Then came a really tragic blow: I was sitting
> At the festival, mouth open for some Aeschylus –
> And what did they announce? 'Theognis next!'
> Theognis! What a chilly blast that was!
> Another good thing: Moschos finished playing,
> And Dexitheos came out to sing a Boeotian song.
> But then, *this* year! I died, I went cross-eyed
> When Chairis slipped that warlike number in.
> But never before, not since I began
> To wash, have my eyes smarted so much with soap
> As now, today: a full Assembly called
> For this morning – and the Pnyx is empty: look!
> They're all in the Agora, chattering away,
> And trying to dodge the rope. Not even

The officials have turned up: they're always late,
And when they *do* arrive, you should see them
Jostling and fighting for the front-row seats,
Like a river in spate. How to make peace?
Never a word on that. O Athens, Athens!
I'm first in the Assembly, every time,
Eagerly waiting. I sit and wait, alone:
I groan, I yawn, I stretch, I fart, I'm bored,
I scribble, scratch, do sums in my head;
I look out at my farm, longing for peace,
Yearning for my village, hating city life –
My village! It's never told me yet, 'Want coal?
Then buy it!' Not coal, or vinegar, or oil –
No buying needed. My village satisfied
My needs itself, without a 'buy' in sight.
So now I'm here to shout and clap and heckle
If anyone talks of anything else at all but peace.
Ah! Here come the officials . . . after noon.
Didn't I say so? Pushing and shoving,
Each of them wanting the same best seat.

A comparison of that soliloquy with those of Harpagon and Howerd shows at once how much closer Aristophanes' style is to the non-literary than to the literary convention. Dikaiopolis mentions real political, literary and social facts in the course of his speech, which is ostensibly that of an old countryman. Later in the play he quotes from and parodies tragedy, in a manner more like that of a literary scholar than an illiterate old man. In the course of the play he also briefly assumes the roles of priest (in the Phallic procession, 242ff.), judge and jury (in the sequences with the Informer, 818–828, 910–951), and persuasive orator (in the central speech, 496–556).

This complexity of role is partly explained by the place of fantasy in the plot. Because of his strange and mighty deed, Dikaiopolis is elevated from his peasant stature to become a kind of surrealist superman, one of whose attributes is the ability to dominate any situation. This protean ability is one of the main qualities of the *poneros* (see p. 55); but it can be readily seen that the *poneria* of Dikaiopolis is more like that of Frankie Howerd than that of Harpagon.

On looking more closely, however, it is clear that the rupture of illusion in the Howerd comedy is in fact very different indeed from that in *Acharnians*. Howerd jumps out of his assigned role simply in order to amuse: his comments and asides are completely non-functional, or even dysfunctional, in terms of the Viking role. But wherever Dikaiopolis ruptures the comic illusion, he does so to make a satirical point which is outside, but entirely relevant to, the plot of *Acharnians*. The Howerd asides have none of the point and satirical relevance of Dikaiopolis' remarks about Kleon, Aeschylus, Chairis and the rest. They are not less funny, but the humour serves a different purpose.

What happens is that instead of stepping out of character to make a topical allusion, Dikaiopolis draws real people and events *inside* the comic plot. They remain real and topical, but assume a role of their own within the fiction. When Howerd describes his audience as tea-ladies and people who have failed to get tickets for Bruce Forsyth, the humour is in the incongruity of the images. But when Dikaiopolis mentions Kleon or Chairis, a precise satirical point is made in addition to that incongruity. This absorption of 'real life' into the fantasy world is a quality central to Aristophanes' comic method, and it is one of his most original contributions to the style of stage comedy as a whole.

The reason for its undoubted success lies, perhaps, in the unity imposed on the plays by their serious themes, which serve to bind and articulate an otherwise random collection of episodes. The technique is familiar today in comic novels (for example *Don Quixote, Gulliver's Travels, Oblomov, The Good Soldier Švejk*), where the underlying seriousness is as much part of the fabric as the comic superstructure. It is hardly ever used, however, in comic drama: satirical sketches nowadays are a separate genre entirely from legitimate comedy. Even comedies with a serious underlying theme (like those of Chekhov, Eliot or Anouilh) studiously avoid breaks in the dramatic illusion, such as are common in non-literary, stand-up comedy. (That this is deliberate can be seen if *Uncle Vanya* is compared with one of Chekhov's short monologues, like the burlesque lecture *On the Dangers of Tobacco*.)

The following passage from Aristophanes' *Peace* (135–179) shows his comic mixture at its most inventive. Trygaios remains in character throughout, as an old farmer. We are conscious all the time that he is about to fly up on a giant dung-beetle to visit Zeus. At the same time, we accept as part of his character the entirely unlikely idea that he is expert enough in Euripides to parody him at some length in talking to his daughter. We further accept the jokes made about the theatrical performance itself. Indeed, the references to the reality of the theatre help us to accept the surrealist invention of the flight to heaven in the first place (see Chapter 5). The beetle is both real (and hungry) and a construction of wood and canvas operated by a careless mechanic; the landing-place is both the home of Zeus and the *terra firma* the actor has been so keen to reach; the audience are not only the war-greedy people of Athens, but also the spectators of this particular piece of staging. The illusion (of an old farmer flying to Zeus) is never actually broken. Instead, everything that has to do with the performance itself is taken in and incorporated as an essential part of that illusion. The theatrical sleight-of-hand is simple, but striking:

CHILD: A wingèd horse like Pegasus would take
            You up to Zeus in far more tragic style.
TRYGAIOS: A wingèd horse? I'd need two lots of food.
            But this way, what I eat myself, in course
            Of time I feed the beetle with as well.

CHILD: What if thou tumblest in the stormy brine?
           How can thy wingèd beetle save thee then?
TRYGAIOS: Canst thou not see I go prepared? Behold
           My oar, erect and ready: *he's* the boat.
CHILD: But dad, what port will take thee, wand'ring, in?
TRYGAIOS: Stag-beetle Harbour, in Piraeus bay.
CHILD: Take care, lest on the road you slip and fall,
           And, lame and limping, give Euripides
           A theme, and end up tragedied in verse.
TRYGAIOS: Yes, I'll take care of that. And now, farewell.
           Ladies and gentlemen, this trip of mine
           Is all for you: don't fart or shit for three
           Full days – for if he gets your wind from up
           On high, he'll throw me off and dive for dinner.
              Gee up now, Pegasus, prance away,
              Pricking your ears to the golden chink
              Of the bit and bridle. Come, away!
              Hey! What d'you think you're doing? Don't
              Divert your nose towards the public bogs!
              Lift yourself cheerfully up, stretch out
              Your fleeting wings, and fly straight up
              To the heavenly courts of Zeus.
              Absent thee from felicity awhile –
              Absent thyself from all thy dungy food.
              Hey, you down there, what are you doing
              Shitting beside that whore-house in Piraeus?
              You'll be the death of me! Dig a hole,
              And bury it under a mound of earth!
              Cover it with funeral wreaths
              And sprinkle perfume over it. If I fall
              And get killed, the Crap-athians
              Will squeeze out an arsetronomical fine
              – And all because of your unruly bum.
           Oh dear! I'm not enjoying this, you know.
           You on the crane, keep your mind on your job,
            Can't you? My navel's knotted up with wind –
           Another lurch, and I'll give the beetle lunch.
           Aha! But this is Zeus' place, methinks.
           Hey, open up! Is anyone at home?

Actors and audience

The last passage shows Aristophanes' blend of reality and illusion at its most subtle. The audience is invited to laugh at Trygaios both as a character in a fiction and as a comic actor playing a part before their eyes. The performance becomes a dynamic part of the fiction, and the fictional elements have a dynamic effect on the style of performance. A similar duality of audience response is solicited throughout the comedies, and enables Aristophanes to shift the emphasis at any moment (and for the briefest of instants) from the point the characters have reached in the plot to the point the actors have reached in the performance, and vice versa. This not only allows him to make whatever topical points or other remarks he wishes without destroying the illusion (for there is no illusion to destroy); it also invests the individual player and indeed the whole performance with a sort of *poneria* of style: that is, the feeling that the occasion is a game whose rules depend on the mood of the moment, and which the players are watching with as much delight as the spectators.

Another example of the juxtaposition, for humorous and didactic effect, of the reality of the performance and the illusion of the play being performed is the sharp visual joke which underlies the whole performance of *Frogs*. As one of the preliminary rites of the City Dionysia, a statue of Dionysos was carried in procession from a temple near the Academy to the Theatre of Dionysos, where it stood in state throughout the theatrical performances.[49] Thus, the buffoon Dionysos of *Frogs* would perform throughout the play in front of his own 'real' image. This places the whole performance of the play Dionysos in a kind of satirical setting of its own – and that setting is then exploited by the actor in passages such as this, where the god-in-the-play makes a burlesque appeal to the real priest of the real god, in his throne on the front row of the theatre (293–297):

DIONYSOS: It must be Empousa.
XANTHIAS: That's right: her whole face
       Is red with fire.
DIONYSOS: Is one leg made of copper?
XANTHIAS: That's right. And the other one is . . . cow-dung.
DIONYSOS: Oh dear, where can I hide?
XANTHIAS (*mocking*):   Where can I hide?
DIONYSOS: Save me, priest, if you want to drink with me.

A similar effect is created in *Peace* by having the whole performance after line 519 take place in front of the rescued statue of the goddess. Here the effect is moral rather than satirical: the benign presence of the rescued goddess permeates every action, every moment of rejoicing now that war is finally gone.

The actors' awareness of their own performance, and their alliance with the audience in watching and enjoying that performance, leads to a particular kind of intimacy between players and spectators. The performers constantly comment on this intimacy, and make full satirical use of it. Direct references to the spectators are a feature of the non-literary comedian's art; they probably came into Old Comedy from the *komos* revelry of the old phallic processions (where, perhaps to avert bad luck, buffoons were posted along the route to mock the worshippers as they passed). In comedy, the humour was often coarse and slapstick. Aristophanes himself implies as much in *Wealth* 795–801 (a passage which gets the best of both worlds, high-minded and lowbrow, since 'figs' was Athenian slang for the genitals):

WEALTH: Anoint me indoors, by the hearth.
That way they can't accuse us of being vulgar.
It isn't dignified for an author
To throw dried figs and sweets to the audience
And try to bribe them to laugh that way.
WIFE: Quite right. Dexinikos is standing up
Already, trying to get his hands on the figs.

As well as wooing the spectators with nuts and figs, it was also common practice for the actors to step out of the dramatic action early in the play, and 'explain the plot'. This is done in *Knights*, *Wasps*, *Peace* and *Birds*, and the opening monologues in *Acharnians* and *Clouds* serve the same function in a less overt way. The most notable use of this 'stepping-aside' technique is Dikaiopolis' central speech in *Acharnians* (496–556) – where the duality between the actor performing in the plot and the actor observing his own performance allows Aristophanes to keep the political commentary light and humorous (as it is not, for example, in the mouths of performers who remain in character, like Lysistrata or Praxagora, or in the parabasis, where the departure from the main plot of the play is more marked).

The spectators were occasionally flattered – usually at the end of long sections of complex discussion which may have bored them – as in this passage from *Frogs*, which follows a 95-line (nearly 10-minute) discussion, in fairly serious terms, of the role played by the artist in society (*Frogs* 1099–1118, in David Barrett's translation):

CHORUS: As for the audience,
You are mistaken
If you think subtle points
Will not be taken.
Such fears are vain, I vow;
They've all got textbooks now –
However high your brow,
They won't be shaken.

No talking down to these:
That's all outdated!
For native wit alone
They're highly rated;
But now they've learnt to read
It's real tough stuff they need;
They don't want chicken-feed –
They're educated!

Passages of explanation or flattery, however, are markedly less funny than those of insult, and are therefore much less frequent. The audience are most often treated as in this passage (*Frogs* 273–276), where Dionysos has just reached the Underworld, and is looking out for the landmarks Herakles has told him to expect:

DIONYSOS: What's over that way?
XANTHIAS: Oh, just dark and dung.
DIONYSOS: Have you seen the parricides down here,
                and the oath-breakers he mentioned?
XANTHIAS (*pointing at the audience*): There: can't you?
DIONYSOS: Oh yes . . . yes, so I can. They're here all right.

In a particularly notable instance of this type of insult (*Clouds* 1087–1104), it is used as the culmination of a burlesque argument (the argument between Right and Wrong). Its style is a parody of the Socratic question-and-answer method, and the joke about the audience comes as a kind of *reductio ad absurdum*, the climax of a 20-minute scene of ever-increasing ludicrousness. The argument ends as follows:

WRONG: What will you say if I convince you?
RIGHT: Nothing more – what else?
WRONG: All right. Tell me,
                Who runs the lawcourts for us?
RIGHT: Buggers.
WRONG: Good. Who writes us tragedies?
RIGHT: Buggers.
WRONG: Good. Who runs on in the Assembly?
RIGHT: Buggers.
WRONG: There you are, then. Don't you see?
                What about the audience out there?
                Look carefully.
RIGHT: All right, I'm looking.
WRONG: What d'you see?
RIGHT: Good lord, most of them are buggers too!
                I know that one . . . and that one over there . . .
                And that one with the shoulder-length hair . . .
WRONG: So what d'you say now?
RIGHT: I'm beaten. Buggers, open up, and take
                My cloak. I'm coming over
                To join you.

Individuals

When the audience is drawn into the action of a play, the actors give it a character to suit the needs of each particular occasion. A different process is used with the individuals from real life who are taken into the plays and mentioned by name. Most of them are used as no more than stock jokes, recurring in the same *persona* on each occasion, and with one predominant feature (lisping, effeminacy, corruption) emphasized above all others. The actors remain within the dramatic action, and the real individuals are lampooned in a dehumanized, mythological way: an instantly recognizable comic impression is given, so brief that it hardly interrupts the flow of the stage illusion.

A good example of this is Aristophanes' treatment of Kleonymos. Whatever else is known about him from other sources, to Aristophanes and his audience he meant one thing only: the fat man who threw his shield away and ran for it. He is mentioned by name, and this lapse is recalled, no less than twenty times, in seven of the eleven plays. Usually the references are very short, and are used in much the same way as metaphors or puns – that is, as one might say 'Croesus-rich' without breaking the stage illusion. This reference, one of three in *Wasps*, is typical (818–823):

PHILOKLEON: Very good: there's just one thing missing.
BDELYKLEON: What's that?
PHILOKLEON: We need a little shrine of Lykos.
BDELYKLEON: Here:
        One shrine. That slave's its patron saint.
PHILOKLEON: O Lykos, lord, I never recognized you.
BDELYKLEON: He looks as big as Kleonymos to me.
PHILOKLEON: True: heroic size, and not a shield in sight.

It is clear that neither Philokleon nor Bdelykleon step out of character here: Kleonymos' size and cowardice have achieved mythical status. He undergoes two even more notable transformations in other plays – again, because of his status as a living myth – without rupturing the stage illusion. In *Clouds* 680 he becomes female; and in one of the most fantastic passages in Aristophanes, he turns into a grotesque, shield-shedding tree (*Birds* 1470–1481, in Arrowsmith's version):

CHORUS: Many the marvels I have seen,
        the wonders on land and sea;
    but the strangest sight I ever saw
        was the weird KLEONYMOS-tree.

    It grows in faraway places;
        its lumber looks quite stout,
    but the wood is good for nothing,
        for the heart is rotten out.

    In Spring it grows gigantic
        with sycophantic green,
    and bitter buds of slander
        on every bough are seen.

    But when, like war, cold winter comes,
        this strange KLEONYMOS yields,
    instead of leaves like other trees,
        a crop of coward's shields.

But the process of dehumanizing and mythologizing goes further even than that. Aristophanes frequently takes real people bodily into his plots, and makes them characters integral to the play and wholly bound by the limits of the stage illusion. Sometimes these creations are two-dimensional, in the same way as the short references to live individuals mentioned above: Lamachos' brief appearance in *Peace* 470–474 (where he does not even speak) is typical. At other times a detailed and rounded comic character is created. Lamachos in *Acharnians*, Kleon in *Knights*, Socrates in *Clouds*, Meton in *Birds*, Euripides and Agathon in *Women at the Festival*, Aeschylus and Euripides in *Frogs* – all these characters are as much part of the stage illusion, and as real within it, as any of the created characters. They have a status like that of the gods who appear (Hermes, War and Quarrel in *Peace*; Iris, Prometheus, Poseidon, Triballos and Herakles in *Birds*; Dionysos, Aiakos and Pluto in *Frogs*; Wealth, Poverty and Hermes in *Wealth*). In the case of the gods, their stage character is often at variance with their attributes in 'real' life. In the case of the humans, one or two real-life characteristics are exaggerated to form a rounded comic whole.

Once illusion has completely swallowed up reality, truth to life becomes a matter of no importance. Obviously there would be no point to the joke unless Socrates, Euripides and the rest retained some part of their real-life characters. But equally obviously, once they become characters in the illusion, they move within the bounds and conventions of that illusion and not those of real life. It is this that makes scholarly pursuit of the 'real' Socrates or Euripides in Aristophanes little more than an after-dinner intellectual game. What truth to reality the characters ever had is as much swallowed up in illusion as that of Freud or Einstein in a comedian's patter today.

The parabasis

The last and in some ways most controversial juxtaposition of reality and stage illusion occurs within the parabasis.[50] In this the Chorus (sometimes in its character according to the plot, sometimes speaking as a comic Chorus in a theatre) performs a fairly long passage (up to 20 minutes) of music, dancing and topical comment. The words sometimes relate to the plot of the play. But often, and for long stretches of dialogue, political and satirical comments are made which are quite external to the play, and sometimes even to the circumstances of the performance at which the parabasis is being performed. (The word *parabasis* means literally 'a stepping-aside', and may refer directly to the dropping of the Chorus' role within the play or its performance, and the assumption of another role entirely, that of a dramatic Chorus in general, the mouthpiece of the god of drama at a dramatic festival.)

Only in *Birds* does the Chorus remain in its stage character throughout the parabasis – and even there 20 lines out of 120 refer explicitly to Athenian politics and theatre practice. The mixture of illusion and reality is more usually like that in the parabasis of *Wasps* (1009–1121). This can be analysed as follows:

1009–1013 Introduction (Chorus-men as wasps, but speaking to 'countless hordes' of theatre spectators): the transition is made from the actors who have just left the stage to the non-illusory material of the parabasis.

1014–1059 The Chorus (speaking as a Chorus, Aristophanes' mouthpiece) speaks of the playwright's excellence, his political enemies, his dramatic rivals, and his hopes for the success of this particular play.

1060–1070 Chorus-men dance, in character as wasps.

1071–1090 The Chorus-men explain to the audience why they are dressed as wasps (the reasons are political). In this section the mixture of real life with theatre illusion is particularly adept. The speakers *are* wasps, but speak of real-life events as the reason for this role.

1091–1121 Two further sections developing the theme of the previous one. The Chorus-men are sometimes wasps, sometimes old men, but generally a mixture of the two; they are as aware as the audience that they are playing a role, and of the metaphorical implications of that role. But they take the role very seriously, and expect the audience to do the same. (The wasp garb is a kind of visual metaphor for the political ambitions of the elderly.)

It used to be argued that the parabasis was a notable interruption of the stage illusion,[51] and thus of the play as a whole. But it seems to me that this belief arose from a fundamental misconception of the true nature of illusion in Greek comedy. There is no break in illusion, because the audience is as much part of the performance, and of the illusion, as the actors. Direct addresses in the parabasis are merely an extension of similar passages in the dialogue. The shifting role of the audience is a deliberate creation; in the parabasis, as elsewhere in the play, the dual relationship between actors and spectators is used as a means both of generating humour and of making serious or satirical points. In fact, like everything else in Aristophanes, the passing from illusion to reality and back is used to serve one or other of his two main purposes: either it emphasizes the serious message which underlies the comic plot, or it is simply there for its own amusing sake.

7

Bawdy

Summary

Bawdy has two main functions in Aristophanes' writing. Firstly, it is used both generally and in detail to articulate the main moral theme of his work, that natural behaviour produces more happiness than artificial systems of thought or action. This is particularly obvious in the peace plays, where bawdy sexuality is one of the principal symbols of the restoration of normality sought by the characters. But in the other plays too, politics, sophistry, science, false religion and bad poetry are all badged with the same restricted, glum view of human life, to which the hero's unabashed and bawdy naturalness offers an exciting alternative.[52]

Bawdy is not, however, only a functional, structural device, a series of controlling images used to articulate moral themes. Its other (equally important) function is that it is funny in its own right – as productive of laughter as any other of the human activities portrayed in the plays, and a primary means of communication between comedian and audience.[53] In this respect Aristophanes is in the mainstream of comic practice the world over. For like double-takes, pratfalls, puns and slapstick, reference to 'taboo' subjects (whether sexual, scatological or of any other kind) is one of the principal *lazzi* or comic routines which lie at the heart of comic performance. Like other *lazzi*, too, bawdy can be used by the comedian in a variety of ways, ranging from outright obscenity to subtle and suggestive irony.

The role of bawdy in comic performance

Part of our delight in watching comedy is in seeing the comedian overstepping the normal bounds and conventions of our own everyday world. He is a kind of licensed buffoon, a scapegoat who confronts and overcomes our taboos. He is free of the complexity of everyday morality; cause and effect are not the same for him as for us; he is as innocent and therefore as harmless as a child – and the fact that he is free of our restraints, but still equipped with all our knowledge, gives him a status almost infinitely fertile for him as a performer of comedy, and no less satisfying for us as spectators. In the character of the *poneros*, knowing innocence reaches a delirious height where (as in the case of tragic heroism) something of the fundamental humanity of man is revealed. Whitman, *ACH*, pp. 259–280, discusses the world of such a man in terms of what he calls 'the higher slapstick'. It is a world, he says (ibid., p. 276), where the spectator is given

> more than a vicarious satisfaction of individual desire; it is a feeling of sublime peace, of an access of knowledge which is true, of a revelation of the nature of things. Custard pie has become a way of life, and the world has been transformed by it . . . The boundless swings into view, and the yearning which is satisfied is too deep and humane ever to be purged from the human psyche. It is the heroic longing, fulfilling its own metaphor of order, its own order, sprouting wings and deposing Zeus.

This is a large claim – but no larger than those involved in theories of tragic catharsis. Ionesco has said that both tragedy and comedy allow us to peer over 'the edge of the abyss'. In tragedy what we see makes us scream with terror, in comedy with laughter, but in each case the effect of catharsis is the same. The beings who enter the abyss on our behalf, the tragic and comic heroes, are stripped down, refined versions of ourselves, freed from the irrelevant trappings of our reality.

Types of bawdy

For the purposes of this chapter the *lazzi* involving bawdy, as used in Aristophanes, are divided into the following groups:

(1) *Explicit bawdy.* The performer uses sexual or scatological words for their shock value. The unexpectedness (and sometimes the unexpected aptness) of what is said arouses the spectator's admiration. Often bawdy puns are used in this way.

(2) *Explicit bawdy prepared.* This is the same as (1) except that the performers lead up to it in advance. The enjoyment for the spectator is partly in the anticipation of bawdy, and partly in the fulfilment of that expectation. The method is sometimes varied by replacing the expected shock with another (often a totally innocent word, sometimes an expressive silence).

(3) *Explicit bawdy involving a third party.* In this one performer uses bawdy language or behaviour to ridicule another. The enjoyment for the spectator lies partly in the bawdy and partly in a feeling of complicity with one performer against the other.

(4) *Secondary bawdy.* In this the performers converse or act together in a bawdy manner. The spectator's enjoyment may be in the agonistic nature of the performance, and may be partly that of a voyeur.

(5) *Double entendre.* This is the largest category, and takes in many of the techniques of (1–4) above. Sometimes it depends on the irony that words or gestures which seem innocent to some or all of the performers are clearly

seen as bawdy by the spectators. At other times all parties are aware of the bawdy overtones, and the performance proceeds, so to speak, on two levels of meaning at once. Double entendre is a particularly satisfying variation of the ridicule procedure described in (3) above, because it replaces aggression with irony.

(6) *Bawdy gesture.* In all the above categories, it is possible for the performers totally to change the meaning of ordinary words or phrases by accompanying them with bawdy gestures. In the fantastic world of the Aristophanic hero everyday objects very often assume a phallic role without a word being said.

It is important to note that practically none of these procedures would work at all (that is, generate humour) if it were not for the distancing effect of the stage performance. In real life, each of the categories of bawdy above might produce embarrassment or anger rather than mirth. The comedian's mask and padded phallus symbolize his escape from the conventions of the 'real' world, and allow him – paradoxically – to enter what may seem a truer, simpler plane of 'reality': that of genuine naturalness as compared with the systems that inhibit the spectators. In fact the total extraversion of comedy at the Athenian festivals gives it a primal, childlike innocence (which affects the politics in the plays as well as the bawdy) – an innocence generally absent in the more inhibited stage drama of the Christian era, though still a feature of non-literary comedy (such as that of fools, jesters, the *commedia dell'arte* and music-hall), where it produces a similarly uproarious and uninhibited feeling of Saturnalia.[54]

Explicit bawdy

In its simplest form, explicit bawdy consists of a single bawdy word or gesture incorporated into an otherwise unbawdy context, which diverts that context into a short, non-functional comic routine. A good example is the last word in *Peace* 42 ('This beast belongs to Zeus, lord of the thunder-crap'). Here a traditional epithet of Zeus, *kataibatou* ('who descends (in lightning)') is modified by one letter to *skataibatou* ('who treads in dung'). The word completes the punch line of a short routine in which the slaves have been trying to guess which god might be the beetle's patron. A similar effect is produced in *Birds* 667–674:

PEISETAIROS: Zeus almighty, what a lovely bird!
                What colour! What a figure!
EUELPIDES: I wouldn't mind getting stuck in there.
PEISETAIROS: Golden! Like a virgin bride.
EUELPIDES: I've got to give her a kiss, at least.
PEISETAIROS: Er, no. The beak, look. You'll regret it.
EUELPIDES. No problem. It's just like shelling an egg.

Here Peisetairos' initial aesthetic appreciation of the flautist nightingale is redirected by Euelpides' bawdy rejoinder into a dialogue in double entendre about the flautist's beak. A scatological joke of the same length is made in *Frogs* 479, where Dionysos replaces the standard formula for pouring offerings, *ekkechutai: kalei theon* ('it's poured; call the god'), with *ekkechoda: kalei theon* ('I've shat myself; call the god'), and leads the dialogue into a passage of double entendre concerning a sponge and the precise location of his heart.

Such routines are short (usually about 5 lines), explicit, and are accompanied by or lead into physical slapstick. In this simple form, frequent in all the plays, the bawdy plays a purely inconsequential role, and exists solely to evoke laughter. In two cases, however, direct functional use is made of explicit bawdy in performance: it is used to make comprehensible what might otherwise seem impossibly fantastic, to reduce the mysterious to the everyday. In *Wealth* the most fantastic section is that in which Karion describes the night spent in the temple of Asklepios (653–767), during which the god appeared and restored Wealth's sight. Karion's bawdy and the reaction of Chremylos' wife serve both to 'distance' the fantasy, by making it seem part of a comic (and bawdy) story, and also to relate the most extraordinary sections of the narrative to everyday matters comprehensible by all the spectators. In addition, the cathartic effect of the laughter induced by the bawdy is that it breaks up the solemnity and mystery of what is being described. Karion inextricably mixes two stories together: that of the healing and that of his theft of the old woman's porridge and its subsequent effect on his bowels. The priest's baffling and mysterious behaviour in the dark temple (676ff.) is glossed by Karion as everyday theft, and leads him to steal the porridge. This theft produces the first bawdy lines, in which Karion describes the old woman's reaction to his hissing (that is, to what she takes to be a fantastic and mysterious apparition, Asklepios' sacred snakes): 'She rolled herself up and lay still, farting sharper than a cat' (693–694). When Asklepios appears – the height of mystery in the scene – Karion himself farts in the god's face (699); the word *apepardon* ('I farted') leads the actors to a routine of 10 lines discussing how the gods reacted. (The use of bawdy to demystify the mysterious is paralleled in the same passage by the way in which the mysterious healing of Wealth is parodied by the wholly naturalistic treatment of Neokleides' eyes, described in 714–726 and brought back in 747 as a kind of punch line that concludes the entire narrative.)

A similar mixture of the everyday with moments of extreme fantasy is Trygaios' flight in *Peace* (154–176, quoted on pp. 85–86). Aristophanes facilitates our acceptance of the fantasy by blending two realistic ideas (the rapaciousness of dung-beetles and the carelessness of crane-operators) with the most unreal parts of the dialogue. Each piece of surreal fantasy is followed by a short passage of realistic, explicit bawdy. Thus, 154–156 (the beginning of the flight: fantasy) leads to 157–158 (the lurch towards the latrines: bawdy); 159–163 (the flight itself: fantasy) leads to 164–171 (the man shitting in Piraeus: bawdy); and 172–176 (Trygaios about to shit in fright because of the wobbling crane, and so feed the beetle by mistake) combines the two elements, and unites real flight and fantasy flight until we happily accept them as one and the same.

The other major use of explicit bawdy is in more extended *lazzi*, where it is used to comment on other characters or statements in the action. In performance the effect is to isolate and ridicule the character so treated, usually by the stock clown's methods of pretending to misunderstand what is being said, or concentrating on matters not apparent to the speaker. The most obvious example is probably *Lysistrata* 1111ff., where the appearance of the desirable young goddess Reconciliation causes bawdy reactions in both the Athenian and the Spartan, and the whole issue of peace and war is gradually reduced to a question of who is to fuck Reconciliation, and how soon (further on this passage, see p. 159). In the same way (though here it is the serious character who uses bawdy to discomfort frauds), Dikaiopolis' bawdy interpolations in the Assembly scene in *Acharnians* are functional rather than inconsequential. His continued implication that the envoys, like the Athenian people they are deluding, are buggers[55] is the burlesque statement of a serious political point, and concerns the underlying theme of the whole play. As in the *Lysistrata* scene, the bawdy here underpins several minutes of the action (it first appears in line 79, and the last bawdy remark is at 161).

The functional nature of bawdy in both those passages is, however, rather uncharacteristic of Aristophanes' use of explicit bawdy. Usually the *lazzi* are not functional ingredients of the plot, but a feature of the way the actors perform the play. The text is merely an indication of how a scene should go; in performance its actual style might depend a great deal on physical action, and additions by the actors (such as vocal volume, funny voices, or pace) which we cannot now recapture. Scenes like Strepsiades' bawdy reaction to the bent-over students in *Clouds* 184ff. and Mnesilochos' approaches to the effeminate Agathon and his slave in *Women at the Festival* 29ff. probably contained a large amount of such physical burlesque. The scene between Chremylos, the old woman and the young man in *Wealth* 959ff. may have depended for its effect on the precarious dignity affected by the actor playing the old woman (see Chapter 10). Certainly there is dignity in her lines, and it is in marked contrast with the suggestiveness of Chremylos or the bawdy buffoonery of the young man (see especially 970f., 1017, 1024, 1037, 1055ff., 1067, 1082f. and 1093).

Secondary bawdy

There are four lengthy scenes of secondary bawdy in Aristophanes. They are the Kinesias/Myrrhine scene in *Lysistrata* (829–979), the unmasking scene in *Women at the Festival* (636–651), the Scythian scene in the same play (1160–1225) and the scene between the young man and three old women in *Assemblywomen* (976–1111). Though all four are different in detail, bawdy is in each case the main point of the scene in performance. However much the action is derived from or integrated with the controlling theme of the play, it is elaborated and developed in performance into a succession of stock comic *lazzi*, until the bawdy element temporarily supersedes the underlying theme.

Of the four scenes, the two in *Women at the Festival* are the simplest and come closest to the sort of primitive, rustic humour Aristophanes and his actors might have learnt from the tradition of improvised comedy. In the first of them, the unmasking scene (where Mnesilochos' female disguise is stripped from him at the festival), structure and language parody a Euripidean recognition scene. From the arrival of Kleisthenes (574) to the beginning of the actual slapstick (634), Aristophanes' parody is concerned with the question-and-answer technique of such scenes, and bawdy is largely absent. But at the point where in a Euripidean scene the characters would reveal their names it is Mnesilochos' sex that is to be revealed, and from this point onwards the scene consists of riotous slapstick in traditional manner, in which the old man's phallus seems to assume a character and identity of its own (638–651, in Barrett's translation):

KLEISTHENES:	Off with that girdle, quick!
MNESILOCHOS:	Oh, what a – you ought to be ashamed of yourself!
WOMAN:	If this is a woman, it's a mighty tough specimen. There you are, you see? No tits like ours at all.
MNESILOCHOS:	That's because I'm barren. I never had a child.
WOMAN:	A moment ago you were the mother of nine.
KLEISTHENES:	Stand up straight! What have you done with it?
WOMAN:	Oooh! He's pushed it through to the back. A beauty, too – such a pretty colour.
KLEISTHENES:	Where? I can't see it.
WOMAN:	It's back in front again.
KLEISTHENES:	No it isn't.
WOMAN:	No, here it is again.
KLEISTHENES:	What is all this, a shuttle service across the Isthmus?
WOMAN:	Oh, the scoundrel! And to think that he was standing up there, abusing us and defending Euripides!
MNESILOCHOS:	Well, this is a fine mess I've got myself into.

The same sort of reworking of traditional material appears in the Scythian scene which ends the play. A burlesque old man chasing a naked girl round the theatre, and being constantly frustrated in his sexual intentions, is standard comic business, as traditional as the idea of a comic foreigner, also used in this scene. Aristophanes makes use of these standard *lazzi* in much the same way as Lope de Vega, Goldoni or Molière incorporated the *lazzi* of the *commedia dell' arte* into literary drama: in this case he adds to them the splendid irony that Euripides has had to disguise himself as a woman (and an old bawd at that) in order to retrieve a situation he himself created by slandering women in the first place. Thus the controlling themes of the play (Euripidean tragedy and the blurring of sexual identity) are blended with standard phallic knockabout to produce an ending as subtle in dramatic technique as it is simple and effective in performance.

Theme and style are blended in the same manner in the Kinesias/Myrrhine scene in *Lysistrata*. The basic routine is that of a comically erect husband frustrated, and incorporates many of the *lazzi* of seduction. But the traditional elements are put to functional use and related to the controlling idea of the whole plot, that war and sex are inimical; that is, the *lazzi* are not only funny in their own right, but also exemplify the general message of the play.[56] The very names of the characters indicate their allegorical status (Kinesias comes from *kinein*, 'to fuck', and Myrrhine means a myrtle-wreath, a standard euphemism for the cunt[57]). Throughout the scene Myrrhine plays the innocent straight-man to Kinesias' *bomolochos*: his is the plight, his the bawdy (869; 873ff., where *katabainein*, 'to go down', is reiterated too often for its double entendre to escape even the densest spectator; 876; 928; 934; 940; 943; 947), and his the comic, bawdy lament with the Chorus when Myrrhine finally deserts him.

The seduction scene in *Assemblywomen* uses traditional routines in a very different way. Although the *lazzi* (basically a reversal of the standard seduction scene, with old hags the seducers and a young man the seduced) are loosely connected in theme with the rest of the play – in the sense that it is Praxagora's new polity that makes this whole episode possible – the scene remains in performance a self-contained comic sketch which could be detached from the rest of the play and performed separately with no appreciable loss. In short, the routines are what matter, and the controlling themes of the whole play are of secondary importance. The *lazzi* here also have to do with the grotesqueness of the old women, and may therefore have depended for their true effect on a guying of the conventions of travesty acting (see Chapter 10). This is further supported by the fact that it is the young man who utters most of the bawdy (for details see Henderson, *MM*, p. 104): the old women are his butts, and preserve the dignity of their language almost intact. Their use of coy euphemisms (for example *katheudein*, 'to sleep with', 1051) or words of whose sexual meaning they seem unaware (for example *koptein*, 'to knock', 976) supports the view that they are trying to be as ladylike as possible – a standard trick of the male actor feigning coy femininity, who is often placed in juxtaposition with a crude buffoon who punctures all his endeavours. The point is that this scene relies almost entirely on stage-craft. It is funny enough, but the faultless stage technique is not put to the service of any deeply felt message, and the whole lacks something of the gusto and spirit of Aristophanes' earlier work. Although they clearly stem from the same tradition – and the same pen – Mnesilochos and these old women inhabit different planes of comic invention. Perhaps

Henderson's analysis of the reasons (*MM*, pp. 100f.) is right; but whatever they are, it should be stressed that this scene is, in terms of stage technique as opposed to comic spirit, one of Aristophanes' most polished and expert performances. (It makes an interesting comparison with *Knights*, for example, which also depends for much of its comic effect on the use of traditional *lazzi*, but which shows as much immaturity in stage technique as it does gusto of theme and style.)

Double entendre

Because of its use of irony, double entendre very closely concerns the relationship between the performer and his audience. Its stock routines are of three kinds. In the first, the double entendre is obvious to the audience but not to the performer; in the second, it is obvious to the audience and to one performer, but not to another; in the third, it is obvious to all the performers as well as to the audience.

The third category is perhaps the simplest, involving as it does the least degree of ironic deception. Words or phrases are used which have perfectly innocent meanings and could be taken by everyone at their face value. But it is obvious that the performers are as aware of the sexual meanings as the audience, and intend those meanings to come across. Thus the language exists quite literally as 'double entendre'; that is, it is heard in two ways at once. Laughter often arises from the juxtaposition of two incongruous meanings, or the incongruity between one of the meanings and the context in which the words are uttered. In performance, the comedian may well signal (by vocal inflexion, or – on the modern stage – by a look) that he is aware that what he says can be taken two ways. The technique is similar to that used when uttering any other puns or plays on words, and the performer's clear awareness of what he is saying is crucial to the effect. A simple, short example is Dionysos' comment on Euripides' Muse (*Frogs* 1308): 'This Muse never used the Lesbian mode. Not once'. Here the word *elezbiasden*, 'used the Lesbian mode', clearly has both an innocent and a bawdy interpretation, but only a fool would assume its meaning to be wholly innocent.

The most extended passage of this kind of double entendre occurs in *Lysistrata* 708–780, the scene in which the women try to slip away out of the Acropolis. The routine used is like that of the buffoon in a double-act trying to do something outrageous and being prevented just in time by the straight man; the variations are first that there are several buffoons, not one, and second that the women's sexual longings are part not only of this scene but of the controlling image of the whole play. Lysistrata herself signals the beginning of the sequence by a word of primary bawdy, *binetiomen*, 'we want to fuck' (715). She then uses several phrases of double entendre herself ('I caught one opening up a hole',

720; 'wriggling about on a block and tackle', 722; and 'making for Orsilochos' place', 725 – where we are not told explicitly that 'Orsilochos' place' is a brothel), and the escaping women each use phrases of ever more extravagant double entendre (moths nibbling wool, 729f.; wool spread out on the bed, 731f.; untreated flax, 735f.; peeling the fibres, 738f.), until the routine is finally capped by physical slapstick with the arrival of the 'pregnant' woman who is in fact carrying Athene's helmet – a subtle juxtaposition of symbols reflecting the principal war/sex antinomy of the play. The portents and oracles then recounted are also in double entendre, both birds and snakes being sexual euphemisms. The whole scene is as graphic an illustration in double entendre of the effects of Lysistrata's plan as the ensuing scene (Kinesias/Myrrhine) is, using explicit bawdy; and like the Kinesias/Myrrhine scene, its effect is particularly marked in that it uses traditional performing routines in an organic way, bounded and controlled by the metaphor of the whole plot.

Double entendre between one innocent and one knowing performer is one of the commonest and most fertile of comic routines. The irony is simple: audience and joker have knowledge not shared by the butt, whose innocence or bewilderment is the main source of laughter. Jokes of this kind are usually short (for example the dialogue about kissing the nightingale, *Birds* 667–674 (quoted on p. 95), or that about the 'plucked' and 'trimmed' plains of the Boeotian and Corinthian girls in *Lysistrata* 85–92). Sometimes these jokes are incorporated into routines of mainly explicit bawdy (for example the old woman/young man scene in *Wealth* 1042–1096, where 'don't bring that torch near me', 1052; 'one spark, and she's ablaze', 1053f.; 'take hold of the nuts', 1056; and perhaps even 'she only has one wedge-shaped (tooth)', 1059, are double entendres). Double entendre seldom sustains a whole scene on its own. But it combines so well with the other attributes of both the *poneros* and the *bomolochos* that it occurs in almost every comic routine in Aristophanes: in fact the shifting between explicit bawdy and double entendre is a major feature of his style.

A remarkable example of how a scene of double entendre can be built into a complex and brilliant routine is the series of jokes about Opora and Theoria in *Peace* 819–909 (where the silence of the girl butts is an essential ingredient in the humour throughout). The first joke is simple and purely visual. The girls arrive with Trygaios, tumbling in as if falling out of the sky. At once Trygaios speaks a line of double entendre: 'I came so fast I hurt my leg' (820). The girls are then totally ignored for 20 lines, both by Trygaios and by the slave – that is, until 842. At once, as in the escaping scene in *Lysistrata*, the beginning of a bawdy routine is signalled by a word of explicit bawdy (*pornoboskousi*, 'they keep whores', 849), and continues in double entendre ('shall I give this one something to eat?', 851f.; 'she'll need something to lick', 855; 'the cake's been kneaded', 869) until Trygaios begins the presentation of Theoria (Holiday) to the Assembly. In this passage, double entendre (compasses, 879; 'I'll put her up', 882; 'he's nodding', 883; lapping soup, 885; lift up legs (for dancing), 889f.; 'look at her lovely oven', 891) is blended ever more intimately with explicit bawdy ('five-year-festival-arse', 876; 'I'm drawing up lines with my cock', 880) until finally, in Trygaios' presentation speech (894–909), both are combined with fantasy images into a whirl of language which depends for effect on speed and the interaction of images rather than on the savouring of each individual image:

> As soon as she's yours you'll be able to hold
> A magnificent, spectacular sports-day, tomorrow.
> First, wrestling on the ground, crab-dancing on all fours,
> Throwing sideways and leaning forward on your knees.
> Then a regular, well-oiled, young man's wrestling match:
> Knocking, poking, flying fists and pricks.
> Then, on the third day, you can go racing:
> Stallions galloping after medallions,
> Chariots rolling over each other,
> Blowing and panting and pushing ahead;
> Some of them will never keep it up –
> They'll fall at the first bend, and lie there limp.
> Gentlemen, here she is! Receive her – Holiday.
> Look how eagerly the President took hold of her.

It is impossible to say, in this passage, which of the games mentioned have explicit sexual meanings, which are double entendres, and which are entirely innocent. In 896 the first phrase, *epi ges palaiein* ('to wrestle on the ground'), is innocent until the second, *tetrapodedon hestanai* ('to stand on four legs'), is uttered, and colours the idea of wrestling into one involving sex as well as athletics. In fact by the time we reach *phusonta kai pneonta* ('blowing and panting') in 903 there is no longer any way of telling how to take the verbs. In such a whirl of language, even totally innocent expressions like 907, 'Look how eagerly the President took hold of her', begin to assume sexual overtones of their own. What began as a scene of simple irony ends with a display of linguistic fantasy, almost certainly matched in performance by movement and gesture, again, no doubt, partly innocent and partly bawdy.

The subtlest kind of double entendre is that in which the performers never make it apparent that they are aware of bawdy meanings in what they are saying. So far as they are concerned their words could be entirely innocent, and all the bawdy is in the minds of the spectators. This is to use the medium of performance itself in an ironic manner, and especially suits the quickly changing character of the Aristophanic *poneros*. In double entendre of this kind we can never be sure, as spectators, whether it is we, the spectators, or the characters onstage who are the butts of the comedian's irony.

The best example of this kind of humour is the Megarian scene in *Acharnians* (719–835).[58] The trigger-word for the routine of double entendre is *choirous* ('pigs/cunts') in 739, and throughout the scene both Dikaiopolis and the Megarian use it in a way which can in every case mean 'pig', but in most cases has bawdy overtones as well. (The words in 760 (salt/prick), 761ff. (garlic/scrotum) and 801ff. (chickpea/erection) have the same characteristic.) In fact the illusion that the actors are talking innocently of pigs is so well sustained that even outright explicit bawdy (like *kerkon*, 'tail', 785, and *kusthos,* 'cunt', 789) can be incorporated into the dialogue without affecting it. The result is that the whole scene, in performance, walks a kind of tightrope between innocence and obscenity – and, as in a tightrope walk, our interest is as much in the near falls as in the successful walk itself. The discussion of tails (785ff.) and of the foods the 'pigs' will eat (800ff.) teeters on the edge of explicit bawdy but never actually crosses it, and the illusion that the characters are innocent allows Aristophanes to incorporate two serious ideas (the threat from the Sycophant and the Megarian's pathetic prayer that he can sell his wife and mother) without breaking the comic mood, and to blend the *choiros* joke at the end with the pathos of conditions in Megara in such a way that neither impedes the effect of the other.

Bawdy gesture

Our knowledge of what gesture was like in the fifth century seems at first sight extremely sketchy. It would be perilous to take the scholiasts' comments as applicable to any kind of stage production earlier than the third century BC; and contemporary vase pictures, though useful, tend to show generalized tableaux rather than gestures related to specific stage events, and where they show movement in comedy – as in the case of the actor (Figure 6; Webster and Trendall, *IGD*, p. 117) or of the two men carrying a cake (Figure 7; *IGD*, p. 120) – it is of a formalized, unspecific kind. The many murders illustrated from tragedy – where, if anywhere, we might expect grandiosity – tend to show comparatively naturalistic, unexaggerated gestures (for example Figure 8; *IGD*, p. 97): although the vase pictures are usually 'stagy' rather than realistic (see, for example, the Pandora illustration, Figure 9; *IGD*, p. 39), they are never so exaggerated that they conflict with Aristotle's general advice (in *Poetics* xvii; compare *Rhetoric* ii) that gesture and movement should harmonize with the general effect of the whole performance.

The size and style of gestures an actor uses must, however, relate to the type of performance he is giving and the nature of the theatre he is in. In general, gestures in tragedy tend to be more stylized than those in comedy; on the other hand, one purpose of comic gestures is to get laughs, and they are therefore likely to be heightened, exaggerated and prolonged. It is safe to assume that in the mock-tragic sections of Aristophanes, just as the style of tragic language was heightened for comic effect, so tragic gestures would be parodied in the same

Figure 6. An actor in the role of Perseus performs on a low stage before two spectators. Detail from Attic red-figure chous, 420 BC (Vlastos Collection, Athens).

Figure 7. Comic scene with two cake-carriers. Detail from Attic chous, 400–390 BC (Agora Museum, Athens).

Figure 8. Medea murders one of her children. Detail from Campanian neck-amphora, c. 330–320 BC (Louvre, Paris).

way. Dikaiopolis' treatment of the brazier hostage (*Acharnians* 331ff.), for example, would be likely to involve gestures as extravagant, and as reminiscent of the tragic gestures used in performing *Telephos*, as his words are extravagant parodies of the same play. Lamachos' ranting entry (*Acharnians* 572ff.) may well have matched the mock-tragedy of the language with suitably outsize gestures and exaggerated movement.

Language and movement are closely related in other sections as well as the mock-tragic. For example, the skirmishes between actors and Chorus in *Acharnians, Wasps, Peace* and especially *Birds* are conducted in highly formal language; and there is more than a hint (for example, lines like 'What are you doing? Don't ruin a fine idea with this dancing', *Peace* 322ff., or 'Get ready to rend and bite; bring up the right wing', *Birds* 352f.) that they also used balletic movement and gesture. Many passages clearly indicate what sort of gestures

accompanied the words (for example the knocking on doors in *Peace* 179 and *Frogs* 37ff. and 460ff., or the beatings in *Frogs* 646ff.). We may presume that gestures were not confined solely to those parts of the plays where they are accompanied by words. It would be ludicrous, for example, to perform *Wealth* (which has very few descriptions of gesture) in a static way throughout. Where gesture and movement are described (as in the passages cited above) there is often a suggestion of noise or exaggeration: we may perhaps infer that extravagant gesture, if not invariable, was certainly not unknown.

The matter is particularly important in the case of bawdy gesture. For a gesture to be funny it must be seen, and seen by all the spectators. Many bawdy gestures in real life, on the other hand, are small-scale and intimate: touching, fondling and stroking for example. Unless gestures of this kind were exaggerated in some way, they would simply be invisible to most of the spectators.

Euelpides' kiss (*Birds* 671ff.) is accompanied by plenty of descriptive language; but even so the removal of the nightingale's mask (and the 'kiss' which probably followed) would have had to be performed with quite a flourish in order to be seen throughout the theatre. Dikaiopolis' feeling of the Megarian's 'piglets' (*Acharnians* 765ff.) cannot have consisted merely of rummaging inside a sack: to be seen, it would be necessary both for him to react in an exaggerated way to what he was supposedly feeling, and perhaps for the daughters and the Megarian also to move and react in a suitable and clearly visible way.

Perhaps there is an analogy to the size of comic gesture in the size of the stage phallus. Whether limp or erect, this seems (on the evidence of vase pictures) to have been between 12 and 18 inches long. In a vase picture it looks as grotesquely out of proportion as the more extravagant features on comic masks. But in the theatre the disproportion between the actor's body and his phallus would have been much less noticeable; just as the mask would appear more 'lifelike' than the actor's own face, so the phallus would assume a size more in keeping with its role in the play.

A possible way in which gesture and costume were used may be inferred from an examination of the clearest and most bawdy comic routine in Aristophanes, the unmasking of Mnesilochos in *Women at the Festival* (636ff., quoted on p. 98). In this sequence Mnesilochos is stripped, first to the waist (636–642), then completely. His phallus is hidden behind him in 644, brought through to the front in 645, moved behind in 646 and presumably returned to the front at the end of the sequence. The removal of the dress would have been clearly visible to every spectator, as would Mnesilochos' total lack of breasts; but even with an 18-inch phallus, the to-ing and fro-ing would not have been visible to more than a minority. Kleisthenes and the first woman, therefore, indicate by their verbal reactions (644–646) what Mnesilochos is doing; it is also clear from the text that Kleisthenes at least runs round Mnesilochos from front to back to front and back again. Thus, the movement of the phallus is indicated not just by the extravagant gestures of one actor alone (Mnesilochos), but also by the words and movements of two others. The sequence is not merely a piece of grotesque bawdy from Mnesilochos (as it might appear to be in the study); it is a carefully controlled and precisely determined 'routine' between all three actors.

This counterpoint of comparatively unexaggerated gestures with a good deal of running about works well in other passages involving bawdy gesture. In *Acharnians* 582–592 Dikaiopolis solicits a breastplate and a feather from Lamachos to make himself sick, and then asks Lamachos to use his sword to circumcise him. On stage, Dikaiopolis probably stands still while Lamachos runs about obeying his instructions, and then ends the routine with an explicit gesture of his phallus (592). In *Peace* 1224ff. (the scene between Trygaios and the Armourer), although it is not clear precisely what Trygaios does with the breastplate, it is clear that his actions are broad and easily visible, and that the meaning of his gestures is enhanced by the reaction of the Armourer. The phallic gestures involving the wineskin (*Lysistrata* 200ff.) and Reconciliation (*Lysistrata* 1115ff.) once again involve a group of actors performing a routine rather than the bawdy gestures of a single individual. Dikaiopolis' final entrance in *Acharnians* (1198ff.) is accompanied by two dancing-girls: their actions at 1214ff. (where they hold Lamachos' leg and Dikaiopolis' prick) are explicit enough, and we may perhaps assume that bawdy gestures also accompany Dikaiopolis' remarks in 1220f. ('I want to go to bed, fuck, have sex in the dark').

Thus, bawdy gesture is used by Aristophanes in much the same way as bawdy language. It is shameless and explicit, ironically combining a kind of childlike innocence and uninhibitedness with full adult awareness and exploitation of the audience's reactions. It is generally functional in use – that is, concerned with the development both of the scene in which it occurs and of the controlling themes of the play as a whole – and it very often brings several actors together in the performance of a single comic routine, and thus links the verbal bawdy of the dialogue with older, non-verbal forms of phallic comedy.

THE ACTORS

8
Leading Actors and Leading Roles

In most of Aristophanes' extant plays, the leading character dominates the action, often speaking between a third and a half of the lines of the play. The leading role usually embodies the main serious theme of the play, and generates most of the comic business. In addition, the leading actor is often given the delicate task of handling those points in the play where stage illusion is balanced against theatrical reality (see Chapter 6).

This chapter examines in some detail the leading actor and the roles he was asked to play. To begin with, the question of his professional status and ability is discussed: for it is clear that he was called upon to show far more expertise than any amateur could provide. One leading part – Philokleon in *Wasps* – is then analysed in detail, to show not only the performing demands made on the actor, but also the way the play is constructed to highlight his part and give him 'star treatment' throughout. The chapter concludes with a more general review of the other leading roles.

Professional status

At first sight, it might appear that there was no such thing as a 'professional' actor in fifth-century Athens: that is, a person who made his entire living from the craft, and practised its skills to a level of expertise not attainable by amateurs with other jobs to do as well. It is a widely-held belief of modern scholars – perhaps arising from the fact that, as in the case of dramatic authors, the position of leading actor was in theory open to anyone who cared to apply – that acting in a Greek comedy on a Greek stage required little more of the actor than the ability to speak clearly, move naturally and wear his mask and costume with distinction. If this were so, then certainly any moderately intelligent person interested in the theatre could have played a leading role – much as university professors today play Socrates or Dionysos in undergraduate productions, and acquit themselves, if not professionally, at least with honour.[59]

But amateurism of this kind, however excellent, was out of place in the Greek theatre. The sheer size of the undertaking is a deciding factor against it. To entertain an audience of some 14,000 at the end of a festival day and in honour of the god of drama himself makes entirely different demands on a performer from those of a small-scale indoor production for a group of colleagues or friends. Under the circumstances of the fifth-century performance – and even working from a script as good as (say) *Clouds* – an actor would need as much professional skill and originality as he could muster. The prizes awarded to leading actors were not for gallant effort: they were for a demonstration of acting expertise at its highest, most professional level.

There is evidence of this expertise in the plays as well. No dramatic author of Aristophanes' skill and experience makes demands of his players which they are unable to meet; on the contrary, he offers them challenges and opportunities to display and extend their professional skill. When Marlowe wrote *Tamburlaine* he had in mind a specific actor, who was able to give a specific type of performance (markedly different, for example, from that required for the leading male roles in his *Dido* or *Edward II*). The rhetorical range and massive physical 'presence' required in performance are apparent from the words the actor was given to speak, the opportunities and challenges afforded him.[60] In a similar way, the demands made musically and rhetorically on the actors in later Euripides are apparent from the text, and differ considerably from those in his early plays. So too with Aristophanes: we can read the parts of Dikaiopolis or Mnesilochos, and deduce from that reading a good deal of what the actor was asked to do. And in the case of Aristophanes' leading actors, just as in late Euripides or Marlowe, the demands are such that although amateur performances are possible, a full and proper performance would require the full expertise, concentration and ability that only a professional – and in some cases a rarely-gifted professional – can provide.[61]

However, if leading actors were professionals, the question remains of how, in the restricted world of Athenian theatre in wartime, they managed to make a living. Even if the leading actor chose and rehearsed the acting-company, and assisted author and backer with recruiting and rehearsing the Chorus, his involvement with any one play, even at a generous estimate, cannot have been for more than six months of the year, and was probably a good deal less. Even if he performed at both festivals, Lenaia as well as City Dionysia, two single festival performances a year would hardly offer him a livelihood.

It is not enough to say flatly that this consideration entirely rules out the existence of professional performers. After all, the opportunities for playwrights were just as scanty, and there were plenty of playwrights producing enough work to be counted as professionals. Like them, actors may have had means of supplementing the income they derived from dramatic employment. Some may have been landowners, like Aristophanes in Aegina; some may have had positions in the religious world, like Sophocles, or in law, like Aeschines in the next century. The 'season' for drama ended as the campaigning and farming seasons began; it would have been no harder for an actor to divide his time between them than for a man to combine acting and oratory.

Two other possibilities suggest themselves. The first is that a leading actor, once chosen, was paid by the state – and paid enough to last him through the summer months as well as the dramatic 'season'. The second is that the other professional occupations known to have been followed by actors in the fourth century were also available to actors in the fifth. These included tours; performances at local, rural festivals; private performances; revivals and the training of pupils.[62]

It is clear that none of these ways of making a living can have been widely practised: they would all be the province of only the most successful of actors. Professional comic actors, like professional playwrights, must have belonged to a small group, well known to each other – and also to the archon's selection committees. The size and importance of the festivals suggests that the chances of the committees choosing leading actors from outside this circle – and especially of selecting amateurs – would be remote. Most probably acting *was* a professional occupation, and aspirants worked their way up from small, silent roles through third or second roles to the top of the profession. Those who were successful may have managed to live off the proceeds; those who were not – and they must have been the majority – probably emulated Aeschines and found other, less chancy occupations.

Philokleon

Viewed from the standpoint of the leading actor, the plays of Aristophanes fall into two distinct groups. Each of the later plays, from *Lysistrata* onwards, has a unique form and style of its own, and therefore makes different demands on its leading actor from all the others. But the earlier plays (perhaps because they conform more closely to traditional patterns of composition) form a reasonably integrated group and share many features of form, type and dramatic style. This means that the technical demands made on the actors who played Dikaiopolis, Agorakritos, Strepsiades, Philokleon, Trygaios and Peisetairos are similar – and the part of Philokleon[63] has been chosen for analysis because it seems not only typical of the group as a whole, but also characteristic of Aristophanes' earlier style at its best and most rewarding to perform.

The analysis that follows makes four presuppositions: (1) that the audience and stage arrangements are roughly those outlined in previous chapters; (2) that the time is late afternoon, not dark but with the shadows lengthening; (3) that the audience is attentive, not restless, and reacts to the jokes – especially the 'stock' jokes – approximately as a modern audience might; (4) that, granted the presence of physical action, dancing and music, it takes about a minute, on average, to deliver 15 lines of the text as we have it.[64]

An approximate time chart of *Wasps* in performance, made on this basis and highlighting the involvement of the leading actor, might be made thus:

113

LINES	DURATION (approx.)	CONTENT
1–140	9 minutes	Prologue (leading actor offstage)
141–229	6 minutes	Slapstick scene: Philokleon tries to escape (leading actor onstage)
230–315	6 minutes	Entry of Chorus (leading actor offstage)
316–525	13 minutes	'Rescue' of Philokleon; preparation for *agon* (leading actor onstage)
526–759	15 minutes	*Agon* (leading actor onstage)
760–1009	13 minutes	Preparation for mock trial; trial scene (leading actor onstage)
1010–1121	7 minutes	Parabasis (leading actor offstage)
1122–1264	9 minutes	Preparation for dinner-party (leading actor onstage)
1265–1325	4 minutes	Interlude and 'messenger speech' (leading actor offstage)
1326–1449	8 minutes	Drunk scene (leading actor onstage)
1450–1473	1½ minutes	Interlude (leading actor offstage)
1474–end	4+ minutes	Finale (leading actor onstage)

The total time required for performance is about 100 minutes, and the leading actor is onstage for about 70 minutes.

Just as, in many 'well made' comedies of the earlier part of this century (such as those of Barrie, Noël Coward or Anouilh), the first appearance of the star is kept back for several minutes, during which the audience's expectation is whetted,[65] so in *Wasps* the first entrance of Philokleon (at line 143) is preceded by nearly 10 minutes of humorous preparation. In particular, from line 88 onwards (that is, once the attention of the audience is fully captured), the effect of Xanthias' long, ludicrous and clinical description of Philokleon as a 'litigious maniac' is principally to whet our eagerness to see this comic prodigy in person. When Philokleon does appear, he comes in not by the drainpipe or through the door (as we have been led to expect), but through the roof. Bdelykleon asks the typical stooge's question, 'Who are you?', and he replies innocently, 'Me? Smoke – escaping'. The comic *poneria* of this first entrance sets the style for all his later appearances, and the economy and effectiveness of the writing are characteristic of Aristophanes at his best.[66]

114

It is apparent from the text that the Philokleon actor was expected to be gifted in three types of performance apart from actual acting: slapstick clowning, dancing and singing. His speeches are full of opportunities for song and dance (see below), and the play contains four notable slapstick sequences: the escape from the house (140ff.), the preparation for the trial scene (760ff.), the preparation for the dinner-party (1122ff.) and the drunk scene (1326ff.). These follow the same constructional pattern as slapstick scenes in later comedy. That is, although the audience sees a continuous sequence of comic routines, the individual actors' parts are 'paced' to give them the chance to catch their breath after each routine and prepare for the next. Usually each slapstick scene is centred on a single serious figure, who is the butt of the humour (in *Wasps* it is Bdelykleon). The clown or clowns make a series of assaults on him, each consisting of preparation, action and reaction. Between each routine and the next there is a moment of rest, during which the audience is prepared for whatever is to follow. Throughout the whole process the clowns and not the butt are the centre of interest. The straight man may be onstage for longer than the clowns, and speak more lines; but his function is principally to provide the moments of rest and preparation without which the scene would degenerate into mindless bustle: in the best slapstick, the correct spacing of the jokes is hardly less important than the jokes themselves.

This process of spacing can be seen particularly clearly in the 'jack-in-the-box' scene[67] which follows Philokleon's first appearance (136–210, in Barrett's prose translation):

BDELYKLEON: Xanthias! Sosias! Are you asleep?

XANTHIAS: Oh lord!

SOSIAS: What's up?

XANTHIAS: It's him. He's awake.

BDELYKLEON: Come round to the back, quickly, one of you. My father's got into the kitchen and he's scurrying about in there like a rat. Keep a watch on the waste pipe and see that he doesn't get out that way. And you, Xanthias, lean on the door.

XANTHIAS: Yes, sir.

BDELYKLEON: Ye gods, what's all that noise in the chimney? Who's there?

PHILOKLEON: Just a puff of smoke.

BDELYKLEON: Smoke? Why, what are they burning?

PHILOKLEON: Figwood.

BDELYKLEON: That accounts for the pungent smell. Pfuh! – Go on, get back inside. Where's the cover? Down you go! I'd better put this log on top as well. Now think of another bright idea. Puff of smoke indeed! They'll be calling me son-of-a-smoke-screen next.

XANTHIAS: Look out, he's pushing at the door.

BDELYKLEON: Hold him, push as hard as you can – I'll come and help. Hold on to the latch – and mind he doesn't pull the peg out.

PHILOKLEON (*inside*): What d'you think you're doing? Let me out, d'ye hear? I must get to court, or Drakontides'll get off.

BDELYKLEON: That'd be just too bad, wouldn't it?

PHILOKLEON: When I went to Delphi, the oracle said that if ever I let a man be acquitted I should just dry up and wither away.

BDELYKLEON: Apollo preserve us, what a prophecy!

PHILOKLEON: Come on, please, let me out: do you want me to die?

BDELYKLEON: I'm not going to let you out – ever.

PHILOKLEON: I shall gnaw through the net.

BDELYKLEON: You haven't got any teeth.

PHILOKLEON: I'll kill you, I will: how can I do it, I wonder? Give me a sword – no, give me a juryman's tablet.

BDELYKLEON: He's up to some real mischief now.

PHILOKLEON: No, no, only I just thought I'd take the donkey down and sell him in the market – and the panniers too; it's the first of the month.

BDELYKLEON: Couldn't I do that for you?

PHILOKLEON: No, not so well as I could.

BDELYKLEON: Much better, you mean. All right, you can let the *donkey* out.

XANTHIAS: That was a subtle one! Just an excuse to get out.

BDELYKLEON: Ha, but it didn't come off: I saw what he was up to. I think I'd better go in and fetch the donkey myself, in case the old blighter slips out. Come on, gee up there, what's the matter with you? Fed up at being sold? C'mern there, get a move on: what are you groaning for? Anyone'd think you'd got Odysseus hanging on underneath.

XANTHIAS: Ye gods, but he has! There's somebody under there, anyway.

BDELYKLEON: Where? Let me look.

XANTHIAS: Here he is, up this end.

BDELYKLEON: Now then, what's all this? Who do you think you are?

PHILOKLEON: No-man.

BDELYKLEON: No-man, eh? Where are you from?

PHILOKLEON: Ithaca.

BDELYKLEON: Well, No-man, you can get back to No-man's-land, sharp! Pull him out from under there, quickly. Oh, the disgusting old rascal – look where he's stuffed his head. I never thought we'd see our old donkey giving birth to a juryman!

PHILOKLEON: Leave me alone, can't you, or there'll be a fight.

BDELYKLEON; What is there to fight about?

XANTHIAS: He'll fight you over the donkey's shadow, like the man in the fable.

BDELYKLEON: You're a nasty, crafty, foolhardy old man.

PHILOKLEON: Nasty? Me? You don't realize how delicious I am: but wait till you've tasted juryman's paunch farci!

BDELYKLEON: Get that donkey back into the house, and yourself too

PHILOKLEON: Help, help! Members of the jury! Kleon! Help!

BDELYKLEON: You can shout as much as you like once I get this door shut. Now, pile a lot of those stones up against the door. Get that peg back into its socket properly – that's right. Now – up with the bar: heave! That's it – and now, quickly, roll that big mortar up against it.

XANTHIAS: Hey, where did that come from? Great chunk of dirt fell right on my head.

BDELYKLEON: Perhaps there's a mouse up there, knocked a bit of earth down.
XANTHIAS: Some mouse! Somebody's pet juryman, more like it. Look, there he is, coming up through the tiles.
BDELYKLEON: Oh, lord, he thinks he's a sparrow, he'll take wing at any moment. Where's that bird-net? Shoo, shoo, get back inside! I'd as soon be keeping guard over Scione as trying to keep this old man indoors.

Only two of those slapstick escape attempts physically involve the leading actor: the smoke and the donkey. Each of them is short and strenuous, and carries a single joke routine from conception to fulfilment. A feeling of climax is achieved in the scene as a whole because its high point, the donkey routine, is longer and more elaborate than what has gone before. The other escape attempts involve noise and perhaps pushing from inside the *skene* (possibly done by assistants); their humour lies in the reactions of Bdelykleon and Xanthias (who at one point, 202f., is showered with dirt, in a routine still familiar to us from Mack Sennett film comedies). In between his two appearances the Philokleon actor is given 30 lines (nearly 2 minutes) to climb down from his ladder or scaffolding under the *skene* roof, and to take up his position under the donkey. The donkey would be played by one or more extras,[68] and it must have taken some time for Philokleon to arrange himself underneath, clinging to the panniers. He has lines to speak as he does so (156–173), but is given a few silent moments (174–178) to organize himself finally for the entrance. The donkey and its burden remain onstage for only a minute or so (18 lines, 179ff.), perhaps because the physical posture was difficult to keep up for longer. Once back inside the *skene*, the actor has plenty of time (119 lines) to change into his wasp costume and climb up to the window in readiness for his next, musical, appearance at 316. (The clattering and heaving from inside that follows his exit was probably done by assistants, as before, to leave him time to change.)

Even though the actor is visible in that scene for only 24 lines out of 93, his position as chief clown is maintained throughout the scene, and he is the focus of attention from start to finish. (The same is true of the later slapstick scenes: see below.) Lines 136–143 announce his imminent arrival; 144–148 contain his appearance as smoke; 149–167 are dialogue between him and the actors onstage, much of which is tragic parody; 168–178 prepare for the donkey sequence, which follows in 179–198; 199–210 are a third escape attempt, this time as mouse or sparrow. The lines which immediately follow the passage quoted (211–229) serve to link the scene, and Philokleon himself, with the imminent arrival of the Chorus.

By the time of the choral entry (230), about 15 minutes into the play, the character of Philokleon has been firmly established. He is primarily a *poneros*, a slapstick clown whose actions are meant to amuse, not to be taken seriously. This establishing of type early in a play is very important to an actor. Whatever he says or does later is viewed by the audience in the light of what they know already. When W. C. Fields performs a difficult juggling act at the end of *The Great McGonigle*, we find it funny because we know Fields is a funny man; it also seems remarkably competent since (so far as we know from the film) he is not primarily a juggler by profession. The same is true of Philokleon's singing and dancing in *Wasps*. He is a slapstick clown; when, therefore, he launches into a display of brilliant singing or dancing, our delight is all the greater because that is not at all what we expect.

This surprised delight is probably the reaction to Philokleon's next appearance, after the choral entry (316). He sings a parody of the monodies typical of Euripides' stranded heroines. Although the non-singing characters rush around, he is allowed to stay comparatively still throughout his operatic performance, and even during the battle scene that follows – to stand still, but still to dominate the action. His behaviour throughout is in deliberate contrast to what has gone before; and yet *poneria* is there, suppressed but only just (for example in 386, 'Lay me out, weep, and bury me – at the court-room bar'; 450,[69] 'Remember that beating I gave you; be grateful'; 510, 'The only gourmet food I ever want is – lawsuits'). It will surface again during the *agon* (the long argument scene, 526–727). Thus, this scene, while preparing the way for the formality of the *agon* structure, still retains enough of Philokleon's character to prepare us for the *poneria* and the supreme ludicrousness which he will use in his own defence.

In passing, it should be said that the protean character of Philokleon's *poneria* is vital to the establishing of the topsy-turvy atmosphere in which the whole plot is to operate. Like *Knights*, *Wasps* eschews overt surrealism: peace treaties in bottles and cities in the sky form no part of the action. Dikaiopolis, Trygaios and the others take us by the hand into a world of complete unreality, a universe where anything at all is possible. Philokleon, on the other hand, invites us to share his own oblique vision of the natural world that surrounds us all. His character (as Dover, *AC*, pp. 125–127 acutely points out) is reprehensible in the extreme; but it is also entirely credible, and even admirable. Admiration is provoked precisely by his protean gusto: he changes his actions to suit each new interlocutor and does so knowingly, brilliantly and with huge enjoyment. With slaves or *alazones* he behaves in a slapstick manner; with the musical Chorus he sings and dances; with the serious Bdelykleon he adopts a serious manner (though continuing to baffle him by making, in a serious tone of voice, entirely outrageous remarks).

By linking the audience's expectations of the performer to the meaning of the character within the play in this manner, Aristophanes uses the nature of theatre (as a performing medium) to indulge in what can only be described as satirical sleight-of-hand. For Philokleon's antinomianism (whether stealing spits or suggesting incest) is in 'real' terms quite indefensible; Aristophanes' satire extends the moral taint in his character to all the jurymen of Athens, the main moral butts of the play. (As often, the lampoon lashes the men within the institution rather than the institution itself.) The taint is spread further, in the same oblique way, by calling Philokleon ('Love-Kleon') and Bdelykleon ('Loathe-Kleon') by those names – at first sight a purely adventitious joke. Kleon, as head of the state where such men as Philokleon wield such authority as these jurymen, is tainted by association. The authorial sleight-of-hand lies in not making these critical points in the overt way of (say) the *Frogs* parabasis, but in absorbing them within a general texture of insouciance and hilarity. To do this requires the use of a performing medium (because it allows the spectators no time to pause and reflect), and also relies heavily on the blurring of the boundaries between real life and stage illusion.

The style of the *agon* or argument scene (526–727) is characteristically formal, and proceeds for the most part in smooth, flowing language. Its content – on Philokleon's side a description of his personal delight in a juryman's life, and on Bdelykleon's a list of the ways in which honest citizens are cheated by corrupt politicians – is interesting enough in itself not to need elaborate staging or physical action. In a passage lasting about 17 minutes, a musical break of about a minute (17 lines) occurs after 7 minutes, and both Philokleon and Bdelykleon end their presentations with the vocal cadenza known as the *pnigos*. (This was a passage of about fifty words, intended to be delivered in a single breath. Its cadenza-like effect would be most marked after a long passage in regular rhythm, and in performance (because it required a forceful delivery lasting anything up to a minute) it could be spectacular to watch.) Apart from this, the main interest lies in the vividness of Philokleon's examples and the way in which he is given the opportunity to impersonate a large number of other characters[70] – the suppliants outside the court, a succession of prisoners at the bar, politicians, and even his own wife and daughter. These impersonations would offer the actor the chance not only to demonstrate vocal expertise, but also to make use of many comic physical routines as well.

So far the play has consisted of three separate sections, in three different styles (slapstick, music and straight acting). From now on the styles are blended, with slapstick as perhaps the predominant mode. The character of Philokleon is further explored: throughout the scenes that follow he is the centre of attention, and the leading actor is given what would nowadays be called 'centre-stage treatment'. In the trial scene for example (760–1008), it is the judge and not the prisoner who is the focus of attention. All the items for the courtroom (soup, cockerel, kneading-trough, pigpen, ladles, potty) are brought out at his insistence or for his convenience; where a joke leads to a punch line, the punch line is usually his (for example the anecdote about fish scales given instead of change in 786–795, with its characteristic 'feed line' from Bdelykleon, 'Go on, what did he say?' (793); or the pigpen joke, 'coming up to scratch' in 844–847); in much of the dialogue Bdelykleon's lines are extremely short, and serve only to 'feed' Philokleon, who retains the comic initiative throughout (for example PHIL: 'Anything you like – except one thing.' BDEL: 'What's that?' (761–762); PHIL: 'Who's going to pay my wages?' BDEL: 'Me.' (784–786); the fish joke mentioned above (786–795); PHIL: 'Where's the bar? That's the most sacred thing of all.' BDEL: 'You're right. It's missing.' (829–833); BDEL: 'What's that?' PHIL: 'The pigpen from Hestia's shrine.' (844); the whole pigpen sequence in 849–855); even when Bdelykleon does have the joke line, Philokleon's next line is often of the sort used by modern comedians to 'top' their interlocutor's laugh ('You don't say?', 'Aren't you the clever one?' and the like: see for example 807–810, 811–813, 820–823, 828–829 and 858–859). Throughout the trial the action is two-sided: Bdelykleon and the dogs maintain a façade of legal procedure, but Philokleon's contribution is a series of self-indulgent jokes in buffoon style – each incident is set up specifically so that he can knock it down. His final breakdown, leading to the dog's acquittal, is couched mainly in mock-tragic language, thus placing the emphasis more on the performance itself than on what is being performed. When Philokleon is finally led out (1008), the character is ostensibly a broken man; but the actor has been given, and has kept, the centre of the action for the whole of this 17-minute scene.

After the parabasis (1009–1121, about 7 minutes) there follows another slapstick scene, first physical (dressing Philokleon in his best clothes) then verbal (discussion of how to behave at dinner-parties). The requirements on the leading actor here are not greatly different from earlier slapstick scenes in the play (for example the escape scene).

From his return at 1326 to the end of the play, however, he is called upon to show considerable technical virtuosity. He makes his entrance, drunk, by one of the walkways, bringing a flute-girl. His first speech (1335–1363) is full of drunken tongue-twisters, some of them (in Greek) not easy to say even when sober (for example *chrysomelolonthion*, 1342; *ean genee de mee kakee nyni gynee*, 1351; *kyminopristokardamoglyphon*, 1357). The scene contains three slapstick contests: the passage with the phallus and the flute-girl, culminating in the black eye he gives Bdelykleon; the *alazon* scenes with the Baking Woman, Chairephon and the Injured Citizen (which allow him verbal as well as physical slapstick); and finally the climactic struggle, at the end of which he is dragged inside to be sobered up, shouting half-lines of tragedy as he goes.

After these 8 minutes of strenuous activity, there is a short choral interlude (1½ minutes), during which the actor would have to remove as much of his costume as would interfere with his dancing (the wasp-sting phallus,[71] and the cloak and shoes put on for the dinner-party). He reappears at 1482, and begins leaping and dancing in a ludicrous – but for the actor, exhausting and difficult – manner. This dancing involves high kicks, contortions of the body, the splits and fast rotation. The actor must speak or sing as he dances (a difficult thing to do when the dancing is so strenuous), and he is eventually joined by 'Karkinos' sons', who perform a 'crab-dance' around him. Whatever the nature of this dance, it certainly includes spinning round and high kicks, and eventually involves the Chorus (and perhaps the other members of the company) as well. The play's conclusion is problematic. It may have ended with a concerted, dancing exit (which fits the surviving text), or it may have closed with a whole suite of dances, perhaps including a performance by the leading actor of the vigorous and obscene *kordax*.[72] Xanthias' claim at the start of the play that 'nothing too weighty' was to be expected (56) is amply vindicated by this ending, which closes both the play and the whole festival day with a suitably cathartic abandonment to Dionysian enjoyment.

Throughout *Wasps* the leading actor is given star treatment, and the success of the entire production depends on his performance: not only the success of winning a prize, but also the successful placing of Aristophanes' serious message in the minds of the audience. The role of Philokleon requires both technical ability and physical stamina of the performer. Out of an approximate running time of 100 minutes, he is onstage for over 70 minutes. He utters nearly a third of the total lines of the play, half of them in forceful lyric metre requiring a stylized delivery. He is required to sing, and to dance in a markedly strenuous way. (The strenuous nature of the part is shown, if by nothing else, by the strategic placing of two lengthy 'rest periods' offstage, at 198–316 (8 minutes) and 1009–1121 (7 minutes). His other stretches offstage are shorter, and were probably filled by changes of costume or preparations for entrance at a different part of the theatre.) Aristophanes' confidence in the stamina of the actor is shown by the fact that the part gets more, not less, demanding as the play proceeds, and ends with a firework display of physical skills.

Apart from athletic slapstick, dancing and expertise in song, the leading actor in *Wasps* is called upon to perform a strikingly large number of impersonations. There is no extended passage in the play where he retains the same character throughout. In his opening scene he impersonates smoke and No-man; in the *agon* he offers a large number of small cameos (all of them contained within the larger impersonation of a speaker in a lawcourt); in the trial scene he shifts constantly between his own character and his assumed role as judge; for much of the final section of the play he is drunk; and throughout the whole performance his lines are filled with shorter or longer sections of tragic parody. The sheer volatility of the part suggests the performance more of a modern situation comedian than of a comic actor, a Groucho Marx rather than a Donald Sinden or an Alan Arkin. The play calls for absolute mastery of comic timing, especially in the trial scene, which demands a precise 'sense' both of the audience and of the other actors, particularly Bdelykleon. If part of being a leading actor consists in having dialogue written to give you every possible opportunity, an equally important part consists in the ability to seize each opportunity and make the most of it.

Other leading roles

The abilities of the leading actor in *Wasps*, and the demands made on him, are duplicated in all the extant plays. Every leading actor in Aristophanes needs good comic timing, self-awareness, slapstick ability and stamina – we may perhaps take it that these were standard requirements of any comedian in any play, and also that they indicate a general level of professional ability at the time. Apart from these qualities, Aristophanes' leading roles reveal a remarkable diversity of technical demands, contained within three broad acting types:

(1) The *poneros*. This acting type conforms to the character type described in Chapter 4 (p. 55). Where he plays a *poneros*, the leading actor governs and controls the whole performance of a play; on his shoulders rest its comic pace and production style; the writing is organized to keep him constantly in command. Such characters are found in the earlier plays: Dikaiopolis, Agora-kritos, Philokleon and Trygaios. From the actor's point of view Strepsiades also conforms partly to this type, and partly to (2) below.

(2) A comparatively serious character, who is not outstandingly funny himself but is the cause of comedy in others. (Strepsiades, for example, surrenders his comic initiative to Socrates for a good part of the central scenes in *Clouds*.) Characters like Peisetairos, Lysistrata, Praxagora and Chremylos are like the 'straight men' in a modern double-act. The comedy happens because they are there, and carries them along with it; but in general the pace and style of the jokes is governed by other actors (notably so in the case of Chremylos, where it is Karion who is the real comedian of the play).

(3) A complex character similar to (1) above, but with a much wider technical range and a greater depth of character. There are only two such parts in Aristophanes, Mnesilochos in *Women at the Festival* and Dionysos in *Frogs*. They are not only the meatiest roles in his plays, but stand out, in terms of technical demands, in the whole literature of comic acting. The parts are analysed, and their most characteristic feature, the close link with the second and third actors, is discussed in Chapter 9.

In terms of technical requirements, the four *poneros* leads can be separated into two pairs. Almost identical technical demands are present in the roles of Dikaiopolis and Agorakritos (*Acharnians* and *Knights* were performed in consecutive years), and these demands differ considerably from those made in the roles of Philokleon and Trygaios (where the demands are again remarkably similar, and again occur in plays performed in consecutive years). In the case of Dikaiopolis and Agorakritos, each has a remarkably long part (Dikaiopolis speaks over 500 lines of *Acharnians*, Agorakritos over 400 lines of *Knights*). Each of them is given a long monologue about half an hour into the performance (Dikaiopolis' speech on the origins of the war, *Acharnians* 496–556; Agorakritos' pseudo-messenger's speech on the assembly, *Knights* 624–682). This is a risky undertaking in comedy. The mood of an audience can never be predicted, and the planting of solo speeches this long (nearly 4 minutes) is a gamble which relies heavily on the actor's ability to control the spectators' mood. The vocal ability suggested by the rhetorical style of these speeches is also evident elsewhere in the plays: in general, the slapstick in *Achamians* and *Knights* lies in dialogue rather than in physical action. Dikaiopolis' tragic parodies (so unlike those of Philokleon or Trygaios), and his agonistic dialogues with Lamachos are very like (and may have inspired) the whole contest in baseness between Agorakritos and Kleon (see further Chapter 9, pp. 129ff.). Physical slapstick for these actors is reserved for their first appearances and the close of the plays; Dikaiopolis has in addition the short scene with the Megarian's daughters in their sack.

If *Achamians* and *Knights* demand actors with good speaking voices, *Wasps* and *Peace* require slapstick comedians who can also sing. Like Philokleon, Trygaios is given a good deal of lyrical or mock-tragic dialogue: the lyrical passages in *Peace* 520–581 and 973–1016 are particularly outstanding. Vigorous physical action is needed in the rescue scene (301–579), and the scene involving the crane (82–179) must have required an acrobat's sense of balance as well as a cool head. Slapstick sequences occur at 82–110 (the beetle fidgeting before takeoff), 435–519 (the hauling on ropes and abortive attempts to pull Peace up) and 956–973 (preparations for sacrifice); and lively verbal humour is present in the two scenes with Hermes (180–235, 361–458) and the long knockabout scene with Hierokles (1052–1126). As in *Wasps*, there are set-pieces involving simultaneous dialogue and movement (887–906, the presentation of Holiday, quoted on p. 102, probably had suitable movements added, like the courtroom descriptions in *Wasps* 547–630; and the balletic skirmish of 301–345 (the Chorus' refusal to stop dancing) involves the leading actor in much the same way as *Wasps* 379–403). The striking similarity in the demands of these two parts – like those of the leading roles in *Achamians* and *Knights* – suggests that Aristophanes may have worked with the same actor for two years running.

The odd man out in the first group – and indeed in Aristophanes' leading roles as a whole – is Strepsiades in *Clouds*. The main difficulty in playing a *bomolochos*/buffoon is that the slightest miscalculation of timing or emphasis can turn the audience's sympathy into exasperation. Unlike the *poneros*, who controls and dominates the stage action, the *bomolochos*, in general, reacts with buffoonery to what happens around him. This puts the actor at the mercy of other people's timing, and makes it far more difficult for him to shape the reactions of the audience. In fact it is remarkable how little time Strepsiades spends at the forefront of the action in *Clouds*. He is silent altogether during the Right/Wrong scene (889–1104), and in much of his dialogue with Socrates (especially 223–803) it is the Socrates actor who has the comic initiative. Only the opening of the play and the knockabout scenes at the end allow Strepsiades to control the flow of the performance. Of all Aristophanes' leading parts, this must have been one of the hardest to perform.

In the second group of plays, those with serious leads, the serious character sets up a situation, and then stands by while a large number of small comic scenes takes place, involving those who are affected by the situation. Most of the play consists, in effect, of knockabout *alazon* scenes, with the leading actor providing a unifying central presence which binds each new comic episode to the basic theme of the play. As was suggested in Chapter 4, this method is sometimes used in picaresque novels; the nearest dramatic equivalents are Ben Jonson's comedies 'of humour', and some British and American radio comedy shows of the last thirty years (for example *ITMA* or *Round the Horne* in Britain, or *The Charlie McCarthy Show* in America). Unlike other types of comedy, this one gives greater scope to the subsidiary performers than to the leading actor, whose position is more that of link-man than principal comedian. His relationship with the audience is one of trust: he acts as a kind of daft but generally reliable spokesman for the ordinary man faced with a lunatic world.

What is chiefly required of an actor playing this kind of paternal role in Aristophanes is an authoritative stage presence. This is necessary for two reasons. In the first half of the play, the 'strange and mighty deed' performed by the character is bizarre and antinomian in conception. Arguing it in logical detail might alienate the audience, and so dramatic sleight-of-hand is used instead to make it seem the inevitable solution to the crisis in hand. A good example is the scene in *Lysistrata* comparing politics to spinning and carding wool (571ff.). The solution proposed to the problem is not the surrealist fantasy of a Dikaiopolis or a Trygaios, but the profoundly shocking notion (to an Athenian male audience) that government should be handed over to women. In the *agon*, therefore, the issue is never properly debated; instead Lysistrata develops her spinning simile at some length, and the real-life aspects of the issue are never discussed – Lysistrata wins the day not by logic, but by the unexpectedness and unanswerability of the simile itself, and by the forcefulness of her own character (a quality which has been well established in the preceding scenes). By the time the Official is bamboozled into abandoning the argument, the audience is as sympathetic to Lysistrata's case as if it had been logically proved. The same technique is used in the *agon* in *Wealth*, though here it is the grotesqueness of the character of Poverty that diverts attention from the questionable logic of what is actually being said. In both cases the vigour of the central performance is crucial to what might be called the 'philosophical' success of the scene.[73]

Once the central deed is done, the 'serious' leading character is used as the unifying link in the rest of the play. This is particularly the case in *Birds*, where no less than seventeen *alazones* appear. Their scenes are usually very short (under 2 minutes each), and a fragmentary effect is avoided only by keeping

Peisetairos' purposes (of sacrificing and of dedicating his city) at the heart of the action throughout, and treating all the *alazon* scenes as interruptions of this purpose. In performance the effect is of one figure constantly on stage, assailed with bewildering frequency by outrageous interruptions of all kinds, but continuing none the less with his self-appointed task. At the end, when the ambassadors from the gods (the last of the *alazones*) appear, the aspirations of the two sides, interrupters and interrupted, are united and satisfied, and the plot moves to its conclusion. Unless Peisetairos is played by an actor of considerable 'presence', the second half of the play becomes dissipated into a pantomime-like series of unconnected – and sometimes not very funny – vignettes. If he dominates the stage, each new *alazon* is seen as just one more piece in a total, and satisfying, mosaic structure.

In *Lysistrata* the organic development of the plot is even more marked. Here the main issue is not decided until very late in the play, and the central character remains in control of the action to the end. It is left to other characters to be funny; but Lysistrata is the stage-manager of everything that goes on, and the dominance of her presence onstage can be seen simply from the size of her part in the dialogue. In *Wealth* unity of a sort is achieved (despite long, set-piece *alazon* scenes) by the alternating presence of Chremylos and Karion, the equality of whose roles was established in the opening scene. The plot of *Wealth*, however, does not develop in the same way as that of *Birds* or *Lysistrata*: the closing scenes have the effect more of illustrating than of developing what has gone before. This is even more the case in *Assemblywomen*. Once the new polity is achieved Praxagora drops out of the play entirely (at 729); the attention of the audience is diverted from the main issue (perhaps too contentious for closer examination?) by the outrageous but philosophically inessential scene between the young man and the three old women (938–1111).

The third type of leading role is scarcely a type at all. It serves to categorize the characters of Dionysos and Mnesilochos (parts analysed in detail in Chapter 9). In these roles, no technique of Athenian comic acting is left unexploited, and the exploitation demands acting skill of the highest order. The first half of *Frogs*, in particular, 'builds' the part of Dionysos consistently and organically, in a way not found again in dramatic literature until Shakespeare. That is to say, the actor is given in the text the means of showing character development even as he plays the character, always a more satisfying thing to do than merely exhibiting the same stereotype throughout, and certainly demanding much greater technical ability. The bluster of 39–48 (where Dionysos pretends that Herakles is afraid of him) and 271–307 (Dionysos facing the imaginary monsters of the Underworld), and its immediate puncturing, develops into the bluster of 460–464 (the knocking at the gates of Hades), with its even harsher result, and from that to splendidly nervous self-assertion in the landlady scene and then the beating scene, where our pleasure at Dionysos' reluctant acceptance of the beating contest is conditioned by his tremulous response to previous challenges. His impersonation of Herakles, sustained with so little success throughout the journey to Hades, leads to the magnificent blurring of identities in 460–673. The verbal repartee of the opening of the play and the dialogue with Herakles and the Corpse lead to the contest with the frogs, the magnificent, quick-fire dialogue of 271–315 (the arrival in the Underworld) and the superb comedy of 549–589 (the landlady scene). Each succeeding scene takes what we know of Dionysos from what has gone before, and extends and develops it. In particular, the whole relationship between Dionysos and Xanthias grows in an organic manner – the simple cross-talk of the beginning leads gradually to a more complex relationship in the clothes-changing and beating scenes, where the two characters become mirror-images of each other. The features of this relationship (repartee, role-playing and the exchanging of character) are transferred to Aeschylus and Euripides in the second half of the play. It is a sign of the strength of the writing, and in particular of the articulation of the comic initiative between all three actors, that we are scarcely worried by Dionysos' relegation to a subordinate position in the second half of the play.

The actor who played Mnesilochos[74] in *Women at the Festival* was called on for perhaps the widest display of technique in Aristophanes. He was expected to be a master of physical slapstick (the shaving and discovery scenes alone show that); he was expected to be adept at comic cross-talk (as in the opening, or the Thesmophoria scene); he was expected to be able to perform in the grandest mock-tragic manner, in both speech and song. Throughout the play his role and that of Euripides blur together, and exchange the comic initiative in a way unsurpassed in Aristophanes, even in *Frogs* (for a detailed analysis, see pp. 133ff.): the actor, therefore, was expected to keep up a difficult, symbiotic relationship with another comedian, in a way different from the whole style of Greek acting, which tended to individuality of performance. And above all, throughout his performance he was called on for that duality of role-playing characteristic of Aristophanes' leading comedians: the ability to enter completely into his role in the play while at the same time retaining his character as an actor who watches and enjoys his own performance, and who shares his enjoyment with the audience. The spectators are enlisted almost as allies in this actor's comic fight against his role, his fellow-actors, the performance and even the very Festival of Dionysos itself. We are invited not only to share the character Mnesilochos' oblique vision of 'reality' within the plot of the play, but also the Mnesilochos actor's oblique vision of the actual reality of his actual performance. In most of the other plays this duality of role serves the purpose of highlighting the serious undercurrents of the action; in *Women at the Festival*, where there is no serious undercurrent, its purpose is purely comic, and the statements it makes are about the nature of comic theatre itself.

9
Characterization in Aristophanes

Stereotype characters

In the majority of Aristophanes' plays there is little or no character development, and practically no organic interaction between leading character and supporting roles. The nature of the leading character is fixed from the start – *Dikaiopolis*, 'Just-to-the-city', *Peisetairos*, 'Persuader-of-companions' or *Lysistrata*, 'Looser-of-armies' – and the whole action of the play relates to that archetype, not developing or influencing it so much as being developed or influenced by it. The other characters relate to it usually by challenging it. The action of the play proceeds by a series of contests, and interest for the spectator lies more in physical or verbal polemic than in the exposition or development of character.

Aristophanes' genius was not, however, limited by this stereotype technique; he turned it into a potent vehicle for moral or political comment. *Knights*, for example, is structured as a series of slapstick contests, unvaried in style or method; but underlying these contests are different and developing views of a serious theme, the corruptness of the real-life Kleon. In later comedy only Molière and Beaumarchais attempt the same mixture with any degree of success. Usually dramatists in this mode avoid social comment altogether, even in cases (such as Wilde's *The Importance of Being Earnest*) where it might well strengthen the comedy. In the majority of comedies the humour lies precisely in character, in the action and reaction of character – our interest in the comedies of Shakespeare, for example, is as much in who the characters are as in what they do (in Aristophanes it is in what they do rather than in what they are).

All but two of Aristophanes' extant plays (*Women at the Festival* and *Frogs*) are of the agonistic and allegorical type. The status of the characters in the play is determined by their status in the allegory, and we know all we need to know about them individually before the action begins. In some cases (for example Dikaiopolis) they reveal their characters in monologue; in others (like the Paphlagonian or Trygaios) they are described by others; in others again they reveal themselves during the opening scene (as in *Lysistrata*, for example). But once revealed, they do not significantly change. Dikaiopolis remains the Dikaiopolis of the prologue throughout the play; the Paphlagonian conforms exactly to the description of him in the prologue; Lysistrata (a more pallid character altogether) reveals no new character traits once the women have sworn their oath. Many characters are defined specifically by their allegorical significance; others are people from real life taken into the action, stripped of their real-life characteristics and given a role (often comic and stereotyped from play to play) within the action (see Chapter 6).

Because of their allegorical function, the majority of Aristophanes' characters remain two-dimensional. Audience reaction to them is conditioned by the point of view they represent, or (in the case of known individuals like Kleonymos or Euripides) by a comic stereotype familar from other plays. Only the heroes are given an extra dimension of character, which lifts them from the two-dimensional state of their adversaries. This quality, *poneria*, enables its possessor to break out of the allegorical confines of the plot, and to assert a protean individuality independent of the main argument. Without *poneria* the plays would often be animated tracts rather than comedies; without *poneria* Dikaiopolis' self-seeking, Strepsiades' obtuseness, Philokleon's antinomianism and the priggishness of Peisetairos, Lysistrata and Praxagora would soon become wearisome. *Poneria* allows them, so to speak, to stand aside from their allegorical qualities, and creates the illusion that they have deliberately chosen those qualities in order to divert both themselves and us. Paradoxically, however, because it frees them from the trap of stereotype into which many of their adversaries fall (for example Lamachos, the Paphlagonian, Socrates, the Athenian Official, Poverty), it weights audience interest in their favour, and hence helps to support their position in the overall moral argument.

The vital, and vitalizing, effect of *poneria* can be clearly seen if we compare Dikaiopolis' interruptions of the Assembly in *Acharnians* with Euelpides' very similar interruptions of Peisetairos in *Birds* 462–602. Euelpides is nothing but a buffoon, a *bomolochos*: his humour is in one vein only, and soon runs out. Dikaiopolis' interruptions, by contrast, are funnier not only because his stance is more significant to the theme of the play, but because he has deliberately chosen to play the part of a buffoon in the Assembly, for specific reasons, and has announced the fact in advance (*Acharnians* 37–39):

> I'm here to shout and clap and heckle
> If anyone talks of anything else at all but peace.

That choice, that statement of intent, is a piece of *poneria* which shapes and frames our response to everything that follows it.

A structure in which all the characters but one are clearly defined and in one mode only, and the exception is the protean hero, is clearly well suited to the top-heavy constitution of an Athenian acting-company. The second, third and subsequent actors had to be versatile, because they played several parts in the same play, often very different in kind – each part was monotypical, and the actor changed his style with each new mask. The leading actor, on the other hand, onstage for most of the action, could build variety into his actual performance, and the scenes were structured to let him do so. Where monotony threatened, interest was shifted elsewhere (as in the insertion of the Myrrhine/ Kinesias scene in *Lysistrata*), a change of theme or pace was introduced (as in the *alazon* scenes in *Birds*), or the leading character was removed from the action entirely (as happens to Praxagora in *Assemblywomen*).

Avoidance of character interaction

Interaction between the characters and the character development that would be consequent upon it are avoided in the agonistic, allegorical plays by the use of two kinds of scene above all. These may be described as (1) the 'tit-for-tat' type and (2) the 'Aunt Sally' type. They are largely absent from the two developmental, non-allegorical plays (*Women at the Festival* and *Frogs*), but provide the greater part of the dramatic structure in all the other plays.

Formality is the essence of the 'tit-for-tat' style. Two adversaries, of more or less equal weight, engage in a ritualized contest, rather like a game of chess. *A* makes a move, then waits to see what *B* will do. *B* makes an answering move, then stands back and waits for *A* to retaliate. (The style is familiar in the 'mutual destruction' sequences of many Laurel and Hardy films.) The humour for the audience consists as much in the formalized 'waiting' periods as in the actions themselves, although scenes of this type reach their climax through the increasing violence, unexpectedness or incongruity of those actions. Dramatic development is entirely independent of the characters; the participants end the contest exactly as they began it – in fact, the more stylized and ritualized the actions are, the more the performers are Bergsonian automata, the funnier the scene. The contest rarely finishes with a true victory: either one participant gives up or the whole affair is interrupted by a third party.

Sometimes the tit-for-tat structure appears in short exchanges only (for example the introductory skirmishes between hero and Chorus in *Acharnians* 284–346 or *Peace* 309–345). Sometimes it forms the backbone of extended scenes, like the argument between Right and Wrong in *Clouds* or the Myrrhine/ Kinesias scene in *Lysistrata*. Sometimes it is the governing structure of an entire play (for example *Acharnians* or *Knights*). Its formality and deliberate pace are often helped by the use of 'long' rhythms (anapaests, for example, rather than iambics), by line responsion and by the use of mock-tragic language. All these assist the artificiality which marks the style. Typical are the magnificent skirmishes between Dikaiopolis and Lamachos (*Acharnians* 572–625 and 1071–1234). In them, although the contestants never entirely drop their overall characters (as *poneros* and *alazon* respectively), the feeling is more of a verbal tennis-match than of a dialogue between two human beings. The following passage is typical, and shows the tit-for-tat style at its best (*Acharnians*

1097–1108, translated by Parker. The scene continues in the manner of this extract for another 32 lines):

LAMACHOS: Break out my fieldpack! Issue Emergency Rations . . .
DIKAIOPOLIS: An emergency's broken out. Bring our largest lunchbasket.
LAMACHOS: Mouldy biscuits, a stack of mildewed hardtack . . .
DIKAIOPOLIS: The fresh-baked bread, the buns, the *petits fours!*
LAMACHOS: . . . some lumps of salt, a bag of wormy beans . . .
DIKAIOPOLIS: That tasty fillet of sole! Never could stand beans.
LAMACHOS: . . . the dried and desicated heads and tails of scrod . . .
DIKAIOPOLIS: The sweetbreads *en brochette* – I'll roast them there.
LAMACHOS: The swirling plumes to deck my hero's helm!
DIKAIOPOLIS: Now for *my* birds. Let's pack those yummy thrushes.
LAMACHOS: Ah, the blazing glint of this ostrich plume!
DIKAIOPOLIS: The delicate, brownish tint of a roasted thrush!
LAMACHOS: Avaunt, Sirrah! Cease your fleering at my panoply!
DIKAIOPOLIS: – Well, tit for tat. You stop leering at my pigeons.

The essential features of the tit-for-tat style are formality and a deliberate pace. The second, 'Aunt Sally' style uses precisely the opposite features: variety and speed. Once again it is a style familiar from later comedy, and particularly from the exchanges between a music-hall comic and his stooge. The joker's adversary constantly sets up new ideas or phrases, only to have them demolished by the joker. In scenes of this kind, although the comic initiative lies with the joker, and exploits his *poneria*, the uncomprehending doggedness of the opponent is also a major part of the humour. As in the tit-for-tat style, this type of humour requires no character development on either side. The repartee exists almost independently of the actors – indeed, the same jokes can be repeated almost exactly by different characters in different plays (Margaret Dumont and Groucho Marx, for example, never alter their relationship from film to film; in Aristophanes, much of the Nikarchos sequence in *Acharnians* 910ff. is repeated – and improved – in the Sycophant scene in *Wealth* 850ff.). Just as the tit-for-tat style may have been developed by Aristophanes from pre-literary agonistic comedy, so the 'Aunt Sally' style is characteristic of another traditional survival, the *alazon* scene. The Megarian scene in *Acharnians* and the first scene with the Official in *Lysistrata* show the way in which the style could be extended, but it is in the *alazon* scenes in *Birds* that it reached its apogee. There are over a dozen of them, and their speed and variety are most marked after the more deliberate pace of the first part of the play. The following short extract, from the Iris scene, is typical of the style as a whole (*Birds* 1229–1236, translated by Arrowsmith):

PEISETAIROS: . . . state your business here.
IRIS: *My* business? Why,
         I am bearing the following message from my father Zeus
         to mankind:

'LET HOLOCAUSTS MAKE GLAD THY GODS
AND MUTTON BARBECUES ON BEEFY ALTARS TOAST,
YEA, TILL EVERY STREET DOTH REEK WITH ROAST
AMBROSIALLY.'

PEISETAIROS: Hmm. I think he wants a sacrifice.
But to which gods?

IRIS: To *which* gods? To *us*, of course.
Who else could he mean?

PEISETAIROS: But that's quite absurd.
You, gods? I mean, really!

IRIS: Name me any other gods.

PEISETAIROS: Why, the Birds, madam . . .

Double-acts

In two of the surviving plays, *Women at the Festival* and *Frogs*, Aristophanes laid aside the stereotyped character-drawing of his other plays, and produced instead comedies of character, in a mode partly like that of late Euripides, and foreshadowing the character comedy which has become the prevailing type of Western literary comedy, especially in the last four hundred years. The reasons for this change of style can only be guessed at. Neither play is an allegory of any kind; both deal almost exclusively with the nature of dramaturgy itself; in both a subsidiary theme is decadence; political comment is almost entirely absent from *Women at the Festival* and in *Frogs* it is reserved only for the generalized comments at the end of the poetic contest (where the point is the ludicrous nature of the lines actually quoted from tragedy, 1427ff., 1431ff., 1443f., 1463ff., rather than their appositeness to the situation to which they are applied), or else it is placed separately from the main action of the play (in the parabasis, 686ff. and 717ff.).

What makes these two plays so alike – and so different from all the others – is not only that the characters develop organically with the plot, but also that there is more than one central character. The double-act between first and second actors in *Women at the Festival* and the interaction between the three main actors in *Frogs* are not only unique in Aristophanes, but represent a peforming style rare in almost all comedy until the present century. Possibly the inference is that Aristophanes had at his disposal in both 411 (*Women at the Festival*) and 405 (*Frogs*) actors who excelled at team performance of this complexity. Certainly in the later extant plays the style is not repeated. *Assemblywomen* partly reverts to the style of the plays before 411 (that is, it has a single hero and stereotyped characters); it also contains a self-contained and brilliantly bawdy sketch, whose style and content are virtually unrelated to the rest of the play. The double-act of Chremylos and Karion in *Wealth* is desultory: the characters do not develop, either individually or by interaction with one another, and after the opening scene, although the two parts are of equal importance, they alternate, never appearing again together – a dramatic structure which surprises as much by its success as by its uniqueness.

Basically, a double-act is created when any two actors perform a scene together. The dialogue flows from one to the other, and comedy often takes the form of banter or mutual insult. The openings of *Knights*, *Wasps* and *Peace* are good examples. In each of them the two characters are independent of one another; they are separate individuals who just happen to be conversing, and each exists in his own right, unattached to the other. In a more sophisticated kind of double-act, two stereotype characters are placed in juxtaposition; here the success of the act depends on both the juxtaposition and the maintenance of the stereotypes. The standard type consists of the fool and his straight man, the con man and the fall-guy. It was well exemplified in this century by Abbott and Costello, and appears in Aristophanes regularly in the *alazon* scenes, and occasionally in more extended sequences such as the opening of *Birds* (where Euelpides is the stock fool and Peisetairos the stock straight man).

In the greatest double-acts of all, the relationship between the characters is symbiotic. Neither exists independently of the double-act, and within the double-act they change and develop as a single character might. The comic initiative is not with one partner alone (as in the fool/straight man double-act): it shifts from one to the other, sometimes separating them into stereotyped situations (as when one partner attempts to 'con' the other) and sometimes uniting them in the face of an adversary from outside. There have been very few successful double-acts of this kind – the greatest was that of Laurel and Hardy, who were so closely linked in people's minds that many of their fans did not know which was which, and who achieved a unity so much greater than the sum of its parts that the many excellent solo films each partner made prior to their association now seem mere curiosities.

It is I think necessary to stress the rarity of this type of performance. The requirement is not just that the material is right (for any pair of comic actors could play Euripides and Mnesilochos – or a Laurel and Hardy script – and get laughs), but that the performers themselves should combine in a way totally unlike the interaction in any other kind of acting at all. Of course we know nothing of the actors who played Euripides and Mnesilochos or Dionysos and Xanthias. The evidence for the chemistry between the performers is in the texts alone – and if Greek comic acting was as formal as some scholars think, then the plays are as funny as, and no funnier than, any pair of gifted comic actors could make them. It is only if we imagine (say) Laurel and Hardy in either of the plays that the difference in scale and stature becomes apparent. This missing dimension – the ingredient put into a performance by the performers themselves – is very easily forgotten in our reading of ancient comedy today; but in reiterating it we are only claiming for Aristophanes' words the same status as those of modern comic scripts (where we do know, and can imagine as we read, the added dimension given by particular performers).[75]

But the leading characters in these plays do not only interact with each other. Their development is also closely interwoven with that of the plots themselves. The plots of the other plays – even those as integrated as *Acharnians* and *Lysistrata* – develop apart from the characters. They have, so to speak, an impetus of their own which takes over from the characters and which, once the strange and mighty deed is done, moves as inexorably to its fulfilment as any tragedy. In *Women at the Festival* and *Frogs* the plot changes as the characters change. The rescue attempts of the second half of *Women at the Festival* are not at all predictable from the opening of the play: they depend on a change in Euripides' character, on a new piece of *poneria* entirely different from that shown previously; and their impetus is governed by the way in which Mnesilochos responds to each of them. The final piece of *poneria*, the outwitting of the Scythian, cannot be foreseen (in the way that, for example, Dikaiopolis' outwitting of Lamachos can); but once it has taken place it seems an inevitable part of the character of Euripides – the plot, in fact, has enhanced the character and vice versa. In the same way, there is nothing in the opening of *Frogs* to prepare us for the magnificent blurring of identities in the scene before Pluto's palace. The logical development of that sequence depends on the revelation of ever-greater *poneria* from both Dionysos and Xanthias, and their *poneria* is only unlocked and revealed by each new twist in the plot as it proceeds. It is obvious that organic growth is present in the plots of *Acharnians*, *Wasps* or *Lysistrata* (as compared with the episodic growth of the other plays); but it is equally clear that it is of an entirely different order from that in the two double-act plays. Not until Shakespeare did such a fusion of character and action appear again.

Women at the Festival

When we read the opening dialogues of *Knights*, *Wasps* or *Peace*, we have no feeling that the participants have any relationship with each other outside of the action we are seeing. They are, so to speak, figures conjured into existence specifically for these scenes, and what they say to each other is entirely determined by and germane to the matter immediately in hand. The spectators are eavesdropping on a specific set of circumstances, articulated in dialogue between two actors (rather than by a single actor in a prologue, for example); the relationship between the characters outside of those circumstances is so irrelevant to us that we never wonder what it might be – we are shown all we need to know, clearly and exactly defined.

When *Women at the Festival* opens, by contrast, we are given only 4 lines of orientation (Mnesilochos asking where he is being taken, 1–4), before we are plunged into the intricacies of a complex relationship which has apparently existed between the characters long before this scene begins[76] – a relationship, what is more, which seems to exist entirely independently of any obvious plot. We are not so much intrigued by what Euripides and Mnesilochos are doing or feeling at this particular moment in the play, as by their relationship to one another. This persists until line 75, when Euripides tells the long-suffering Mnesilochos (and us) the problem at the heart of the plot. By this time we know a great deal about the respective characters of the two men, and about their relationship with one other person (Agathon's servant). That knowledge is crucial to the development of the action, and affects our reaction to everything that follows, particularly the announcement of Euripides' plight.

This effect is achieved first by the pseudo-philosophical discussion about the nature of hearing and sight (5–21), which tells us something of Euripides' character (he is the wily word-monger and thought-bender familiar from his other appearances in comedy), and then by the discussion of who Agathon actually is (25–35), which establishes the inconsequential bawdy that is a main characteristic of Mnesilochos (and incidentally begins the questioning of identity in terms of sex that is a main theme of the whole play). The two of them then crouch down to listen together, and react together, to what Agathon's servant is going to say. The sequence (1–38) runs as follows:

MNESILOCHOS: Zeus, will spring never come? This man'll be
The death of me: he's been lugging me around
Since breakfast-time. Oi! Before I finally fall to bits,
I'd like to hear where you're taking me, Euripides.

EURIPIDES: You can't use the word *hear* of things
You're going to *see*.

MNESILOCHOS: Eh? Say that again.
I can't *hear* –

EURIPIDES: What you're going to *see*.

MNESILOCHOS: Ah! And I can't *see* –

EURIPIDES: What you ought to *hear*.

MNESILOCHOS: Sounds wonderful, but what does it *mean*?
I'm not supposed to see *or* hear – is that it?

EURIPIDES: No no. They're entirely disjunct phenomena.

MNESILOCHOS: Not hearing and not seeing?

EURIPIDES: Exactly.

MNESILOCHOS: How d'you mean, disjunct?

EURIPIDES: Like this. When the atmosphere first split
And stirred itself and gave birth to all creation,
For *seeing* it devised the eye,
A sphere in imitation of the sun,
And for *hearing* the tube we call the ear.

MNESILOCHOS: A tube, eh? And that's why I mustn't see or hear?
Well, I'm glad I found out. What a thing it is
To go around with a professor all my own.

EURIPIDES: Stick around, and I'll teach you plenty more.

MNESILOCHOS:	Let's stop here, then, and you can teach me
	And the nice ladies and gentlemen how to be
	A beggar, like those people in your tragedies.
EURIPIDES:	Come here, and pay attention.
MNESILOCHOS:	There.
EURIPIDES:	D'you see that door?
MNESILOCHOS:	Er . . . I think I do.
EURIPIDES:	Don't talk about it.
MNESILOCHOS:	Don't talk about the door?
EURIPIDES:	Listen.
MNESILOCHOS:	Listen, and don't talk about the door?
EURIPIDES:	Inside that house lives Agathon,
	The famous tragic poet.
MNESILOCHOS:	Agathon, eh? What's he look like?
EURIPIDES:	Well, he's –
MNESILOCHOS:	Suntanned? Ever so strong?
EURIPIDES:	That must be someone else. Haven't you seen him?
MNESILOCHOS:	Big, bushy beard?
EURIPIDES:	Haven't you *seen* him?
MNESILOCHOS:	No – not to recognize him again, anyway.
EURIPIDES:	You may have fucked him once. You must have done.
	Come over here, and crouch down. A slave's coming
	With a fire-pot and myrtle-twigs.
	Looks like he's going to sacrifice for inspiration.

The basic character types revealed in this sequence are those of *alazon* (Euripides) and a combination of *eiron*, *bomolochos* and *poneros* in Mnesilochos (who dissembles his real understanding, as an *eiron* does, in 6–18, plays the *bomolochos*/buffoon in 25–34, and reveals *poneria* in the punch lines 'professor all my own', 21, 'a beggar, like those people in your tragedies', 24, and 'Don't talk about the door', 28, all three of which show that the qualities shown in the lines leading up to them were assumed *in order* to make the joke, and were not inherent either in his character or in the situation).

Both characters in this opening are playing roles, not only for the benefit of the spectators, but also for each other and as part of their developing relationship with each other. Mnesilochos – as his reactions show – is well used to *alazon*-style lectures from Euripides; Euripides – as his parade of rather dogged patience shows – is well used to the exuberant insouciance of Mnesilochos. Neither of them seems at all concerned with the presence of the audience (as the slaves are in *Knights*, *Wasps* and *Peace*, where the opening dialogue is closely related to the plot); instead they seem engaged in a long-standing dialogue which is entirely private. It is easier to suspend disbelief in the 'reality' of these characters than in that of any others of Aristophanes except those in *Frogs* (where the same sort of private debate occurs: see below).[77] Neither is exclusively comic or straight man: the humour of 1–21 (up to the 'professor all my own' joke) is governed by Euripides' pomposity (which Mnesilochos'

135

obtuseness is designed to throw into high relief); in the rest of the sequence quoted the roles are reversed, and Mnesilochos' *poneria* governs the humour while Euripides acts as feed.

In the rest of the opening scene Euripides and Mnesilochos react together to Agathon and his slave. Euripides' *poneria* begins to assert itself in the mock-tragic language of 76ff. (the description of his fears about the Thesmophoria), and in the nature of the strange and mighty deed he is proposing (for someone else to perform, we note). It continues – again largely in mock-tragic style – as he sets out his scheme to Agathon (173–192), and is replaced by a kind of mock-tragic buffoonery when Agathon refuses to take part in the scheme (202 and 209). Mnesilochos acts splendidly as buffoon during and after Agathon's song, but takes over as *poneros* from Euripides at 200, and reaches a high point by volunteering at last to go to the Thesmophoria in Agathon's place (212f.). Throughout the scene the question of identity has been explored. Agathon's appearance is so feminine that the *poneros* Mnesilochos takes some time to admit that he is really a man; Agathon and Euripides converse with each other (in mock-tragic language) like professors playing some learned game; the sequence ends with Mnesilochos offering to undergo a transformation of sex for Euripides' sake.

The shaving scene (the 'masking' of Mnesilochos, which is balanced later by the similarly constructed 'unmasking' at the Thesmophoria, 589ff.) is played with Euripides as con man and Mnesilochos as comic stooge, in a more straightforward double-act style. The scene (213–276), taken on its own, would be as simple as (say) an Abbott and Costello dialogue; but taken in context, and bearing in mind what we already know of Euripides and Mnesilochos' relationship, it is clearly yet another example of their role-playing with one another. Euripides' conning of Mnesilochos is kept fairly straightforward, but Mnesilochos is well aware that he is being conned, and shows this by unexpected moments of *poneria* that lie outside the range of an Abbott and Costello dialogue: 232 'I'm being shaved for battle', 235 'It's not me in the mirror, it's Kleisthenes!' and in particular 245f. 'Phew, what a stink of soot! You've carbonized my crutch!' (Barrett's translation) – these are the remarks of someone agreeing to play the stooge rather than someone bewildered and unaware of the true nature of what is happening to him.

Thus, by the time of Mnesilochos' major impersonation (during the Thesmophoria scene) he has been established as an extremely complex character: a *poneros* who is happy to play the buffoon whenever he wants, an *eiron* who is all the time conscious of the qualities he is dissembling. This self-awareness and self-enjoyment, this willingness to drop in and out of a stereotyped role whenever it pleases him, lays an important foundation for his female role-playing in the rest of the play, which will be just as casually (and just as fleetingly) assumed or abandoned whenever the comic mood takes him. The character of Euripides has been more consistent; for his true *poneria* – the use of rescue scenes from his own plays, and the impersonations it will entail – is still to come. He has kept up his role in the relationship (basically that of an *alazon*, but with elements of *poneria*) in much the same way throughout; his lapses into deliberate and self-aware role-playing have been kept mainly to his exchanges with Agathon. We can now anticipate the sort of comedy we are to see from Mnesilochos as the play proceeds. Our anticipation is a creative thing (that is, it generates enjoyment and conditions our reaction to what follows): we expect Mnesilochos to show delightful diversity of character – a quality very different from the (equally delightful) *sameness* of character we expect from Dikaiopolis after the Assembly scene in *Acharnians*. In the case of Euripides all options are open, and we have still to discover his full comic potential; our anticipation here involves discovery rather than the fulfilment of expectation. It is also noteworthy that the outcome of the plot itself is still entirely mysterious – a very different state of affairs from the earlier plays, where the accomplishment of the deed is an end in itself rather than the means to further development.

In fact what happens next is a cunning manipulation of one of the conventions of Greek stage performance: doubling. Mnesilochos' change of sex has taken place before our eyes, and he remains onstage, transparently disguised, and maintaining his female role in the Thesmophoria with obvious difficulty (279–294). The Euripides actor meanwhile goes offstage and changes mask[78] and costume, ready to appear as the First Woman at 380.[79] If – as is argued in Chapter 10 – the audience was aware of doubling on the Greek stage, then the single word *ego* ('I') (380), announcing not so much the appearance of a new character as the reappearance of the same actor in a new costume, would exploit the doubling convention in a way which is both funny and explicitly to do with role-playing. The actor then launches into a monologue in true Euripidean style (383–432), to which Mnesilochos makes an appropriately Euripidean reply (466–520). There follows a short argument, in which we see the same double-act characteristics as at the start of the play: a kind of ritualized, largely irrelevant 'scoring of points', in this case beginning with high Euripidean argument (540–550, on whether or not Euripides' heroines are shameless creatures) and ending with scurrility ('I'll make you shit that sesame-cake you ate', 570). After this follows the Kleisthenes scene (574–654), a parody of a Euripidean recognition scene, and structured between the three actors in a way remarkably similar to the earlier Agathon scene (146ff.). The Thesmophoria sequence concludes with an extended parody of Euripides' *Telephos*, the First Woman throwing in parodies of distraught mothers for good measure (for example at 659–661, 695–698). Thus, although the *character* Euripides has temporarily disappeared from the action, the *fact* of Euripides has remained prominent in our minds throughout.

It is a sign not only of Mnesilochos' *poneria*, but also of the insubstantial morality of the whole plot, that he is so little worried by the failure of his impersonation.[80] If Trygaios' strange and mighty deed (for example) had failed as miserably, we should have had tragedy instead of comedy. But *Women at the Festival* is pure entertainment, and almost entirely lacks a moral dimension. The introduction of the Euripides parodies in this scene (culminating in the Palamedes impersonation) not only sets the plot on another course but also moves the location of the play beyond the 'real' setting of the mock-Thesmophoria to a more fantastic country, the imaginary world of Euripidean drama.[81] This is the only point in the play where fantasy does take over. The physical 'scene' remains realistic to the end (the theatre; the Thesmophoria), but the mind now enters a realm of boundless possibility similar to that produced by the surrealist deeds of the heroes of the moralistic plays. The contrast between this fantasy world and the 'reality' of Mnesilochos' situation is the generating theme of the rest of the play (as the contrast between the hero's fantasy world and his rivals' reality is in the other plays); but *Women at the Festival* differs from the moralistic plays (and even from the other plays rooted in reality rather than fantasy or allegory, *Wasps*, *Clouds* and *Lysistrata*) because there is no synthesis at the end, with the hero's fantasy world totally engulfing reality. In this play fantasy fails, and earthy reality (sexual titillation – yet another form of role-playing) takes over instead.

Mnesilochos' lament, and his decision to invoke Euripides' *Palamedes* (765–785), is not merely the hinge on which the rest of the plot will hang, or the point in the play where reality is finally superseded by fantasy. It is also, in terms of dramaturgy, one of Aristophanes' finest inventions. The character of Mnesilochos and the direction in which the plot is moving fuse together and produce a single magnificently comic and superbly generative idea, that of using Euripidean methods to escape from a situation brought about by Euripides in the first place. The triumph consists in the fact that for this character to have this idea at this point in the play is not the logical outcome of the action thus far, but seems instead an inspiration of the moment, a flash of comic insight wholly appropriate to the character of Mnesilochos as we have seen it unfold before us. These moments of fusion between plot and character are rare in drama: this one, for sheer ludicrous rightness, for self-conscious, generative *poneria*, is hardly matched until the Gadshill sequence in *Henry IV Part I* or the plot against Malvolio in *Twelfth Night*. This is to place Mnesilochos, as a comic character, in the highest company – and the fact that he seems as much at home there as Dikaiopolis, Agorakritos or Peisetairos do not, shows something of the character and quality of the play.

In the two rescue scenes the double-act of Euripides and Mnesilochos is once more paramount. They stand apart from the other characters in a simple and obvious way: they are parodying Euripides, and the Priestess and Scythian are not. This simple separateness is best seen in the first parody, where the partners in the double-act ignore the Priestess altogether, except where the Euripidean lines allow her a momentary entrance into the conversation (for example at 896–899, or the splendidly mock-tragic 920–924). Separateness of a more complex kind (where the double-actors seem to be indulging in a private discussion or argument, independently of the main action) occurs especially in the Echo scene: the success of 1072–1081 in particular depends on joint timing by the two actors and on their clear awareness of each other, especially if the sequence is to build quickly enough to allow Euripides' taunting of the Scythian (1082ff.) to form the climax of the whole exchange.

The effect of climax through the parody scene is achieved in several ways. Firstly, there is the nature of the parodies themselves. In the *Helen* scene the Euripidean lines are quoted verbatim, but chosen more or less at random, and usually lead to disgruntled or angry comment from the Priestess. Lines 855–868 are a good example of the way this is done (the translation is by Barrett):

MNESILOCHOS:	Here flows the Naiad-haunted stream of Nile,
	Whose waters, spreading o'er the shining plain,
	Do duty for the showers, and bring relief
	To Egypt's constipated citizens.
PRIESTESS:	You're up to no good, I can see that all right.
MNESILOCHOS:	Great Sparta was my home, and great the fame
	Of Tyndareus my father.
PRIESTESS:	Well, if your father was famous, I can tell you what he was famous *for*.
MNESILOCHOS:	Yes, my name
	Is Helen.
PRIESTESS:	At it again – pretending to be a woman! Before you've even been punished for your first little game!
MNESILOCHOS:	And many lost their lives
	On grim Scamander's banks, because of me.
PRIESTESS:	A pity you didn't lose yours, I'm thinking.
MNESILOCHOS:	And here I sit: but of my darling spouse,
	The wretched Menelaos, there's no sign.
	Why am I still alive?
PRIESTESS:	Don't ask me, ask the crows.

An even more effective form of the same 'puncturing' joke is 906–916, where 7 lines of *Helen* – with one change, in 910 – are uttered in the grand manner, only to collapse into the obviously hammed-up 914–916 ('Take me, take me, husband. Embrace me. Let me kiss you. Take me, take me, take me, away, away at once'), a real gift to the Mnesilochos actor. Secondly, there is the character played by the third actor. In the *Helen* parody he plays a straightforward role, that of the Priestess,[82] who speaks like a conventional comic old woman, in buffoon style, throughout, except for one mock-tragic outburst in 920–923. In the *Andromeda* scene, however, the third actor plays the splendid

Scythian, an *alazon* figure striking both for his bad Greek (always a fertile source of humour in Aristophanes) and for his dull wits. Thirdly, the *Andromeda* scene unlike the others is full of opportunities for physical knockabout, from Euripides' overflight on the crane and the mock-battle of the Echo scene to the passage at 1110ff., which is built out of increasingly bawdy knockabout, and ends with the Scythian chasing Euripides from the stage.

After a choral interlude (1136–1159) just long enough for the Euripides actor to change from his Perseus costume to that of the old woman,[83] he returns, capitulates to the women of the Chorus, and brings on the Scythian's dancing-girl. In a play concerned throughout with illusion and reality, Euripides is compelled finally not only to apologize to the women he has maligned, but actually to assume as his final role that of a woman himself. He and the Scythian dominate the final knockabout (Mnesilochos only speaks twice in 90 lines). The play ends in fast, bawdy slapstick – and in a final Chorus (1226–1231) which unites the real Thesmophoria with the actors in the theatre, and so brings reality and illusion together in triumphant synthesis.

Just as the first half of the play allowed Mnesilochos to assume the dominant role in the double-act, by means of the physical changes in the Euripides actor (from Euripides to Priestess and back again), so in the second half Euripides becomes dominant, because of the physical restraints on the Mnesilochos actor (who is guarded, and later strapped to a plank). The first, Mnesilochos-dominated, half of the play is concerned with 'reality' (the obvious problems, and bawdy implications, of a man playing a woman); the second half, the Euripides half, is concerned with 'illusion' – Euripidean drama – though the earthy dimension is not entirely lacking. The fact that the first and second actors clearly functioned as a double-act rather than separate individuals gives point and articulation to these basic contrasts within the underlying structure of the play.

Frogs

The symbiotic double-act at the heart of *Women at the Festival* (with the third actor used mainly as a foil to this partnership) is replaced in *Frogs* by a tripartite relationship. The first, second and third actors are given parts of equal weight and technical difficulty. Throughout the play the most animated scenes are those involving all three of them (the Herakles scene, the beating scene, the poetic contest); where extended dialogue occurs between any two actors, it is as likely to be between second and third actors as between second and first actors. In the first half of the play the main double-act dialogue is between Dionysos and Xanthias (first and second actors); in the second half it is between Aeschylus and Euripides (second and third actors). Throughout the play, the fourth actor (who is given a fair amount to do, more than in any other extant play) plays the foil or extra partner to these three: characteristic examples are his appearances as Plathane in 549–577 and as Pluto in 1414ff.

The most striking difference between the three main actors lies in the depth of characterization they are asked to give their parts. Leaving aside the many minor figures, too small to give much of a character dimension (for example Charon and the landlady), or simple stereotypes like Herakles and Aiakos, we are left with the characters of Dionysos (first actor), Xanthias and Euripides (second actor[84]), and Aeschylus (third actor). Of these parts, the two tragedians are far less developed characters than Xanthias or Dionysos; the third actor, therefore, is asked overall for less depth of characterization than the second or first actors. The tragedians' roles are agonistic, and a certain amount of two-dimensional stereotype is important in creating this effect: Aeschylus is mainly an *alazon* and Euripides an *eiron*, and this difference is several times mentioned by the Chorus (for example 814–829, 900–904, 1099–1108).

The characters of Xanthias and Dionysos are more fully developed. Of all the characters in the play, they conform most closely to the double-act style of *Women at the Festival*. Their opening dialogue (1–35) is as irrelevant to the action as that of Mnesilochos and Euripides, and the comic initiative moves from one to the other in the same way. This shifting relationship is carried on in the magnificent scene at the edge of the Underworld (271–315), and is given physical shape in the changing of clothes and identities in 460–673. As in the Mnesilochos/Euripides double-act, neither is exclusively comic or feed; the symbiosis of their relationship is complete, and (again as in the earlier play) seems at times to exist in its own right, independent of the action of this particular play. (Xanthias is not, for example, exclusively the archetypical *poneros* slave, as Karion is in *Wealth*; equally, Dionysos is never just the foolish old master, as Chremylos is in the same play, at least in his relationship with Karion.)

A striking difference between this double-act and the one in *Women at the Festival* is the way in which third characters are regularly brought into it. In the earlier play such characters (Agathon, Kleisthenes and the Priestess) remain outside the double-act, and act as foils to it; in *Frogs* the third characters (Herakles, Aiakos and the landlady) are brought completely into the act, and temporarily replace one or other of the partners. In 38–164 (dialogue between Dionysos and Herakles) Xanthias takes practically no part; in 503–521 (dialogue between Xanthias and Aiakos) Dionysos is silent; in 549–578 (the landlady scene) Xanthias speaks only inconsequential asides. In the beating scene this process is taken a stage further: the double-act becomes a triple-act, and the interest is less in seeing Dionysos and Xanthias reacting together as one to Aiakos, than in seeing the initiative shift from one to another of all three actors. In his short scene alone with Aiakos (738–813, on the delights of being a wicked slave) Xanthias shows few of his characteristics from earlier in the play:

in fact this scene as a whole is different in style from anything else in Aristophanes, and looks forward more to the two-dimensional, stereotyped world of Roman New Comedy.

Of the two parts, Dionysos and Xanthias, Xanthias is far less developed than Dionysos. *Poneria* is his chief quality: he is almost the cunning slave of Roman comedy, except that he is far more closely involved in the action. In Roman comedy the slaves tend to stage-manage the plot, with particular objectives in mind: their own role-playing is undertaken principally to further those objectives, and failure often leaves them at the mercy of their masters. Xanthias, in contrast, plays roles to suit himself, and with little concern for the outcome: this can be seen most clearly at 637ff., where imminent exposure as slave, not god, is greeted with cheerful acceptance and even anticipation of the interesting scene that is bound to follow. Insouciance of this kind, the stock-in-trade of the Aristophanic *poneros*, is rarely found in Roman comedy.

Dionysos – as befits a god in his own theatre at his own festival – is a character of considerable depth and complexity. For most of the play he is an *eiron*, dissembling his true divine character: it is revealed only at the height of the argument over identity in the beating scene (631 – where no one believes him), and at the close of the poetic contest (1488f. – where he refers to his role as saviour of the city[85]). He is equally, in the first half of the play, an *alazon*, vainly trying to claim for himself the qualities of Herakles. He is alternately Xanthias' stooge and the comedian to Xanthias' straight man. In his dealings with Herakles and Aiakos he is predominantly a *bomolochos*/buffoon, though blessed with sudden flashes of *poneria* that lift his character out of that potentially tiresome rut. (Examples are the dialogue about the size of his desire for Euripides, 52–66; 'Make your route short; I'm not much of a walker', 128; and his pretence not to feel the blows in the beating scene, 646ff. – and compare, in the poetic contest, 847f. 'Bring in a black lamb; there's a storm blowing up'; 1169 'Brilliant! I don't understand a word'; 1471 'My tongue swore – but I choose Aeschylus'). His character develops between the opening scene and the beating scene (see pp. 125ff.), and although his approach in the poetic contest is largely that of a pure *bomolochos* (see for example the pointless Theramenes joke in 968ff.; 'He was talking to the dead; even saying it three times, he'll not get through', 1175f.; his reaction to the drum-beats in 1278ff. and Euripides' Muse in 1308; and the dialogue about which politicians the city prefers, 1451–1466), very often what he says is not just buffoonery *tout court*, but makes an ironical comment on the pretensions of Aeschylus and Euripides — the discussion of the poet's duty to society (1004ff.) shows this particularly clearly.

The fact remains, however, that *Frogs* is not a play with a single leading role (except technically, in that the leading actor played Dionysos). The 'star' role is Dionysos until the parabasis – but even so, the comic initiative lies as often with other characters as it does with him. In the poetic contest the initiative shifts between the three main characters in a way unparalleled in ancient comedy. Dionysos dominates 640–694, Euripides 905–991, Aeschylus 1004–1098, Euripides 1119–1176, Aeschylus 1177–1250, Euripides 1261–1295, Aeschylus 1269–1368, Dionysos 1369–end. When to this we add the importance of Herakles in 38–164, the scene between Xanthias and Aiakos in 738–813, and the tripartite structure of the humour in 605–673, it is clear that just as *Women at the Festival* centred on a double-act rather than a single protagonist, so *Frogs* is a 'company play', where the interaction between the three comedians far outweighed their relative status in the acting-company.

10

The Dramatic Use of Stage Conventions

The nature of stage conventions

Of all the performing arts, the theatre makes most use of conventions. This is because its nature is deictic rather than descriptive: it shows the representation of an action rather than the action itself. (Even the rupture of illusion in comedy is *acted*: there is, by definition, no intrusion of genuine reality into a stage performance.) Without well established and well understood conventions, even the simplest kind of theatre would disorientate and confuse its audience, just as unheralded role-playing (such as suddenly feigning illness in the street, or breaking into song in the doctor's surgery) would in real life.

The conventions that build up in theatre practice are often extremely subtle; their origins cannot clearly be traced. Not only that, but they change from epoch to epoch, country to country, stage to stage. Hence, the conventions of Greek theatre must today be approached with caution. Since the essence of a convention is that it is unwritten, we run the risk either of missing a Greek convention entirely, or of reading into Greek conventions meanings extrapolated from those of our own theatre (as happened in the case of Greek stage illusion, where the misunderstandings of generations of scholars have only recently begun to be cleared up).

For example, all that we know of Greek theatrical style suggests that it was highly spectacular, totally unlike the realistic drama of today. The size of the theatre, costumes, masks, music, the presence of a Chorus throughout the action – all these might suggest to us the trappings not of a play, but of a far more convention-ridden modern form, grand opera. The danger is that we may go on to assume that the Greeks reacted to their plays as we do to grand opera, and base our interpretation of the plays on this (possibly false) assumption.

The risk of such a large general misapprehension is perhaps so obvious that it rarely happens. But the same thing applies to much smaller, less obvious conventions. A good example is weeping on stage. Because of films and television we are accustomed today to the idea that when a character in a play weeps, he looks like someone weeping in real life, even down to the tears running down his cheeks. But not all actors can weep real tears to order, and in films and television plays the 'tears' are often applied by make-up (drops of glycerine) before the camera starts turning. On the stage, where it is not possible to stop the action in the same way, a convention has arisen that when a character covers his face with his hands and shakes his shoulders, he is weeping. Often his own words or those of other characters help the illusion by referring explicitly to weeping. If a reference is made, later in the play, to 'cheeks wet with tears', the actor may contrive, while covering his face with his hands, to wet his cheeks with glycerine or other means. In Greek drama weeping is extremely common,[86] and it is obvious that it could not have been shown in any realistic way, because of the masks. The convention used seems to have been a bent head, with the arm upraised so that the robe falls to cover the face; as in modern drama, the character himself or other characters help the illusion by referring specifically to tears or grief. The danger for a modern commentator is in assuming that the Greek convention is somehow more 'theatrical' and less convincing than the modern one. To a Greek audience, an upraised arm and a bent head would be no more obtrusive or 'hammy' than the covering of the face is to us.

In serious drama the whole point of a convention is that it should not be noticed. Its purpose is to provide both actors and audience with a convenient signal that a particular action is being represented, and it should be no more obtrusive on the stage than the real action would be in life. On the modern proscenium stage, for example, both actors and audience have been trained to observe the 'fourth wall' convention (where the actors always act facing outwards, towards the audience, which is as it were eavesdropping through the fourth wall of a room) to such an extent that we are quite unaware of it. Indeed, both actors and spectators are often disconcerted by their first experience of performances 'in the round', where the actors inevitably turn their backs to many spectators for much of the action.

In comedy a very frequent source of fun is the ridicule of stage conventions, usually by exaggerating them or referring expressly to their existence – that is, in each case, by pointing out that they are artificial and illusory and so destroying the semblance of reality they were designed to create. In a recent one-man show, for example, a well-known English comedian (Max Wall) announced to the audience, 'I shall now execute a tap-dance I used to do when I was ten years old. In those days I did it from right to left. But nowadays I always do it from left to right. That way it feels better – and in any case, the right-hand profile is my handsome one.' This patter relies not only on sexual double entendre, and on the audience's knowledge of the comedian's battered, grotesque leer (which follows the last line quoted), but also neatly guys the fourth wall convention, and the equally conventional notion that there is an unseen barrier between the 'reality' of the performer and that of the audience, a barrier which is not to be crossed.

The most frequent use of convention to produce humour is in parody. Here the conventions of one style of performance are taken over and ridiculed by their incongruous position in another: a ballet-dancer in a brothel or a whore in *Swan Lake*, for example. The language and declamatory style of tragedy lend themselves particularly well to parody, because of the association of comedy with the puncturing of pomposity (an association which is itself conventional). Sometimes the declamatory style is used on comic words, with suitably incongruous results; at other times quotations from actual tragedies (complete, truncated or adapted) are spoken as if they are natural to the comedy, and the incongruity arises from their totally irrelevant tragic associations.

This particular convention, the irrelevant association of tragic and comic styles, was especially fruitful in the Greek theatre. Part of the reason was the metrical formality of tragic language compared with comic. But in addition, the simple order of plays on the programme was conventional, and could be used for comic effect. If the opening line of the first play on a given day was, 'I come, the son of Zeus, to this land of Thebes',[87] then − because the first play was always, by convention, a tragedy − the audience would know that this speaker was a serious figure, and their reaction to all his subsequent remarks would be adjusted accordingly. The same line at the start of a satyr-play or comedy at the end of the day would clearly be parody, and would evoke an entirely different mood. The openings of *Acharnians*, *Women at the Festival*, *Assemblywomen* and even *Knights* depend entirely on this convention for their effect; in the same way, many of Euripides' opening lines could lead as easily to comedy as to tragedy.[88]

Faced with most of the conventions of the Greek theatre, it is comparatively easy to see what is going on, and to reinterpret the style in terms of today. We can make enough of an imaginative leap, for example, to see that the Greeks were as little conscious of masks as we are of make-up, as little worried by the absence of realistic scenery as we are by three-sided rooms with all the furniture facing the missing fourth wall, as willing to accept the fact that if a play said so, it was dark even in the blaze of afternoon sun, as we are willing to accept the highlighting and changing lights in modern theatres. We can imagine, with a fair chance of being right, what the presence of the Chorus did for a play, or the effect of a long messenger's monologue after several scenes of lively dialogue.

There are, however, two conventions which need closer examination, those of doubling (where the same actor plays more than one part) and travesty (where male actors play female parts). The reason is that both are still used on our own stage. Parts are doubled, if not often at least sometimes, and authors have even used the convention for dramatic effect (for example Anouilh in *Ring Round the Moon*, in which the leading actor plays twins, or Ray Cooney in his farce *One for the Pot*, in which the leading actor plays four separate parts). Travesty acting has been a feature of the modern theatre since well before Shakespeare, and (in the form of 'drag' acting) had a remarkable burst of popularity in the late 1960s and early 1970s.[89] Because the conventions are still alive, they have particular

146

associations for us today; and we must consider carefully whether those associations were the same for Aristophanes' audiences, and from there what effect the conventions had on the performance and meaning of his plays.[90] The question is particularly important because of the way comedy treats stage conventions: it is hard to believe that Aristophanes, who clearly got so much mileage out of other conventional devices, should have ignored these two altogether. It may be, in fact, that if we try to find the sort of effect doubling and travesty acting had (whether done 'straight' or burlesqued), we may find that an entirely new dimension is added to the plays, a dimension hitherto ignored (on the assumption that the Greeks were so used to the conventions that they failed to notice them too), or misunderstood because of the very different associations of those same conventions on the modern stage.

Doubling

On the modern stage there are two sorts of doubling, and the audience reacts to each in a different manner. Small companies presenting plays with large casts often double several of the smaller parts – and usually when they do they are not particularly concerned that the audience should be aware of it. Often the actor's make-up and costume are completely changed, and he plays each part in an entirely distinct way. In this case it is possible for the audience to remain unaware that doubling has taken place. Often the only indication is to be found in the programme, and the effect on the production is exactly the same as if two separate actors had taken the doubled parts.

The second method involves trumpeting abroad the fact that parts are being doubled. The doubling is made an essential part of the production style, and part of the audience's expectation is to see its effect on the balance and meaning of the play. The parts of Claudius and the Ghost in *Hamlet* are often played by the same actor – and clearly, if the audience is made aware of the fact, it makes a significant contribution to the meaning of these characters within the action. In an experimental production of *Medea* (at Guildford, England, in 1970) all the male parts were played by a single actor, who wore a different mask for each part but in other ways was completely recognizable. This made an explicit comment on Medea's view of men, and the doubling was vital to the meaning of the production. Doubling of this kind (like another modern practice, the alternation on subsequent nights of a pair of actors in such roles as Iago and Othello, or Richard II and Bolingbroke) adds extra resonances to the play in performance, and it is then essential that the audience should be aware of the doubling in advance.

In the Greek theatre the audience *always* knew about the doubling in advance. Since it was not a necessary procedure – there were certainly enough actors about to operate a system of one man one part – we must assume that it was felt to be either an inalterable or a desirable part of the effect of Greek drama. It is not sufficient to say that in a large theatre a change of costume and mask, coupled with homogeneity of performing style, would be enough to make doubling unnoticed by the audience. If that were the case we should need to be told why doubling was used at all – for it cannot be explained on the grounds of economy (which was not a feature of the production style in any other way) or ritual necessity. We know that the audience were well aware of the identity of their actors: the existence of prizes for performers shows that. We know that certain actors were famous for particular abilities (for example vocal expertise, or success in female parts).[91] It is logical to assume that the audience were not only well aware that doubling was taking place, but that they also knew, by and large, which individual actors were playing which parts at any given moment.

This is not to say, of course, that the dramatist necessarily took such doubling into account when he wrote the play. King Oedipus, for example, is not significantly changed in meaning if the parts are taken by three rather than eight actors. If it were, then – taking Jebb's distribution of parts for the sake of argument – we should expect to be able to detect from the writing some connection between the parts of Creon, Teiresias and the messenger from Corinth (all played by the second actor), or Jocasta, the priest, the messenger from the palace and the servant of Laios (all played by the third actor). There is no such connection, and to make one is to add gratuitously to Sophocles' text (unlike the doubling of the Ghost and Claudius in Hamlet, which seems rather to bring out a resonance of meaning already implicit in the play). What the audience saw in King Oedipus was a convention: Jocasta goes offstage, and the actor reappears later as a messenger, to announce her death and Oedipus' self-mutilation; Creon has an angry scene with Oedipus, then the same actor reappears as Teiresias for another angry scene. It seems reasonable to suppose that the spectators were aware of the doubling, but paid it no particular heed: at most, they might have been impressed by the versatility of the second and third actors. So far as the tragic dramatist is concerned, the main – and major – effect of doubling is to isolate, in performance, the leading actor, the only actor who does *not* play several roles; and this isolation of the actor clearly mirrors the domination and isolation of the main character which is a feature in Greek tragedies generally.

In comedy, however, conventions are not always taken for granted by author, performer or spectator. They are frequently exaggerated and ridiculed, and the expectation of such ridicule is one of the main pleasures of the genre. Aristophanes ridicules the conventions of masks, costumes, stage machinery, diction, music, dancing and the Chorus; he even parodies the whole convention of an actor giving a performance, and allows his characters to make fun both of themselves (as actors in a comic show) and of the spectators watching that show. It is hard to believe that he would have left un-ridiculed such an obvious and important convention as the doubling of subsidiary roles.

We should also consider the difference between tragic and comic acting. A tragic actor generally assumes his role completely: his own personality is entirely submerged in that of the stage character. When we think of Laurence Olivier, for example, it is probably not as an actor who cleans his teeth and holds political opinions like anyone else, but as the embodiment of Hamlet, Richard III, Archie Rice or Heathcliff. A comic actor, on the other hand, is usually funny in himself, and his own stage personality reappears, virtually unchanged, in play after play. When we think of (say) Zero Mostel or Richard Briers, it is in terms of general comic qualities rather than as the embodiment of particular roles. Margaret Rutherford is basically the same whether she is playing Lady Bracknell or Miss Marple. The further we go towards stereotype comedy, the more this is the case. The great film comedians – Langdon, Keaton, Fields, the Marx Brothers, Tati – play essentially the same part in film after film. Even Chaplin is recognizably himself in *Monsieur Verdoux*, *Limelight* and *A King in New York*, despite his shedding of the Little Tramp role.

If the same thing was true of Athenian comic acting – and given the other similarities between Aristophanic comedy and that of our own era, it is likely that it was – then the effect on the doubling of parts is immediately obvious, and very striking indeed. The spectators were not seeing, in the doubled parts, a succession of completely different characters all of which just happened to be played by one versatile actor (as they were with the doubled parts in *King Oedipus*): they were seeing a known comedian, a Hermon or an Apollodoros, playing a succession of different parts. The comedian's own character was naturally subsumed in that of the people he was portraying (as Fields' is when he is Mr Micawber or The Great McGonigle); but recognizable elements of his own large stage persona remained, whatever the particular mask and costume he happened to be wearing.

This thesis is supported rather than challenged by the use of masks in Greek comic acting. For a comedian of this type, facial expression is only one of many personal characteristics. The faces of many great comedians are mask-like, in that they remain the same in part after part. With Langdon, Ben Turpin, Keaton, Fields, Chaplin, Laurel and Hardy, Groucho Marx or Tati we are aware of their changing expressions (since our drama contains the convention of a mobile face), but they are not comic in their facial expressions only. Each of them has a distinctive set of physical mannerisms, a physical presence which is funny in its own right. Laurel and Hardy in Scottish costume (or Swiss, or in the uniform of the Foreign Legion) are still recognizably Laurel and Hardy. Chaplin in *Limelight* wears a different facial mask from all his earlier films, and yet he is still recognizably Chaplin. I believe that the same thing was generally true in Aristophanes' theatre: each actor was known to the audience in his own comic persona, and that persona was apparent throughout, whatever part he was actually playing.

There is no certainty either about the number of actors in comedy or about the way in which the parts were distributed among them. The whole question is extremely contentious.[92] The most that can be said with certainty is that comedy, like tragedy, employed doubling; that some of Aristophanes' plays can be performed with a minimum of three actors, while others require four; and that extra performers, speaking only a few lines, could be used when necessary. It seems logical to assume that the leading actor played the leading part on stage throughout, and that doubling was generally done by the other actors. The isolation which this produces in the leading character is important to those of the comedies with an allegorical theme, but less so in the plays after *Lysistrata*. In the two fourth-century plays the type and style of acting is very different, and it is likely that all the actors doubled parts.

If the theory that the audience could recognize an individual actor despite his changing roles is reasonable, we should expect to find at least some supporting evidence in the texts. Since, for example, loud parts are not generally written for quiet actors, we should be able to trace some stylistic similarity in parts presumed to have been played by the same actor. We should expect this similarity to be less apparent in the allegorical plays than in the later ones, where the characters are less stereotyped and the technique and individual ability of each actor is called upon to a greater extent.

In the three simplest plays (technically speaking), *Knights, Wasps* and *Peace*, the minor parts are so devoid of character that stylistic analysis is hardly possible. The slaves and *alazones* who appear are stock figures, and if the audience noticed the doubling in these plays at all it can only have been in passing – the doubling makes no significant contribution to the style or meaning of the performance. In *Acharnians, Clouds* and *Birds*, on the other hand, the audience's awareness of the doubling could have played a considerable part in the whole effect. For example, if the same actor played both Euripides and Lamachos in *Acharnians* (both parts in mock-tragic style), then a satirical point would be made by the performance style alone: that Lamachos is a Euripidean character remote from true reality, and Dikaiopolis – for all his borrowing of Euripides' costumes – is not. If a dialect comedian performed as the Megarian and then almost at once as the Theban, the juxtaposition of performances would not only sharpen the audience's appreciation of his skill, but would also help to 'frame' the scenes as performances rather than reality – as, so to speak, cartoon-like demonstrations of the effects of war (a main strand in the argument of the play). In *Clouds*,[93] if the Socrates actor also played Wrong, then a significant satirical point about the integrity of the real Socrates would be made, and made in performance alone. In *Birds* the effect is different, and doubling is used for slapstick rather than for satirical effect. Assuming that the leading actor took no other part but Peisetairos, there are no less than twenty-one speaking parts to be divided among the other actors, as well as several non-speaking roles for extras. Seventeen of these parts occur after the parabasis: that is, in the last hour of the play. Whether these seventeen parts were divided among two or three actors, the effect in performance would still be one of a delirious kaleidoscope of characters – and would be all the funnier if each actor was also recognizable as himself throughout.

Like the two fourth-century plays, *Lysistrata* poses special problems of casting. So far as doubling is concerned, the main interest for the audience would consist in seeing each of the actors (possibly including the leading actor, if he also played the Spartan youth in 1242–1320) playing both male and female roles. Certainly there is very little stylistic affinity between one part and another; perhaps the tight construction of the play and the unusually organic development of its plot would strike an audience more forcibly than whether *X* or *Y* was playing a given part. *Lysistrata* is the first genuine 'company play' in Aristophanes, and the individuality of each actor is less important than what he contributes to the whole. It is also a play whose humour derives from situation rather than from character, and as such would suit straight comic actors better than the individual comedians of the other plays.

From the actors' point of view, *Assemblywomen* and *Wealth* are differently structured from all the other plays. *Assemblywomen* is in two distinct – and indeed, almost entirely self-contained – halves. Four actors are required for the seduction scene, three of them playing grotesque hags (see below). There is not sufficient individuality in the characters of the first half of the play for stylistic links to be made between them and the characters of the second half. Blepyros is the most rounded (and most grotesque) of the early characters: perhaps, therefore, his part was doubled with that of the most grotesque of the hags, the third. *Wealth* divides up between one 'straight' actor, two comedians, and a fourth, 'straight' actor playing small roles. There is some stylistic affinity between the parts of Poverty and the old woman, and between those of the Sycophant, the young man and Hermes. But the links are not strong enough to allow even the most conjectural distribution of parts on stylistic grounds.

In *Frogs* the leading actor played Dionysos throughout, and the second and third actors clearly each played one of the two tragedians. The Xanthias actor cannot have played any of the subsidiary characters in the first half of the play, as Xanthias is onstage all the time. This means that he can, in fact, only have played two parts altogether: Xanthias until 813, and one of the tragedians thereafter. This leaves the third actor the parts of Herakles, Charon, Aiakos and the landlady in the first half of the play, and the part of the second of the two tragedians thereafter.[94] The common denominators of the first four of these parts are (1) that three of them are mythological figures of a notably awesome kind, and (2) that three of the four parts, as written (Herakles, Aiakos and the landlady), are blustering characters in *alazon* style. Now, noise and bluster are characteristics frequently attributed to Aeschylus by the Chorus, who characterize Euripides, on the other hand, as a slippery, wily *poneros* – a similar character to that of Xanthias. This suggests that a good casting of the tragedians would be to give Euripides to the second actor and Aeschylus to the third. What happens now is that the recognizable and recurring physical traits of a particular actor – let us say for the sake of argument that he was large and loud – are put to dramatic use, and constitute an element in the comedy which would be obvious on the stage, but is not so apparent in the written text. First of all the third actor appears in three mythological disguises, Herakles, Aiakos and Charon, and browbeats the Dionysos actor in each of them; he caps this by making his next appearance in 'drag' as a blustering landlady; and finally his physical and stage presence are put to specific dramatic use in his appearance as Aeschylus. The critical point this casting makes about Aeschylus' character is paralleled by giving the part of Euripides to the actor who has played the *poneros* Xanthias: in short, the general argument of the second half of the play is first prefigured and then embodied in the actual staging of the performance.

In *Women at the Festival* only three actors are needed, except for the brief scene with the Prytanis and the Scythian (which requires a fourth actor, speaking only 8 lines, to play the Prytanis, and a silent extra to appear in the Scythian's mask and costume until the part is taken over by the third actor at 1001). If the first actor played Mnesilochos throughout, and the second actor doubled the parts of Euripides and the (extremely Euripidean) first woman, then the third actor is left with Agathon's slave, Agathon, the second woman, Kleisthenes, the third woman and the Scythian.[95] What is immediately apparent in this list is effeminacy: with the exception of the Scythian, all the parts are actual females or men so sympathetic to women that they can dress as women and pass for females. Agathon even sings like a woman, and his song leaves Mnesilochos in a state of considerable sexual excitement (130–133). (Agathon's servant also sings, and may well – like Kephisophon in *Acharnians* – have aped his master's effeminate dress and manner.) It is attractive to surmise that the third actor in this particular play was an accomplished musician, and also adept at female roles. If he was known to the audience, and always recognizable as himself whatever part he played, then his appearance as the tough, brutish and totally masculine Scythian would have produced a marked comic effect. Even funnier than a blusterer playing a blusterer is a limp-wristed effeminate playing a blusterer – and the ironic edge such an interpretation gives the last scene is wholly in keeping with the blurred and ambivalent attitude to sexual role-playing which is such a feature of the play.

Travesty acting

There can be no doubt that Greek audiences fully accepted travesty acting. In extant Greek tragedy eighteen leading and forty-five subsidiary roles, and in Aristophanes two leading and twenty-five subsidiary speaking roles, are female. Some of these parts – especially some of the leads – are dominant, masculine women; but many of them are entirely feminine in character and exhibit no masculine traits whatsoever. They range in age from youthful figures like Deianeira or Ismene to old women like Atossa or Hecuba; there is however a slight preference for women of the mature middle years, such as Jocasta, Phaedra or Medea.

In tragedy the femininity of these women is never questioned: it would destroy the illusion completely if they were thought of for one moment as male. In performance the convention must have been simple: if the character was dressed as a woman and identified by the other characters as a woman, then that was all that was required for the audience to ignore the actual masculinity of the actor. This is similar to the convention in Shakespeare's plays (both in the professional productions of his own day and in modern productions in boys' schools); as in the case of Shakespeare, some advantage would be gained if the actor happened to look or sound more female than male, but this would be of little importance to the overall effect of the part in performance. Indeed, doubling in the Greek theatre often involved the same actor in playing male and female parts in the same play, and it is unlikely that he made any great physical distinction between the performances. Probably female parts were played with a slightly altered tone of voice, and no more: the vocal expertise of Greek actors was one of their chief attributes,[96] and several actors were renowned for their skill at playing women – which implies that a particular skill, almost certainly vocal, was in fact required.

In comedy the range of female parts is considerably wider, and offers greater scope for speculation about the nature of the performing conventions. At one end of the scale, it seems likely that real girls were used in many of the plays in non-speaking parts. They may have appeared naked, and generally represented abstract, allegorical figures such as Reconciliation or Harvest. It cost only nine obols (that is, about one thousandth of the total production cost) to hire a girl for the day. Some scholars[97] object that in a March/April festival it was too cold to appear naked, but it is doubtful whether slave-girls at nine obols a time would be allowed to notice the fact. Such girls might appear as Dikaiopolis' dancing-girls (*Acharnians* 1198ff.), the Spondai (*Knights* 1389ff.), the flute-girl (*Wasps* 1326ff.), Holiday and perhaps Harvest (*Peace* 520ff.), Reconciliation (*Lysistrata* 1114ff.), the Scythian's girl (*Women at the Festival* 1175ff.) and the Muse of Euripides (*Frogs* 1306ff.). Next after them come speaking characters who are clearly thought of as female throughout: there is for example no suggestion of homosexual attack against them, as there is with characters whose femininity is in some doubt. The plays of 411 (*Women at the Festival* and *Lysistrata*) are particularly rich in these parts, and this suggests that Aristophanes had actors at his disposal that year who were adept at the skills required – and, perhaps, therefore, that skills of a particular sort *were* required. This second group includes the large majority of Aristophanes' female parts, ranging from the tiny role of Dikaiopolis' daughter (*Acharnians* 245–279) to leading parts like Lysistrata or Praxagora. A third group consists of characters whose femininity is in some doubt (see below). These parts appear only in the late plays, and consist of the three old women in *Assemblywomen*, and Poverty and the old woman in *Wealth*.

The vast majority of Aristophanes' female roles are in the same acting category as those in tragedy. That is, there is never any doubt but that the character is a woman. Femininity is established at first entrance, and the convention is accepted unquestioningly by all the other characters. This acceptance is crucial to most of these parts: it would be fatal for the whole masquerade in *Assemblywomen*, for example, if we were encouraged to doubt Praxagora's femininity; the unmasking of Mnesilochos is funny only if his acting of femininity has been less effective than that of the actors playing the first and second 'real' women; the Myrrhine/Kinesias scene in *Lysistrata* would not work unless Myrrhine is thought to be not only feminine but attractive as well.

The convention of travesty acting is used at three different levels in *Women at the Festival*, depending on the humorous effect required. At the primary level the convention is the same as in earlier plays: characters who appear to be women *are* women. This applies to the female herald, the first and second women and the priestess. At a second level come characters who are assuming the roles of women, but who must be shown to the audience as men in disguise. Agathon and Kleisthenes come into this category. They presumably follow the established conventions of travesty acting (a beardless mask, a female costume without the phallus, a light tone of voice) so exactly that without help from other characters we would undoubtedly accept them as entirely feminine. Agathon's first appearance, however, is prefaced and followed by robust remarks from Mnesilochos (96–100, 130–145), which tell us exactly what to think of the imposture being played and the reasons for it. The case of Kleisthenes is even more interesting. He is seen approaching by the Chorus, who mistake him for a woman (571–573). It is not until his own second line of dialogue (575, 'I'm your (male) friend: you can see by my chin') that we learn that he is a man, and some minutes pass until we hear his name (634).[98] The fact that he is thought a woman until he speaks suggests also that there was some convention of movement to indicate femininity. At a third level, the conventions are not followed simply: they are guyed and exaggerated. Mnesilochos himself does this in the rescue scenes. But we must surely imagine that his performance as a woman in the Thesmophoria scene was equally exaggerated, and that its success (he goes undetected from 279 until Kleisthenes' arrival in 574) is due not so much to his own accurate following of the conventions as to the obtuseness of the other characters onstage – an irony likely to be very funny to the watching audience.

This Mnesilochos performance, where the audience are informed of the coming imposture before it happens, might lead us to ask if the travesty conventions could be guyed to some extent *without* prior warning: if, in fact, exaggeration of the conventions was enough to evoke humour in its own right. A modern female impersonator or pantomime dame often has inflated breasts, extra-long eyelashes, a wiggle to his walk and a manner of performance which offers a kind of cartoon femininity – of which there need be no indication at all in the written script. This is surely the kind of performance given by Mnesilochos; and it seems reasonable to assume it possible in the two late plays as well. Certainly it would increase the humour of the seduction scene in *Assemblywomen* (877–1111). Here the part of the young girl is clearly to be played 'straight', and the conventions are followed throughout. But what of the old women? Was their increasing repulsiveness achieved entirely within the conventions – or were the conventions exaggerated and parodied to produce the effect? If this happens – if the old women are as transparently male as Mnesilochos – the whole tone of this seduction scene changes. If the old women are 'real' women, then they are indeed repellent – as many commentators have remarked – and the humour is savage and distasteful (in a way wholly unlike the rest of Aristophanes, whose most bilious satire otherwise preserves, in every case, an element of either fantasy or surrealism which is lacking here). But if they are clearly male, similar to modern pantomime dames, then the joke moves from the text of the play into its performance, and the grotesquerie is hilarious rather than pathetic, with the young man's distaste and horror arousing mirth rather than agreement.

Questions of a similar kind arise in connection with the parts of Poverty and the old woman in *Wealth*. Everything about Poverty is exaggerated: we are told, for example, exactly what to think of her vocal ranting in the remarks made by Chremylos and Blepsidemos in 422–437. If the exaggerated grandeur of her diction was matched by an exaggeration of the conventions of travesty, the comedy of the part would be greatly enhanced, and the actor could deepen his interpretation from the shallow *alazon* stereotype he is otherwise offered. In the case of the old woman the question is even more crucial to the actor's interpretation of the part. If she is female she is a figure to be pitied as much as mocked; but if she is clearly male, a pantomime-dame figure, the tone of the mockery becomes ironical instead of bitter, and the character's complaints and self-conceit hilarious rather than pathetic. If she is a 'real' old woman, then this is undoubtedly the cruellest scene in Aristophanes. The Megarian scene in *Acharnians*, ostensibly as heartless (the daughters are sold, and the gleeful

Megarian makes similar plans for his wife and mother) is not cruel because it happens not in the 'real' world but in the fantasy world of Dikaiopolis, where causality – and therefore suffering – does not exist. The Sycophant scene in *Wealth* is not cruel for the same reason: the character is a fantasy figure, exaggerated and changed into a cartoon figure whose downfall is inevitable but hardly pathetic. But the old woman (so far as the words alone tell us) is not a cartoon figure: the text is remarkable for its realism. This means that unless a cartoon-like dimension is added in performance the scene is too close to real life to be properly funny, and is a remarkable lapse of taste and technique on Aristophanes' part. It therefore seems possible, at least, that the stage conventions of travesty were guyed in order to add the necessary dimension of unreality, a dimension which affects not merely this character in this scene, but the comic style and meaning of the whole play.

The problem for modern commentators is that our evidence is limited to the text alone, and the text gives no hint of any such guying of the conventions of travesty. But Aristophanes' text does show us that scenes as distasteful as this are far from the norm, and that cruel satire is normally softened by a clearly established dimension of unreality. It used to be held that *Wealth* generally, and this scene in particular, reveal a slowing-down of Aristophanes' comic invention, perhaps even second-rate work composed after a debilitating stroke. But there is no textual evidence for this either, and it is more attractive to suggest that the ageing comedian fell back on stage technique when his verbal and plotting abilities began to slow down, and that this and other scenes in *Wealth* rely on theatrical rather than scripted pyrotechnics to make their proper effect.

11

Conclusion: the Art of Aristophanes

The excellence of Aristophanes

Aristophanes did not invent written stage comedy: he was born two generations too late for that. But he is the first comic author whose works survive, and one of the supreme masters of the genre. Whether we regard them as inexhaustible mines of humour, worked over the centuries by most of the great writers and performers of Western comedy, or simply as masterpieces in their own right, his plays stand in the same relationship to comedy as Homer's poems do to epic, Aeschylus' plays to tragedy or Herodotus' investigations to history.

Over the years, Aristophanes' greatness has never been denied. But few attempts have been made to describe it, to isolate its components in a way familiar to students of other literary genres. Perhaps this is due to a continuing scholarly reluctance to discuss comedy in depth at all: it still tends to be regarded as an insubstantial and essentially secondary form of literature. Others again may feel that laughter is too precious a butterfly to break on the wheel of analysis. Whatever the reason, judgments about Aristophanes are rare, and his excellence is usually taken as read, in a kind of unspoken agreement between one enthusiast and the next.

There are three features of Aristophanes' style which I believe place him among the highest masters of comic drama. These are *comic metaphor*, *language* and *stage sense*. After two and a half thousand years and ten thousand refinements in the comic art, they are still fresh and clear; they are essential ingredients – perhaps *the* essential ingredients – of his greatness; they are easily perceived in the surviving texts.

Comic metaphor

Aristophanes well understood that the principal need, in comedy, is for clarity of theme. However rich and dense the detail of his plays – and few other playwrights offer cakes so stuffed with plums – the themes, the controlling images, the fantasy and even the jokes themselves have a broad simplicity, a largeness of vision that in the theatre carries all else before it. Dikaiopolis' private treaty, Strepsiades' attempts to learn, the strike in *Lysistrata* and the

157

rescue attempts in *Women at the Festival* (to take four plays at random) – these are universally comprehensible ideas, whose grandeur and elegance evokes an immediate response. There is nothing hermetic here.

There is nothing miraculous or unique, either: large gestures are the common stock of all great comic playwrights. If there is a miracle, it lies in the precision of Aristophanes' thought. Broad and clear each theme may be; but it also hits a precise moral and didactic target. The brilliance of these controlling themes, their pungent aptness, is perhaps the most striking feature of Aristophanes' work. He instructs and entertains in a single moment, irresistibly.

The art is one of metaphor. Aristophanes looks at one human activity (for example, politics enslaving the state), and sees another (for example, slaves bullying a foolish old master). He then treats them as one and the same. The result is a kind of poetry of situation – and like the poetry of words, it is at once simple to understand and rich in evocations and overtones. Like Aeschylus, Aristophanes rarely philosophizes, rarely explains: philosophy and explanation vibrate in the actions and words themselves. In both artists, the polished intellectuality and elegant pattern-making of Sophocles or Euripides are replaced by rawness, illogicality, feeling itself. Our interest focuses not so much on the forces at work on man as on man himself: protean, creative, unpredictable.

None of this would work if the metaphors were flabby, if the linkage of ideas seemed adventitious or unconvincing. Aristophanes is not concerned with unravelling complex situations (as are, for example, Sheridan, Wilde or Feydeau): his interest is in the precise moments of vision, the points of balance themselves. Watching each of his plays, we first share with the hero his blinding instant of vision, then (with him) settle back to enjoy its consequences.

In plays where the hero's vision, the informing metaphor, is pin-sharp, the crucial factor is fantasy. With Trygaios' decision to fly to heaven and argue with Zeus, or Peisetairos' plan to build Cloudcuckooland, there is no arguing. Their schemes need no justifying, because they are self-evidently *right* – and what makes them so is the liberation from everyday restraint which fantasy gives them.[99] In *Acharnians, Peace, Birds, Women at the Festival* and *Frogs* the controlling metaphor is one of action: the hero's exuberant deed and its consequences make the play. In *Knights, Clouds, Wasps* and *Lysistrata* the deeds are less fantastic, and exuberance lies instead in character and consequence. The last two plays, *Assemblywomen* and *Wealth*, seem to me to lack exuberance of either action or character. The deeds are unreal, but are made to seem surprisingly ordinary in their execution; the characters (save for those in the second half of *Assemblywomen*, where the full vigour of Aristophanes' earlier style is once more present) often lack that element of self-delighted joy which so engages us in the earlier plays. In fact the interest in *Assemblywomen* and *Wealth* is chiefly in stagecraft, excellence of technique – and it can be argued that this quality is not always enough to hold a reader's interest, though both plays are generally highly successful in performance.

Once the action of the play has been articulated by a single large, controlling metaphor, it is fuelled and propelled by a series of smaller metaphors, which reinforce and develop the same lateral view of the moral situation at the heart of the plot. It is fitting, for example, that Dikaiopolis' private peace in *Acharnians* should be embodied in a skin of wine: the metaphor is a symbol not only of the unconstrained enjoyment peace brings with it, but also of the god who presides over that enjoyment, Dionysos himself (to whom Dikaiopolis leads a procession of thanksgiving in 237ff., and in whose honour, at the Feast of Cups, Dikaiopolis downs his goblet first, as the climactic action of the play). Socrates' muddled philosophy in *Clouds* is symbolized by his worship of the spirit *Dinos* ('rotation') – and this is embodied in a visual metaphor, the placing of a large pot (also called *dinos*) outside his door in the place usually reserved for the statue of the guardian god of a household: in this Blaboratory, confusion rules. In the same way, the cushions and food with which Demos ('the people') is bribed in *Knights*, the domestic issues tried in Philokleon's court and the rescue in *Peace* of a statue and two girls by physical effort in a theatre instead of Peace, Harvest and Holiday by political effort in real life, are metaphors for real behaviour outside the theatre, and reflect the moral aptness of the central symbol of each play. In *Assemblywomen* Aristophanes goes further: the whole seduction scene is itself a metaphor for the kind of freedom and reasonableness proposed by Praxagora – a devastating point, since, despite all the drunken bustle, chaos and disintegration are the results of this strange and mighty deed instead of the usual delirious success.

The best and most characteristic propelling metaphor of this kind occurs in the Reconciliation scene in *Lysistrata* (1112ff.). Here the antinomy between frustrated war and liberated peace is symbolized by using as a map on which to plot truce terms not a piece of paper or leather, but the contours of a desirable girl, Reconciliation herself. When the Athenian and Spartan lust for the girl, they are lusting for reconciliation: as always the point is simple, but the moral overtones (and their relation to the controlling theme of the play) are rich and resonant. That the scene also offers unlimited opportunities for bawdy jokes and puns, lascivious gesture and seductive double entendre is a bonus exploited to the full. The fusion in this scene of theme, idea and stage action shows Aristophanes' genius at its most brilliant. Here is the second half of the scene, building to its climax (1147–1187):

ATHENIAN: Lysistrata, they shouldn't be doing that.
SPARTAN: No, we shouldn't. But it's such a sweet behind.
LYSISTRATA: D'you think I'm letting the men of Athens off?
Don't you remember how the Spartans came along
In the old days, when you were slaves

Of Hippias the tyrant and all that crew?
They stood by your side in the battle-line,
Slaughtered the enemy (Hippias' crowd and those
Thessalians) and set you free, dressed you
In free men's clothes. Have you forgotten that?

SPARTAN: What a woman! The best I ever saw.

ATHENIAN: What a cunt! The nicest I ever saw.

LYSISTRATA: Each side's helped the other, many times.
So give up this pigheaded war. Make peace!
Go on, make a treaty. What's stopping you?

SPARTAN: We would, if someone gave us back
That promontory.

LYSISTRATA: What promontory?

SPARTAN: Pylos. Er . . . there.
We've been starved of that for long enough.

ATHENIAN: You're not getting your hands on that!

LYSISTRATA: Oh, let it go.

ATHENIAN: But how do *we* manoeuvre then?

LYSISTRATA: Ask for another stretch of land instead.

ATHENIAN: Right. We demand in exchange for that
This flat plain here, this gulf,
This round entrance here, these legs –

SPARTAN: You're crazy! You can't have all of that.

LYSISTRATA: Oh, let it go. Don't fight over a pair of legs.

ATHENIAN: I want to strip off and plough this territory.

SPARTAN: I've got some fertilizing to do as well.

LYSISTRATA: Make a proper treaty, and then it's yours.
If you're decided, call a delegate conference,
Consult your allies.

ATHENIAN: Consult our allies?
We can't hold out that long. In any case,
The allies will back us to the hilt.

SPARTAN: Ours too.

ATHENIAN: Every man of them wants union, now.

LYSISTRATA: All right. Go and solemnify yourselves;
Then we women, all over the city,
Will regale you with everything we have
In our treasure-chests. Go and make your oath;
Swear to keep faith; then each of you
Can take his wife and go back home.

ATHENIAN: Let's go, quick as we can.

SPARTAN: Any way you like.

ATHENIAN: This way, then. Hurry!

Language

The most remarkable thing about Aristophanes' language is how unremarkable most of it is. The plays are studded with puns, lyrics, parody and neologisms. But the basic flow of language is extremely simple and unobtrusive. Its function is to propel the play along, to support a baroque edifice of ideas, actions and jokes. In the plays of Aeschylus (as in those of Shakespeare) poetic language has a major role of its own to play – sometimes, indeed, it entirely dominates the effect of a scene or materially alters our view of an action or a character.[100] In Sophocles (as in Racine) language also dominates, though in a different way. Here there is conscious limpidity of style, a kind of literary elegance and homogeneity of utterance which throws emphasis less on character than on idea and motive, the philosophical rationale behind the drama. But in Aristophanes (as in Euripides or Chekhov) the language is principally a vehicle for expressing other things. When it does stand out (for example in a punning or lyrical sequence) our interest and admiration usually remain for the characters who can say such things, rather than for the words they say them in.

An excellent – and characteristic – example of plain language supporting character and humour is the opening dialogue of *Knights*. Here, with remarkable economy, Aristophanes establishes not only the characters of the two slaves who are speaking, but also the didactic and humorous character of the play we are about to see. The passage is full of jokes, slapstick and arresting ideas; but its fundamental language remains simple and functional. Here are the opening lines of the scene (1–36), from the moment when the slaves tumble out of the stage house as if hurled out on their ears:

DEMOSTHENES: Owwwww! Ohhhhhh! Ouuuuuuuuuuuch!
Damn! Damn! Damn that new slave, that Paphlagon.
Him and his tricks. Damn him, damn him to hell.
Ever since he arrived, he's brought nothing
But trouble and beatings for all the rest of us.
NIKIAS: Owww! That Paphlagon. Ohh, that lying swine.
DEMOSTHENES: There, there. Where does it hurt?
NIKIAS: Everywhere. Same as you.
DEMOSTHENES: There's only one thing for it. A little duet.
You know the one I mean. Are you ready?
BOTH (*singing mournfully*): Moo moo moo moo moo mooh.
DEMOSTHENES: Ah, that's no good. There must be some other way.
NIKIAS: Well?
DEMOSTHENES: Well, what?
NIKIAS: Go on. I'm listening.
DEMOSTHENES: No no. After you.
NIKIAS: It was your idea.
DEMOSTHENES: I've *no* idea.
NIKIAS: 'Speak now, or forever hold your peace.'
DEMOSTHENES: Eh?
NIKIAS: 'To be or not to be, that is the question.'
DEMOSTHENES: No it bloody isn't. What good will *that* do?
Oh, I don't know. Can you spare me the next dance?
NIKIAS (*breaking free of the dance*): No no no.
Just a minute. Say 'purr'.

DEMOSTHENES: All right. 'Purr'.
NIKIAS: Good. Now 'wheel-scar'.
DEMOSTHENES: Eh?
NIKIAS: 'Wheel-scar'.
DEMOSTHENES: 'Wheel-scar'.
NIKIAS: Very good. Now try them both together,
One after the other, faster and faster,
As though you were jerking off.
DEMOSTHENES: Purr. Wheel-scar. Purr. Wheel-scar. Purr.
Wheel-scar-purr. Wheelscarpurr . . . wheelscarpurr . . .
WE'LL SCARPER!
NIKIAS: Good idea?
DEMOSTHENES: Oh yes. Except for the wine.
NIKIAS: What wine?
DEMOSTHENES: My whine, when they catch us and beat us up.
NIKIAS: There's only one thing for it, then. Your knees.
DEMOSTHENES: Pardon?
NIKIAS: Get down on your knees, and pray.
DEMOSTHENES: You don't mean you still believe in the gods?
NIKIAS: Of course.
DEMOSTHENES: And how d'you know the gods exist?
NIKIAS: Simple: just look at the way they're treating me.
DEMOSTHENES: Oh, very clever. There must be some other way.
I know. Shall I put it to the audience?

Subtlety of rhythm, a major part of the effect of Aristophanes' language, can be blurred to us today, especially in translation. Greek audiences were more sensitive to rhythmic nuance than we are in English, where rhythms other than 'free verse' tend to sound formal or artificial in the theatre. The rhythms of Greek verse depend firstly on stress and tone, and secondly on complex arrangements of short and long syllables. Spoken stress and syllable stress are very often at variance (as in the English line 'To be or not to be; that is the question', where the spoken stress is by no means on every alternate syllable): part of the poet's skill is in manipulating the tiny moments of clash, tension and resolution, in patterns which satisfy the ear. In addition, the various metres had conventional and musical associations for the Greeks that they do not for us: elegiac, threnodic, martial, and so on. Once again this allowed a poet tremendous subtlety of allusion – the meaning of a line or scene could be changed by the use of rhythm in ways we can now only dimly perceive. (The possibilities of ironical inflection through rhythm, for example, are likely to have been as fully exploited by Aristophanes as the other means of irony we can still perceive today.)

Perceptible still, and a notable feature of Aristophanes' art, is his use and blending of three kinds of metre above all. They are *iambics* (used for the fastest moving, most everyday dialogue, about half of each play), *anapaests* (used for formal argument scenes like the *agon*, and also a main feature of the parabasis) and *lyrics* (used mainly for poetic interludes, particularly from the Chorus). The juxtaposition of these three metres and the performing styles they suggest (ordinary speech, formal rhetoric and lyrical song) is a vital and dynamic element in the structure of the plays. Its articulating effect can be seen at its best in the Right/Wrong scene in *Clouds* (889–1104), in Praxagora's exposition of the benefits of her new state in *Assemblywomen* (583–710) and, finest of all, in the poetic contest in *Frogs* (830–1410).

Because the main 'poetical' element lies elsewhere (in situation, plot metaphor and comic detail), there is surprisingly little *verbal* poetry in most of the plays. A large number of 'literary' passages (that is, passages in heightened language) are little more than functional doggerel, whose purpose is to punctuate the action and move it along, and to which a kind of surface poeticism is added by the use of neologisms or unexpectedly graphic words. Characteristic examples are the passage about the audience in *Frogs* 1099–1118 (quoted on p. 88), or this short chorus from *Clouds* (700–705):

> Ponder, consider, roll yourself up in a ball
> And whirl about, any way you can. And if you fall
> Into perplexity, jump quickly off on another line
> Of thought. Don't let sleep,
> Honey of the soul, take its place on your eyes.

The charm of passages like that lies in their wit and freshness; but (unlike true poetry) they offer little else. Their meaning *is* their form; their content *is* their style. The same is often true of more closely integrated sections, where the verse takes off into a sudden brief whirl of words, into fantastic images which attract partly for their own sake, and partly because of their unexpected aptness – that is, they are not intrinsic to the character or situation, but once heard seem delightfully apposite. Their function is decorative, not constructive (as the images in true 'poetry' tend to be). Examples abound: 'I stuck my bum through the fence, opened up and yelled . . .' (*Knights* 640ff.), 'My long-haired son rides, drives chariots, dream-buys-and-sells horses' (*Clouds* 14ff.), 'Where can I find a ten-thousand-wine-jar phrase to welcome you?' (*Peace* 521f.), 'A city soft as a blanket to curl up in' (*Birds* 121f.), or the untranslatable dish at the climax of *Assemblywomen* (1169ff.), two dozen ingredients cooked together into a single monstrous, orgasmic word:

> *lopado-temacho-selacho-galeo-*
> *kranio-leipsano-drimypo-trimmato-*
> *silphio-tyro-melito-katakechymeno-*
> *kichl-epikossypho-phatto-perister-*
> *alektryon-opte-kephallio-kinklo-*
> *peleio-lagohio-siraio-baphe-tragano-pterygohn.*[101]

This kind of fast, witty verse gives way to real poetry in two plays above all, *Peace* and *Birds*. In them, the literary language is not an addition, a decoration:

it is used to articulate the major message of the play. There is a yearning in this poetry; the words, the metaphors reach out and express emotion and atmosphere conveyable in no other form. The ache for peace, and the deep satisfaction of everyday pursuits, are expressed in many of the lyrics of *Peace*, and give the action of the play an ambience all its own; in the same way, the inconsequential grace and elegance of bird life are related in the lyrics of *Birds* to one of man's most fundamental pleasures, perception of the harmony of all created things. The same feeling, the same yearning, appears in the hymns and religious passages of some of the other plays (notably the Initiates' hymns in *Frogs* 316–459). Perhaps Aristophanes is using poetry to express the inexpressible; certainly these passages stand out from the plays, colouring and influencing the action around them. It is tempting to quote as an example the much-anthologized opening of the *Birds* parabasis ('Come, creatures of shadow, like children of leaves', 685ff.); but I choose instead a less well-known passage, part of the chorus of welcome to the rescued goddess of plenty in *Peace* (582–597):

> Welcome, welcome! How we smile, dearest,
> Now you are here. I was gnawed with desire for you,
> Longing for blessings to glow through the countryside.
> You are our greatest gift;
> We longed for you, we who work the land.
> All that was sweet, delightful, free,
> Came to us from you. To farmers
> You were porridge and salvation in one.
> Now our vines, our young fig-shoots,
> All growing things, will take you and laugh with you.

Stage sense

As we read or see Aristophanes' plays today, the overwhelming impression is one of rightness. Language, stage action, controlling themes and metaphors all combine to make a single, unified entertainment. Many stage comedies, including some of the finest (*The Alchemist, The School for Scandal, She Stoops to Conquer, The Government Inspector*), tend to sprawl, to tug in several directions at once. In Aristophanes the dramatic 'line' of each play is clear and straight; it binds a dozen diverse elements into a coherent whole. Even characters or scenes which at first seem to be there solely for their own sake (such as Euripides in *Acharnians* or the Myrrhine/Kinesias scene in *Lysistrata*) in fact fit into and help to shape dramatic unity.

Good examples are the last two surviving plays. At first sight, *Assemblywomen* might seem to be broken-backed and *Wealth* pallid and dramatically half-hearted. Not so; in these much-criticized plays Aristophanes' sense of theatre is as sure as ever. If we ponder the plot of *Assemblywomen*, we might say that after the long account of how Praxagora's new state is to work, what is needed is a demonstration of its effects on the individual – and that is exactly what the seduction scene provides. On the other hand, after the theorizing and political philosophy of the first two-thirds of the play, we want to end with slapstick and unintellectual buffoonery – and that again is exactly what the final scene provides. So the critic explains or justifies. But in performance the play's single 'line' is perfectly apparent, and needs no justification. Its form is unusual (a diptych), but no less satisfying for that. In the same way, the reader of *Wealth* may feel that there are too many similar characters, and in particular that the main generators of humour, Chremylos and Karion, are not sharply enough characterized or differentiated from one another. In the theatre, where we can *see* the difference, this 'problem' disappears. The plot moves like a Swiss weather-house: there are two kinds of action, each with its own protagonist, and they appear in alternation. But a single line of logic binds them together; the play is articulated not for reading but for performance, and its line is a performing line. Again there is a parallel in fine art: this time a series of panels illustrating different aspects of a single progressing theme.

At the beginning of his career, Aristophanes' dramatic technique was by no means as skilled as this. His early plays derive unity not from 'company' articulation, from a precise sense of how a scene will 'play' in the theatre; instead we are dazzled with bravura themes and bravura central roles. *Acharnians*, *Knights*, *Clouds* and *Wasps* offer the actors parts of barnstorming virtuosity, and in the theatre that virtuosity carries all before it. The main character is a figure of huge gusto, with hundreds of lines to speak. Even though his colleagues often have juicy roles of their own, the success of the play rests mainly on the performance of the leading actor. And the acting technique required is one of surface brilliance rather than the subtler style needed for the later plays. Only in *Peace* and *Birds*, ostensibly in the same style, is performing brilliance balanced and deepened by theme and atmosphere: in the other early plays, however important the themes, these qualities take second place in performance to theatrical pyrotechnics. This is a characteristic of the work of many dramatists at the start of their careers: they are often interested mainly in 'theatre', in performers in the grand manner, in the art of acting itself. The same kind of bravura parts, requiring the same gusto of performing style, are found in Shakespeare's early plays, notably *The Taming of the Shrew*, *Romeo and Juliet* and *Richard II*.

In his 'middle' plays, Aristophanes demands a less febrile style of performance. Starting with *Lysistrata*, the plays show a perfect integration of theme and style, of company acting and individual performance. There is plenty of bravura still (the parts of Mnesilochos and Dionysos alone show that), but it is now governed by the line of the whole performance, instead of governing it. Kinesias in *Lysistrata*, Agathon and the Scythian in *Women at the Festival* and Xanthias in *Frogs* yield nothing in gusto to such earlier characters as Lamachos and

Pseudartabas in *Acharnians*, the slaves in *Knights* or Hermes and War in *Peace*; but although what they say (and the way the actors say it) is in the same mode as the earlier plays, the effect is completely different because of the binding unity present in the plays. The same thing is true in Shakespeare: 'middle-period' plays like *The Merchant of Venice, Henry IV, Henry V, Julius Caesar* or *Twelfth Night* are full of bravura roles in the older style, but these roles are bound in with the unified themes of the plays, and with a 'company performance' articulation of those themes, in a way not present in the early work.

What is remarkable about all this is not that Aristophanes' work shows development, but that at each stage his technique precisely suits his themes and comic style. The huge, clamorous themes of *Acharnians* and *Knights* and the aggressive anger that fuels *Clouds* and *Wasps* demand breadth and arrogance of performance; the wider vision (often of the same themes) in the 'middle' plays is more suited to a relaxed, ironical style; in the last two plays, where the themes are perhaps a little tired, rock-solid technique is put to work, and works. In all these 'periods', the art is one of balance. The components of each play, lyric, slapstick, irony, satire, music and dance, are precisely placed together to make a seamless and congruent whole. Intellectual rationale, the 'vision' for which Aristophanes is famous, is matched by a theatrical vision, a craftsman's awareness of his medium, an ability to push actors and staging to dizzy heights where meaning and form become a single, dazzling object of delight.

Notes to the Text

Full details of books referred to in the notes by their initials will be found in the bibliography on pp. 177–178

1 This intrusion of seriousness into farce is often held, for example, to be a major blemish of Chaplin's full-length films. *The Great Dictator*, the nearest thing to an Aristophanic comedy Chaplin made, shows this weakness in many places: the serious themes and the farce get in each other's way, instead of blending seamlessly as they do in Aristophanes.

2 A convenient source for the tradition of literary comedy between Terence and our own day is the summary in G. E. Duckworth, *The Nature of Roman Comedy* (Princeton 1952), Chapter 15. A more general view is included in G. A. Highet, *The Classical Tradition* (Oxford 1949), and a short account for students appears in my *Roman Comedy* (London 1976).

3 In fact we know that vocal expertise was one of the main qualifications required of a Greek actor. See Pickard-Cambridge, *DFA*, pp. 167ff.

4 See A. B. Gascoigne, *World Theatre* (London 1968), Chapter 1, for examples of such performances in cultures other than that of Greece. The Greek tradition is dealt with in some detail in Pickard-Cambridge, *DTC*, in the opening chapter of G. Norwood, *Greek Comedy* (London 1931), and, most satisfactorily, in Lever, *AGC*, Chapters 1 and 2.

5 Further on this, see the illustrations in Gascoigne, *World Theatre*, pp. 46, 102, 104, 111 and 112. A. Nicoll, *Masks, Mimes and Miracles* (London 1931), is the standard work on the subject.

6 Solomos, *LA*, p. 7.

7 The best accounts are in Lever, *AGC*, Chapter 4, and Ehrenberg, *PA*, Chapters 10–13.

8 If these plays show the sort of experiment that might win favour, the later plays of Euripides, with their ambivalent attitude towards the gods, show experiments that survived the selection process and the actors (the latter perhaps because of the superb parts Euripides wrote for them), but which did not always find favour in the theatre itself.

9 On this collaboration, see the interesting comments in Solomos, *LA*, Chapter 6.

10 The view that the play was incomplete at this stage is supported by the story of Eupolis' and Aristophanes' collaboration in the early stages of *Knights*. When, if not at this stage, did their collaboration take place, and when, if not now, to allow Aristophanes time to complete the play as we have it, did it break up? See *Clouds* 553f., and Solomos, *LA*, Chapter 6.

11 R. Meiggs and D. Lewis (eds), *A Selection of Greek Historical Inscriptions*

(Oxford 1969), no. 79A, lines 34–49, pp. 241–242, 247.

12 In Demosthenes' *De Corona* in particular. See Pickard-Cambridge, *DFA*, pp. 133ff.

13 See Lever, *AGC*, p. 112; C. Bailey, 'Who Played Dicaeopolis?', in *Greek Poetry and Life: Essays Presented to Gilbert Murray* (Oxford 1936), pp. 231ff.

14 See Pickard-Cambridge, *DFA*, pp. 263–265.

15 Aelian, *Various Histories* ii, 13.

16 The standard work is Pickard-Cambridge, *TDA*; Chapters 1–3 present the evidence in comprehensive detail. A simpler and slightly clearer account appears in Webster's invaluable *GTP*, pp. 1–20. C. W. Dearden, *The Stage of Aristophanes* (London 1976), offers one interpretation of the evidence; it will be seen that in many places I tend to prefer another.

17 Based on that on p. 16 of F. H. Sandbach's excellent short introduction, *The Comic Theatre of Greece and Rome* (London 1977).

18 Over the centuries, more controversy has attached to the *skene* than to any other part of the Greek theatre. The problem is that no *skenai* of the fifth century survive, and all ancient writings on theatre refer to buildings of the following century, or later, and thus correspond with the extant remains, which are generally of the same period. By that time the word *skene* had come to mean a stone platform on top of which the actors performed. In the Theatre of Dionysos it was 66 feet long, 9 feet wide and 13 feet high. There was a rigid division between it and the area used by the Chorus (the reduced dancing-circle and the inner ends of the walkways, an area at this time called the *thymele*). It used to be held that this kind of staging was also used in the fifth century; but the consensus of modern scholarship is that fifth-century practice was entirely different, and that the theatre buildings were very much simpler.

19 *Skenai* are mentioned, for example, in *Peace* 731. Here they are probably huts at the outer ends of the walkways, used by the Chorus as dressing-rooms.

20 I see no need for the higher raised stage suggested by some scholars. To have a dais before the central entrance, with two or three steps leading up to it, is quite sufficient – this is used in modern productions in the theatres of Epidaurus and Delphi, and works perfectly well, allowing total visibility from all parts of the house. In fact a high raised stage, cutting the actors off from the Chorus, would hamper the production of very many plays. Three of Sophocles' plays (*Ajax, Philoctetes* and *Oedipus at Colonus*) and nine of Euripides' (*Hecuba, Madness of Herakles, Hippolytus, Helen, Ion, Iphigeneia in Tauris, Phoinissai, Rhesus* and *The Suppliants*) require actors and Chorus to mingle freely in a way impossible with a raised stage. In Aristophanes, the battle between Dikaiopolis and the Chorus (*Acharnians* 280ff.), the freeing of Philokleon (*Wasps* 316ff.), the rescue of Peace (*Peace* 459ff.), the attack by the birds (*Birds* 337ff.), the whole effect of the speeches and unmasking scene in *Women at the Festival* (295ff.), Dionysos' encounter with the frogs (*Frogs* 209ff.) and Karion's Homeric dance with the Chorus of *Wealth* (295ff.) all depend for their effect on close interaction between actors and Chorus. Other passages in the plays (for example, Euelpides' attempt to unmask the nightingale in *Birds* 671ff. or Dionysos' appeal for help to his own priest in *Frogs* 297) suggest that actors and Chorus not only performed on the same level, but used each other's area of performance – usually with the actors entering the dancing-circle, but sometimes with the Chorus pressing forward to the stage house.

References to 'climbing' or 'going up' are explainable by the fact that the walkways sloped upwards from their entrances to the level of the dancing-circle.

21 Adapted and considerably modified from Dearden, *The Stage of Aristophanes*, p. 35.

22 Carl Ruck, 'Euripides' Mother: Vegetables and the Phallos in Aristophanes', in *Arion*, n.s., 2/1 (1975), pp. 13–58, says that the word *anabaden* ('raised up') is a synonym for 'erect' (pp. 20ff.). He refers also to the Agathon passage as one of complex sexual symbolism. Certainly this explanation is as attractive as the raised-stage explanation of the nineteenth century.

23 The same is true of *Ajax* 346ff. In *The Madness of Herakles* 1029ff., however (a similar scene of mass slaughter), the references are again to the 'folding back' of doors.

24 This is the solution suggested by K. J. Dover in his edition of the play (*The Clouds*, Oxford 1968, p. 119). I would make Socrates' door the central entrance to the *skene*, and Strepsiades' door a temporary structure to left or right, and I would imagine a *dinos* of the same size as Strepsiades' Herm; but in all other respects I agree with Dover's solution. The refutation in Dearden, *The Stage of Aristophanes*, p. 67, not only presupposes the existence of a raised stage, but seems to show remarkably little stage sense, whether for the Theatre of Dionysos or anywhere else.

25 Pickard-Cambridge, *TDA*, pp. 100ff., is disinclined to accept the existence of a revolve in the fifth century at all. He accepts the use of wheeled furniture in *Acharnians* and *Women at the Festival* (though his suggestion of an upper-level appearance in *Acharnians* seems unlikely, particularly as it depends on a rather forced interpretation of the words *katabaden* and *anabaden*). He rejects the revolving scenery postulated by the scholiast in *Clouds*. Wheeled furniture and movable screens are acceptable, and seem most appropriate both to the staging as envisaged elsewhere in the book, and to the language in the plays themselves. Once again, I can find very little sense on this subject in Dearden, *The Stage of Aristophanes*.

26 That is, unless some of the mock-tragic lines (for example 225, 228ff.) are Euripidean in origin.

27 Dover, *AC*, or the introduction to Barrett, *FOP*, give a brisk but coherent account of the state of the evidence. More information can be found in Cornford, *OAC*, which should perhaps be combined with a reading of Pickard-Cambridge, *DTC*.

28 Full analyses of all the plays are given in Pickard-Cambridge, *DTC*, pp. 213–229. An earlier section of the book, 'Excursus on the Form of the Old Comedy as seen in Aristophanes' (*DTC*, pp. 194–212), discusses the use of formal structures in Aristophanes with admirable clarity.

29 The nature of illusion in the parabasis has been much discussed. See above, Chapter 6, pp. 91ff., and also Sifakis, *PAC*, *passim*, and especially Chapters 1, 3 and 4.

30 Excluding the many lyrical choruses, which often fulfil the same function of establishing or maintaining a mood, the list of examples would include Dikaiopolis' procession (*Acharnians* 241–279), the dialogue between the Chorus and the Boy (*Wasps* 248–265), part of the serenade scene in *Assembly-women* (952–968), and the Homeric dance of Karion and the Chorus in *Wealth* (290–315).

31 On this use of people as metaphors, see above, Chapter 6, pp. 89ff.

32 The passage quoted is the third of three balancing sections. The others

deal with the coward Kleonymos and the highwayman Orestes. The Kleonymos passage is quoted on p. 90 above.

33 None the less, although he much developed the traditional stereotypes of comic character, Aristophanes was not really concerned with the creation or development of dramatic characters as such. See above, Chapter 8.

34 The ancient Greek name for the quality of *poneria* was *metis*, 'cunning intelligence'. Its nature is thoroughly discussed in M. Detienne and J.-P. Vernant, *Cunning Intelligence in Greek Culture and Society* (London 1978).

35 See W. Arrowsmith, 'Aristophanes' Birds: The Fantasy Politics of Eros', in *Arion*, n.s., 1/1 (1973), pp. 119–167.

36 See C. P. Segal, 'The Character and Cults of Dionysus and the Unity of the Frogs', in *Harvard Studies in Classical Philology*, LXVI (1961), pp. 207ff.; Lever, *AGC*, pp. 88–96. Dionysos is also celebrated in *Clouds* 595ff. and *Women at the Festival* 985ff.

37 Further on this, see Ehrenberg, *PA*, pp. 184ff., and the penetrating article by K. J. Dover, 'Greek Comedy', in M. Platnauer (ed.), *Fifty Years of Classical Scholarship* (Oxford 1954), pp. 96–129.

38 It is likely that Greek playwrights, like modern ones, had a 'reading public' in mind as well as a 'theatre public'; certainly parts of the meaning of their plays would only be apparent to such readers (see Webster, *GTP*, p. xiii). But even so, the primary aim of a Greek dramatist must have been to make his philosophical meaning as clear as possible to the spectators at the original, festival performance.

39 Good general treatments of cosmic order in tragedy can be found in E. R. Dodds, *The Greeks and the Irrational* (Berkeley 1951), and in H. Lloyd-Jones, *The Justice of Zeus* (Berkeley

1971). The theme is discussed, for specific plays, in H. D. F. Kitto, *Form and Meaning in Drama* (London 1956) (*Agamemnon, Eumenides, Philoctetes, Antigone, Ajax* and *Hamlet*) and *Poiesis* (Berkeley 1966) (*The Persians, Women of Trachis* and *Oedipus the King*). An entirely opposite, and not universally accepted, view of the function of Greek tragedy can be found in B. W. Vickers, *Towards Greek Tragedy* (London 1973), and in J. Kott, *The Eating of the Gods* (London 1974). Readers seeking more detailed information on specific plays are referred to the bibliographies of these books, particularly those of Kitto and Vickers.

40 On Aristophanes' unique blend of fact and fantasy, see Ehrenberg, *PA*, pp. 26–30. The whole nature of fantasy in Aristophanes is examined in detail in Whitman, *ACH*, Chapter 8, and briefly discussed in Dover, *AC*, Chapter 3.

41 This example is borrowed from E. W. Segal, 'The Menaechmi: Roman Comedy of Errors', in *Yale Classical Studies* 21 (1969), pp. 85ff. The same author's *Roman Laughter* (Cambridge, Mass. 1968) discusses the dramatic use of Saturnalia in Plautus in considerable detail.

42 On this ritual aspect of Aristophanes' inheritance, see Cornford, *OAC*, pp. 9–26.

43 The splendid phrase 'litigious mania' is borrowed from Barrett, *FOP*, p. 42.

44 For Greek women, of course, taking an active part in politics would itself have been a 'strange and mighty deed'. The 'unreality' at the start of *Lysistrata* and *Assemblywomen*, for a Greek audience, would have been greatly increased by the fact that all the actors playing women dressed as men were men in the first place. The blurring of sexual identity at the start of these plays, before the audience knew the plot, must have been very striking indeed, and have produced an

'unreal' atmosphere only partly realized today, when we read the plays
in the study or see them performed by
actors of both sexes.

45 For an excellent and concise discussion of this convention, see Dover,
AC, pp. 41–45.

46 Aristotle, *Nicomachean Ethics* 1108ᵃ 21;
Rhetoric iii, 18. See also G. Kaibel,
Comicorum Graecorum Fragmenta i, 52 (=
Tractatus Coislinianus 6). The discussion in Cornford, *OAC*, though
savaged by Pickard-Cambridge in the
first editions of *DTC* and *DFA*, is once
again of remarkable general interest,
in view of recent writings on the medieval Fool (for example W. Willeford,
The Fool and his Scepter, Washington
1969).

47 The differences are described with
exemplary clarity in P. D. Arnott, *An
Introduction to the Greek Theatre* (London
1965), Chapter 1, and in Sifakis, *PAC*,
Chapter 1. On stage illusion in general,
see J. L. Styan's excellent discussion
in *Drama, Stage and Audience* (London
1975).

48 Further details on this and many
other presentational matters raised in
this chapter can be found in V. M.
Roberts, *The Nature of Theatre* (New
York 1971), especially Chapter 2.

49 See Pickard-Cambridge, *DFA*, pp.
59ff.

50 Generally on the parabasis, see Dover,
AC, pp. 49–53. The whole question of
the shedding of illusion in the parabasis is dealt with in Sifakis, *PAC*,
Chapters 1–5, and pp. 103–108.

51 See, for example, Norwood, *Greek
Comedy*, pp. 11f.; Pickard-Cambridge,
DTC, p. 199; Cornford, *OAC*, p. 10.
All of them describe the parabasis as
'non-dramatic' and 'an interruption'
of the play. Lever, *AGC*, pp. 110ff.,
writes sound sense on the whole
matter.

52 The dramatic function of bawdy in
Aristophanes generally, and in each
individual play, is discussed in Henderson, *MM*, which is surely destined
to become a standard work on this
aspect of Aristophanes' bawdy.

53 It is only in the last few years that the
integrity and inoffensive funniness
of Aristophanes' bawdy have been
generally admitted. The muscular
Christians in whose hands classical
learning once reposed found it a distasteful, unholy blemish on the plays;
often they performed surgery on the
texts, and declared them healthier for
the wholesale removal of those lines
and themes which caused offence. In
places such nineteenth-century teaching attitudes (and the mutilated texts
they produced) linger sadly on. But it
can be argued, too, that our own age's
obsessive interest in displaying sexual
freedom has led us to distort Aristophanes' meaning just as much in
the other direction, by overstressing
the bawdy in performance or in critical
writing. Of all the features of his style,
bawdy is still the least understood.
Henderson, *MM*, puts the matter into
some kind of perspective, and more
generally, the whole subject of Greek
sexuality has been excellently treated
by K. J. Dover. (See especially, his
articles 'Classical Greek Attitudes to
Sexual Behaviour', in *Arethusa* 6
(1973), pp. 59ff., and 'Eros and
Nomos', in *London University Bulletin
for Classical Studies* 11 (1964), pp. 31ff.)
See also Dodds, *The Greeks and the
Irrational*, Chapter 2, *passim*.

54 On the status of the fool, and his interaction with society, see Willeford, *The
Fool and his Scepter*, Chapter 2 discusses
the phallic associations of the jester.
A detailed discussion of the social
function of jokes, from the psycho-
logist's point of view, may be found in
S. Freud, *Jokes and their Relation to the
Unconscious* (trans. J. Strachey, London 1960), Chapter 3, sections 2–3;
Chapter 5, *passim*.

55 See Henderson, *MM*, pp. 57–60, and especially p. 59.

56 Henderson's remarks on this scene are particularly pertinent: *MM*, pp. 95, 98.

57 See Henderson, *MM*, pp. 134f.; Carl Ruck, 'Euripides' Mother: Vegetables and the Phallos in Aristophanes', in *Arion*, n.s., 2/1 (1975), pp. 13–58, especially the comments on wreaths on p. 17.

58 For penetrating analyses of this scene, see Dover, *AC*, pp. 63ff.; Henderson, *MM*, pp. 6of.

59 Leo Aylen, *Classical Drama and its Influence* (London 1965), p. 87, mentions an illustrious impersonation of this type (Kitto as Socrates in *Clouds*). The context tells us about the gusto of the performance, and the rapture with which it was received; but it also makes clear that this was a good amateur production, in no way comparable with that of a professional company.

60 His acting style is probably parodied by Shakespeare, in the lines given to Ancient Pistol. These again suggest beyond reasonable doubt the kind of performance required.

61 A moment's consideration of the parts of Hamlet or Volpone will show at once the kind of differences between a good amateur performance and that of a leading professional.

62 That a living could be made from these activities in the fourth century is apparent from such passages as Demosthenes' reference to Theodoros in *de Falsa Legatione* 246 (See O. J. Todd, 'Tritagonistes. A reconsideration', in *Classical Quarterly* 32 (1938), pp. 30ff.). Admittedly in Theodoros' time old plays were more frequently revived than in the fifth century. But the absence of fifth-century plays from any of the great centres of culture except Athens suggests either that all playwrights submitted their work for the Athenian festivals, or (less likely, on the face of it) that when plays were performed elsewhere, they were the work of the great Athenian dramatists. Plutarch, *Nikias* 29, is evidence for the extraordinary interest in Athenian drama shown in fifth-century Syracuse. As to private performances, the actor on the Anavysos *chous* of 420 BC (Figure 6 above; Trendall and Webster, *IGD*, p. 117) may as easily be giving a show before a single patron (and friend) as in a theatre.

63 See also D. M. MacDowell's excellent remarks on the character in his edition of *Wasps* (Oxford 1971), pp. 7–12.

64 The modern verse comedies of Christopher Fry take about a minute per page (25–30 lines); but they lack music and dancing, and contain little slapstick. At 15 lines a minute, *Wasps* (a longer play than most) would take about 1¾ hours to perform. This accords well with the total time available to perform five plays in the daylight hours of one festival day. See P. Walcot, *Greek Drama in its Theatrical and Social Context* (Cardiff 1976), Chapter 1.

65 That is, preparatory scenes build their expectation to a climax, on which the star enters. A similar procedure is used in the off-camera 'audience warm-ups' before television comedy shows. There, however, the 'warm-up' material is extraneous to the comedy it precedes.

66 The 'warm-ups' in *Knights* and *Peace* are very similar to this. Clearly the humour of the leading actor's first line is materially enhanced if the performer is someone well known to the audience (as it would be today if the line was delivered by a Zero Mostel or a Frankie Howerd rather than by a total stranger). Aristophanes' audience *did* know whom to expect: the names of play, playwright and actors were announced some days before the performance, during the *pro-agon* (see Pickard-Cambridge, *DFA*, pp. 67f.).

67 The phrase is part of MacDowell's enthusiastic description of the scene (*Wasps* edition, p. 149). Whitman's comments, *ACH*, pp. 162f., are characteristic of his excellent critique of the whole play (*ACH*, pp. 143–166).

68 See P. D. Arnott, 'Animals in the Greek Theatre', in *Greece and Rome* vi (1959), pp. 178–179.

69 There is, as MacDowell (*Wasps* edition, p. 188) notes, considerable dramatic weakness in this scene. Either the text as we have it is incomplete in some way, or there was some non-verbal 'business' in 437–455. Philokleon's speech at 448–452, and especially 448, suggests that the slaves may have been grotesque in size or appearance, and that physical knockabout was in full swing at this point. It is certainly surprising that the text offers the leading actor so little to do at this stage. Perhaps his costume (or that of the slaves) offered comic possibilities of which we know nothing.

70 Impersonation is an essential characteristic of the *poneros*. See Whitman, *ACH*, Chapter 2, especially pp. 43–53.

71 I find unconvincing MacDowell's assertion (*Wasps* edition, p. 11) that Philokleon was not dressed in the same costume as the Chorus (at least after 430). He is on his way to work, after all, and would naturally wear the same as his fellows. In the trial scene he is still acting as a juryman, and the humour of the dressing-up sequence at 1122ff. would be materially enhanced if he was still wearing his wasp outfit underneath.

72 On this dance, see T. B. L. Webster, *The Greek Chorus* (London 1972), pp. 184–185.

73 The technique is familiar in other contexts, and is indeed a standby of political oratory. Aristophanes uses it again in the parabasis of *Frogs*: the simile between men and money, though attractive in the theatre, would hardly stand up to sustained examination outside it.

74 Some scholars object to calling him by this name, and prefer a generic title like 'The Relation'. But I prefer to name him, even if manuscript support for the name is suspect.

75 Those who remain sceptical about this symbiotic relationship are invited to compare Xanthias' conversation with Aiakos (*Frogs* 738–813) with his dialogues with Dionysos. The difference is not in the quality of the writing, or in the type of jokes; the Xanthias/Aiakos scene is different principally because we have hitherto seen Xanthias only in terms of his relationship with his master. Separated from Dionysos, he seems a different character entirely. I believe that the reason for the insertion of this non-functional scene was to break up the mood of close unity established in the first half of the play, ready for the more stereotyped, agonistic confrontation of Aeschylus and Euripides. (In this contest, too, Dionysos, shorn of the dimension given him by Xanthias, becomes a pallid, two-dimensional buffoon.)

76 Clearly, one cannot assume anything about the characters in a play outside of the specific action of the play itself, and to do so has rightly been regarded as a solecism of the worst kind. This being so, the irrelevance of what Mnesilochos and Euripides reveal of their relationship at the start of this play, and the depth of the relationship itself, are all the more striking. It is as if Aristophanes himself was caught up in the documentary fallacy.

77 In the same way, Laurel and Hardy first appear in *Way Out West* (1936) in a situation which has nothing to do with the plot (of which the audience has already seen five minutes), but everything to do with their relationship to each other. Laurel is leading a

loaded mule, and himself carrying a heavy rucksack; Hardy is reclining at ease on a hurdle dragged by the mule, which Laurel's careless driving causes first to bump over some large rocks, and then to sink several inches into a large, muddy creek (which he himself and the mule, because they are on foot, have negotiated with ease). The likeness of this opening to the beginning of *Frogs* is most marked – and was apparently intentional.

78 I am assuming that the actor wore a portrait mask throughout his performance as Euripides – which gives extra ironical point to the impersonations in the rescue scenes (871ff.). He would naturally replace it with an old-woman mask for the Thesmophoria scene. That he changed costume is suggested by the length of time he is offstage (100 lines before the Thesmophoria scene, 106 lines after it).

79 There can be no doubt that this was the part he took. It is not only that the character is onstage for longer than the others, and speaks more dialogue (a characteristic of parts assumed to have been played by the deuteragonist), but also that the relationship in style and mood of the scenes between Mnesilochos/First Woman and Mnesilochos/Euripides is far closer, far more coherent, than those involving Mnesilochos and any other character.

80 His actions during the unmasking scene (i.e. 635–650) are in the careless, self-indulgent style of the true *poneros*, as is his inconsequential, mock-tragic lament (650–651) when they fail. His threat to the wineskin is *poneria*, and culminates in the magnificent paratragedy of 752ff., and the characteristic insouciance of 756 and 758 (two lines of very self-conscious role-playing). Even when threatened by the majesty of the Prytanis, he does not cower, but seizes the opportunity for another mock-Euripidean lament, embarking on his ludicrous – gloriously, self-evidently ludicrous – invocation of Palamedes.

81 For the existence of Euripides' style as a kind of spatial dimension in its own right, the actual fantasy world in which most of *Women at the Festival* operates, see Whitman, *ACH*, pp. 216–227. In no other play of Aristophanes is there such blurring of the distinction between truth and illusion.

82 I am presuming that the Prytanis in 929–946 was played by a fourth actor, and that the (silent) Scythian in the same lines was played by an extra. The third actor is given 54 lines (947–1000: 4 minutes) to change from the Priestess' robe and mask into those of the Scythian.

83 I imagine him here wearing the costume of an old woman, but retaining the Euripides portrait mask.

84 There is no saying which tragedians the second and third actors actually played. I have allocated Aeschylus to the Herakles actor (the third, who also played Aiakos) on the grounds of similarity of physical appearance and vocal style in the parts; in the same way, Xanthias and Euripides share a certain slippery dexterity with language.

85 See Lever, *AGC*, Chapter 4, *passim*. On the character of Dionysos, see further E. Lapalus, 'Le Dionysos et l'Héraclés des Grenouilles', in *Revue des Etudes Grecques* XLVII (1934), pp. 1ff.; C. P. Segal, 'The Character and Cults of Dionysos and the Unity of the Frogs', in *Harvard Studies in Classical Philology* LXV (1961), pp. 207ff.; Whitman, *ACH*, pp. 228–258, and especially pp. 232ff.

86 Pickard-Cambridge, *DFA*, pp. 171f. cites four examples from Aeschylus, five from Sophocles, and no less than twenty-six from Euripides.

87 In fact, the first line of Euripides' *Bacchae*.

88 We share today the Greek convention here: before ever we begin to read a play by Euripides or Aristophanes, we are conditioned to expect either tragedy or comedy. An uneducated reader or spectator might react quite differently – a point forcefully made about *Medea* in Jules Dassin's film *Never on Sunday* (1961), where the uneducated whore, who never missed a production of the play, had always taken it for hammed-up farce until the earnest American scholar shattered her illusion, and her enjoyment of the play, for ever.

89 The all-male *As You Like It* done by the English National Theatre Company in 1974 was the most notable example of many on the London stage since the war. The Englishman Danny la Rue and the American Charles Pierce have both made flourishing stage careers out of female impersonation.

90 One might ask the same question in an even starker form: what is the difference in effect between Medea or Antigone when performed by a man, and by a woman? A male actor today, perhaps, would produce the same initial shock and curiosity as a female actress would have done in the fifth century.

91 See further Pickard-Cambridge, *DFA*, pp. 167ff., 272ff.

92 Pickard-Cambridge, *DFA*, pp. 149–153, gives a convenient summary of the evidence, though there is much to quarrel with in his distribution of the parts. The books and articles referred to in his note 4 (*DFA*, p. 149) are vital to the discussion, though not to the solution, of this fascinating and thorny problem.

93 *Clouds* is the most problematical of the plays, from the point of view of charac-ter distribution. See C. F. Russo, *Aristofane, autore di teatro* (Florence 1962), pp. 155–171; Dover, *AC*, pp. 103–108; Dover, *Clouds* edition, pp. lxxviiff.

94 A fourth actor is needed during the landlady scene, and he is normally allocated – on grounds both of logistic and of dramatic sense – the parts of the Corpse, Pluto's servant in 503–520, Plathane in the landlady scene, and Pluto.

95 Possibly the fourth actor played some of these parts, for example Agathon's slave and one of the women; but even if he did, the argument is unaffected.

96 See Aristotle's comments in *Rhetoric* iii and *Poetics* xix. Other classical references to the effectiveness of the actors' vocal skill are collected in Pickard-Cambridge, *DFA*, pp. 167ff.

97 See Whitman, *ACH*, p. 311, note 31.

98 He may, of course, have worn a portrait mask, in which case all the doubts as to his real identity, and especially those of Mnesilochos in 592–594, gain an extra ironical and satirical tone.

99 Most other stage comedy makes its humour from causality, from the constraints placed on the characters; the parallel with Aristophanes' comedy of freedom comes in the non-literary tradition, and reaches its apogee in the fantastic, inconsequential world of slapstick film comedy.

100 The plainness of Iago's language, contrasted with the poetic richness of Othello's, is an example of how this happens in Shakespeare. In Aeschylus, notable passages where poetry takes over and impels the dramatic action include Prometheus' description of Io's wanderings, the Cassandra scene in *Agamemnon* and the whole central section of *Seven Against Thebes* (the description of the champions).

101 Obviously untranslatable. Douglass Parker opts for a Dylan Thomas-ish, Colonel Sandersy mishmash which he calls 'One-dish madness':

It's hors-d'oeuvre-dotted-delicious
    with heart-of-the-briny oysters
and sea-tangy fishlets oh-so-zestfully
    nestled in clusters
on spry-as-the-morning, utterly udder-fresh
    goat-good cheese,
caressing a lip-smacking, tooth-tensing medley
    Of goodies like these:

alabaster-bosomed pigeon with bee-sweet-
    honey-drenched thrush,
do-it-again-love dove and the brown-basted,
    burst-breasted gush
of thick-thighed chicken, the let-us-be-truly-
    thankful amen
of gobbet-good bloblets of squab, hard by the
    hit-me-again
of ever-so-finely-filleted, palate-proud
    mullet, new-speared,
with gusto-lusty sweetmeats, crunch-yummily
    kitcheneered
to rush the most reluctant tooth to the gnash . . .
    In short, it's Heavenly Hash.

Select Bibliography

The main purpose of this bibliography is to lead interested readers to books which either cover essential background matters left out of this one, or which take further some of the issues raised in these pages. Scholars will have ready access to complete bibliographies of Aristophanes; other readers will find most helpful the lists in Dover, *AC*, or Henderson, *MM* (see below).

The Greek text referred to throughout this book is that of Hall and Geldart (second edition, Oxford 1906–1907). The Oxford University Press is in the process of publishing a complete critical edition of the plays: at the time of writing (early 1979), *Wasps, Clouds, Peace* and *Ecclesiazusae* (*Assemblywomen*) are available.

The plays are translated in several versions. I would particularly recommend those of William Arrowsmith and Douglass Parker in the Mentor series (Ann Arbor 1961–1967): they come nearest to the spirit of the originals, without sacrificing too much of the letter. Of the Penguin Classics versions (Harmondsworth 1964–1978) the best are by David Barrett, and particularly those in *The Frogs and Other Plays*. Cambridge University Press are in the process of publishing translations of my own: the first volume (1980) includes *Clouds, Knights* and *Assemblywomen*.

The essential background books are *Aristophanic Comedy* by K. J. Dover (London 1972), which deals succinctly with all matters to do with the plays, but avoids literary criticism throughout, and *Aristophanes and the Comic Hero* by C. H. Whitman (Cambridge, Mass. 1964), which deals in depth with Aristophanes' character-drawing, political and moral writing, and fantasy. These books are referred to in the text and notes as Dover, *AC*, and Whitman, *ACH*, respectively.

Other important books frequently cited in the text and notes are:

Cornford, *OAC*: F. M. Cornford, *The Origin of Attic Comedy* (ed. T. H. Gaster) (Gloucester, Mass. 1968)

Ehrenberg, *PA*: V. Ehrenberg, *The People of Aristophanes* (Oxford 1942)

Henderson, *MM*: J. Henderson, *The Maculate Muse* (New Haven 1975)

Lever, *AGC*:   K. Lever, *The Art of Greek Comedy* (London 1956)

Pickard-Cambridge, *DFA*: Sir A. Pickard-Cambridge, *The Dramatic Festivals of Athens* (second edition, Oxford 1968)

Pickard-Cambridge, *DTC*: Sir A. Pickard-Cambridge, *Dithyramb, Tragedy and Comedy* (second edition, Oxford 1962)

Pickard-Cambridge, *TDA*: Sir A. Pickard-Cambridge, *The Theatre of Dionysos in Athens* (Oxford 1946)

Sifakis, *PAC*: G. M. Sifakis, *Parabasis and Animal Choruses* (London 1971)
Solomos, *LA*: A. Solomos, *The Living Aristophanes* (Ann Arbor 1974)
Trendall and Webster, *IGD*: A. D. Trendall and T. B. L. Webster, *Illustrations of Greek Drama* (London 1971)
Webster, *GTP*: T. B. L. Webster, *Greek Theatre Production* (second edition, London 1970)

All other books and articles cited are accompanied by full bibliographical details as they occur, either in the text or in the notes.

Index of Lines Referred to in the Text

General Index

Abbott and Costello 55, 132, 136
absurd deed 66–76, 84, 124, 136, 138, 158
Absurd Drama 20, 67
Acharnians, The 33
  absurd deed in 69–72, 74, 84, 124, 158
  alazones in 54, 56, 129–130
  alienation in 68–70
  Aristophanes revealed in (?) 57
  bawdy in 97, 102–103
  bawdy gesture in 105, 107, 108
  characterization in 88, 128, 129, 130, 133, 137, 138, 165
  Chorus in 42, 105
  comic metaphor in 157, 158, 159
  doors in 44
  double entendre in 102–103
  doubling in 150
  farce in 16
  fifth-century performance of 28, 31–32, 35, 45, 46
  illusion in 88
  lampoons in 17, 31–32, 52, 83–85, 91
  language in 58–59, 105
  lazzi in 20
  leading role in 112–113, 122–123, 127–129, 165
  Lenaia in 28
  naked women in 153
  parabasis of 57
  philosophy of natural order in 59
  poneros in 55, 56, 84, 127, 128, 129, 133, 137
  religious aspect of 58–59, 76
  skene roof in 43
  structure of 52, 122–123, 129–130, 133, 164–165
  theatre convention in 83–85
  travesty acting in 154
acrobatics 18–20, 93
Acropolis 35, 39, 44

actor, fourth 33, 128, 140–141, 151, n. 82, n. 95
actor, leading 32–34, 111–126, 127, 128–129, 131, 140, 149, 165
  in Aristophanes' plays: *Acharnians* 112–113, 122–123; *Assemblywomen* 122, 125; *Birds* 122, 124–125; *Clouds* 112, 122–124; *Frogs* 122, 125–126, 151; *Knights* 122–123; *Lysistrata* 122, 124–125; *Peace* 122–123; *Wasps* 111, 113–121, 122–123; *Wealth* 122, 125; *Women at the Festival* 112, 122, 125–126
actor, second 33, 113, 128, 131, 140, 148, 151, n. 79, n. 84
actor, third 33, 113, 128, 131, 140, 148, 151, n. 84
actors, and acting 17–18, 21, 25, 32–34, 111–126, n. 62
  and audience 17–18, 21, 79–81, 83, 86–89, 100–103, 126, 147–148, 150, 153, n. 66
  and comedians 81–83, 84, 94–95, 122, 149, 151
  in comedy 79, 149
  distribution of parts between 150–152, n. 79, n. 82, n. 84, nn. 92–95
  and doubling 21, 137, 147–152
  in Euripides 112
  use of gesture 103–108, 145
  at rehearsals 33–34
  selection of 32–33
  skills of 18–19, 111–121, 153, 154, 165, n. 89
  status of 111–113
  in theatre 39, 41–42, 44, 48–49, n. 20
  touring 33–34, 113
  in tragedy 21, 149
  travesty 97, 99, 147, 153–156
  SEE ALSO actors, fourth; leading; second; third; comedians;

Aristophanes (cont.)
  producing in name of Kallistratos
    30
  rivals 14, 26–27, 36, 52
  traditional forms, use of 14, 19–21,
    50–54, 76, 98, 99, 108
Aristotle 32, 103, n. 46, n. 96
Arkin, Alan 121
Arnott, Peter n. 47, n. 68
Arrowsmith, William 73–74, 77–78,
  90, 130, n. 35
Assemblywomen 22, n. 30
  absurd deed in n. 44
  alienation in 68
  bawdy in 98, 99–100
  characterization in 128, 131, 151,
    158–159
  comic metaphor in 158–159
  doors in 44
  doubling in 151
  farce in 16–17
  gods in 59
  illusion in 88
  language in 163
  lazzi in 99
  leading role in 113, 122, 125
  parody in 146
  philosophy of natural order in 59,
    76
  poneria in 128
  reversal of reality in 70, 72, 74–75
  spoudaios in 54–56, 122
  structure of 125, 129, 131
  travesty acting in 154–155
As You Like It n. 89
Athens 11–12, 26–27, 59–60
  Assembly in 83–84
  SEE ALSO play production;
    playwrights; Dionysos,
    Theatre of
Attic comic traditions 14, 19, 50–56,
  76, 87–88, 98
audience
  composition of 35
  effects of plays on 35, 161
  expectations of, in fifth century
    14–15, 55, 111–113, 123, 146
  expectations of, today 13–15, 17,
    41, 79–82
  and judging 36
  as participants 79–92
  relationship with characters 79–82,
    128, 135, 150
  relationship with performers 17,

    21, 79–82, 86–90, 100–103, 119,
    126, 147–151, n. 66
  seating and vision 40–41, 153
  SEE ALSO Dionysos, Theatre of;
    festivals, dramatic
L'Avare, Harpagon in 81–82, 84
Aylen, Leo n. 59

Babylonians, The 26, 58
Bacchae, The 58, n. 87
backer (*choregos*) 25–26, 29–33, 112
Bailey, H. C. n. 13
Barrault, Jean-Louis 18
Barrett, David 88–89, 98, 115–117,
  136, 139, n. 27, n. 43
Barrie, Sir James 114
bawdy 17, 21, 37, 93–108, n. 53,
  n. 54
  to achieve alienation 96
  in Aristophanes' plays: *Acharnians*
    97, 102–103, 105, 107; *Assembly-
    women* 98, 99–100; *Birds* 95–96,
    101, 105, 107; *Clouds* 97;
    Frogs 96, 100; *Lysistrata* 97, 99,
    100–101, 108; *Peace* 95, 96–97;
    Wealth 96, 97, 101; *Women at the
    Festival* 98–99, 107, 140
  double entendre 94–95, 100–103
  explicit 94, 95–97
  gesture 95, 103–108
Beaumarchais, Pierre-Augustin
  Caron de 55, 82, 127
Beckett, Samuel 20
Bells, The 80
Benny, Jack 82
Bergson, Henri 67, 129
Bernhardt, Sarah 80
Birds 28, 33, n. 20, n. 35
  absurd deed in 70, 73–74, 158
  alazones in 54, 75, 124–125, 129,
    130–131, 150–151
  alienation in 68, 69
  bawdy in 95–96, 101, 106, 108
  bawdy gesture in 106, 108
  bomolochos in 55, 56, 128
  characterization in 128, 131
  Chorus in 42, 91–92, 105
  comic metaphor in 158
  crane in 47–48
  door in 44, 46
  double-act in 132
  double entendre in 101
  doubling in 150–151
  farce in 16